FROM

In this
decad
emplo
group
world.

Since
tempo
in the
menta
comp;
of de]
setting
enviro
group;
of stu
conce;

ERIC N
Progra
of Org
Rural
Organization.

FROM DEPENDENCY TO AUTONOMY
STUDIES IN ORGANIZATION AND CHANGE

ERIC MILLER

'an association in which the free development of
each is the condition of the free development of all'

Free Association Books / London / 1993

First published in 1993 by
FREE ASSOCIATION BOOKS
57 Warren Street, London W1T 5NR

A CIP catalogue record for this book is available
from the British Library

ISBN 1 85343 335 7 pbk

Produced for Free Association Books by
Chase Publishing Services, Fortescue, Sidmouth, EX10 9QG
Digitally Reprinted in the European Union by
Antony Rowe Ltd, Eastbourne, England

CONTENTS

FIGURES

PREFACE

One paper (Miller, 1980) not included in this volume discusses the 'politics of identity', a subject which has long intrigued me. Goffman wrote about it in *The Presentation of Self in Everyday Life* (1956); Heider had something useful to say in *The Psychology of Interpersonal Relations* (1958); Rice and I discussed aspects of it at the level of inter-system relations (Miller and Rice, 1967; Rice, 1969); and Andrew Szmidla, a one-time associate of mine, developed an interesting framework though regrettably never published it (see Miller, 1977, pp. 60-1). It is a subject that nestles on the boundaries of micro-sociology, social psychology, psycho-dynamic psychology and political science. It also feels very relevant, in at least two ways, to the process of assembling a selection of one's papers for publication.

First, this is a self-indulgent – even narcissistic – process. It is an opportunity to say: 'Look at me: see how clever I am!' It also, however, raises uncomfortable questions: Who is this 'I'? What 'self' do I want to indulge? Along with that goes a risk: the collection is one presentation of me; for the reader, my writings *are* me. So as a statement of identity a volume of papers is non-negotiable; others will use it to make judgements about me, positive or negative, and there will be no further chance for me to influence those judgements by saying 'Yes, but . . . '

Second, my own professional identity does not itself fit within any neat disciplinary boundary. Faced with forms asking for 'profession or occupation' I am never sure what to enter. 'Social anthropologist'? That's something I was but am no longer. 'Organizational consultant'? But that's only part of what I do. 'Social science practitioner'? Rather a mouthful, and it still doesn't seem right.

This comes of spending most of my working life at the Tavistock Institute of Human Relations. It is an institute that defines itself as multi-disciplinary. Furthermore, for more than forty years it has struggled to occupy a space between academic social science on the one side and a commercial consultancy practice on the other. This was a transposition into the social sciences of clinical research in medicine. The Institute emerged in 1946 out of the Tavistock

Clinic, which was, and still is, a psychoanalytically oriented out-patient clinic also engaged in training of mental health professionals. Members of the founding group were a mixture of pre-war Clinic staff and (mainly) social scientists from elsewhere who were brought together by the War Office during World War II as a resource in tackling large-scale problems – problems that included but also went way beyond treatment of the large numbers of psychiatric casualties. (For a full account see Trist and Murray, 1990.) Based on this experience, they saw a role for themselves in the period of post-war reconstruction. And, by analogy with clinical research, they argued that social scientists could gain access to critical aspects of the functioning of social systems only from a professional role in which they were helping these systems to tackle real issues of development and change. 'No therapy without research; no research without therapy.' So action research was to be central to the Tavistock Institute's mission: to advance the social sciences through involvement in practical human problems and concerns. And action research, by its nature, is problem-centred, not discipline-centred.

Remarkably, this stance has been maintained. To be sure, few projects have an even balance of consultancy and research objectives. Nor are the research questions always formulated in advance. However, even where there is no explicit research component, nearly every piece of consultancy uses a scientific method. It goes through the phases of collection of data, the generation of working hypotheses, and the testing of these against more data, preferably through the implementation of a change in the client system. The client is an active collaborator in what is a learning process for both parties. Psychoanalysts tend to use the term 'interpretation' rather than 'working hypothesis' and they do not use the written word, but their basic methodology is much the same. To me, action research *is* clinical research. Very little of my own or others' work at the Tavistock Institute has had purely research objectives. Equally (though we sometimes regret it) we have resisted the financial temptation of a purely commercial practice as 'expert consultants'.

Management consultancy was one such opportunity forgone. One innovation of the war-time group had been the creation of the

War Office Selection Boards (WOSBs). These had the dual function of broadening the social class base for recruitment for a vastly expanding army and of providing a selection process which would allow candidates to show their talents in realistic situations. In this, the use of leaderless groups was an important innovation. It recast the conventional conception of leadership: the focus shifted from the qualities of an individual in isolation to the demonstration of actual behaviour in relation to others. TIHR developed this approach, combining intellectual and projective tests with group exercises, for processes of management selection. During the 1950s and early 1960s the demand was considerable – a market ripe for commercial exploitation. But that was not TIHR's style. Once the development phase was complete, the conceptual challenge evaporated: no one on the staff wanted to be a full-time practitioner. Much the same happened with consumer research (see Menzies Lyth, 1989). Innovative studies of unconscious responses to various products were both exciting and lucrative; the commercialization of the field was left to others.

Thus, although the Institute has succeeded in establishing a reasonably distinctive identity, it has always seemed precarious. It reminds me of Chile, with its long narrow strip of habitable land between the peaks of the Andes and the Pacific Ocean. Perhaps the same uncertainty applies to those who joined the Institute. How far were we making a positive choice and how far were we refugees – people who didn't quite fit in the domains of either academia or commerce? Those who left invariably opted for one or the other. Perhaps we who stayed were perennial misfits.

I suppose I was a refugee. I arrived having had temporary identities in both domains. And in retrospect it feels as if there was a kind of inevitability about my joining the Institute.

Unknowingly, I had my first brush with the future Institute early in 1943. At the end of 1941 I had been awarded an exhibition in Classics at Cambridge. Still seventeen, I could spend a year at university before joining the army. It was not a productive year: I did the minimum of study, rowed, and worried about the future. Once in uniform, I underwent my basic training for about six weeks and was then dispatched to this mysterious two-day event called a WOSB. My recollections are fragmentary: being shown a series of fuzzy pictures plus one blank page and told to write stories about them (the Thematic Apperception Test, as I was to learn later); swinging on a rope across a brook; and also being with a group of others inside a tennis court, where various lengths of timber were lying around and we were instructed to escape without touching the wire, supposedly electrified. A few months later I acquired the identity of a junior officer in the Royal Artillery.

It was service in India and, towards the end of the war, in Burma that steered me towards my next identity. I was posted to an artillery unit that was quite unusual in two ways: first, it was a field battery that the Maharaja of Gwalior had – literally – lent to the Royal Indian Artillery for the duration of the war; and second, the troops were a mixture of Hindus and Muslims. Neighbouring units included Sikhs and Gurkhas and then, when the war ended, the Burmese came out of the jungle and there were the surrendering cohorts of Japanese to add to the cultural *mélange*. Returning to Cambridge, I abandoned classics for anthropology and two years later saw me back in India with a degree and funding for field research, this time with my first wife and fellow anthropologist, the late Kathleen Gough.

The timing was exquisite – a month after India had gained independence in August 1947. And the subject of the study was change in the traditional social system in Kerala, where substantial Muslim and Syrian Christian minorities lived alongside the highly stratified caste structure of the Hindu majority. I revelled in my two years there and besides the thesis produced at least one good paper about caste that yielded a crop of citations.

For my post-doctoral research the Foreign Office gave me a one-and-a-half-year studentship for field work in the far north of Thailand among the Black-bottomed Lao. (Traditionally the men were solidly tattooed from waist to thigh, so that, when stripped, they looked from the rear as though they were wearing navy-blue trunks.) I chose them as a peasant society with an economy broadly similar to that of Kerala but with a contrasting social system, reputed to be 'loosely structured'. This research nearly didn't happen: the Korean crisis blew up and the War Office put me back into my role as artillery officer. A tussle went on over my head and

I was just going on embarkation leave when the Foreign Office won and I sailed for Bangkok instead.

It was an intriguing society and once I was reasonably proficient in the local dialect I made some good and useful relationships. But there was more than an undercurrent of violence: three unexplained murders; myself the rather bloody victim of an attempted robbery. In my innocence, it took me a long time to realize that I had settled close to the edge of what was later called the Golden Triangle. The men who paddled their little boat-loads of vegetables or charcoal, whom I watched from my riverside hut, perched on stilts, were often carrying other cargo as well. Some were also becoming consumers.

As my time in Thailand drew to an end, I realized that the identity of 'academic social anthropologist' was becoming less and less attractive. The next step would be to become an assistant lecturer and send out another cohort of young anthropologists to do their field work and get their doctorates . . . and so on. In the face of the social problems I had seen in India and Thailand I was no longer content with the role of observer, albeit participant observer: I wanted to do something with my anthropology. (The fact that termites had fed themselves proudly on some of my fieldnotes – they seemed especially partial to red ink – possibly added to my disenchantment.) So I wrote to Meyer Fortes, then professor at Cambridge, asking for ideas and went on holiday to Australia.

There followed a chain of events of a kind that makes one wonder about predestination. Based in Massachusetts was a family-owned jute company, Ludlow, which had several jute mills in the US and a large one, with 8000 employees, in India. The executive vice-president, Peter Stone, was tuned into the latest trends in industrial psychology and was also a concerned employer. He had funded a team from the Harvard School of Public Health to survey the Indian work-force. Their conclusion was that the major source of sickness absence was malaria; if only the workers could be persuaded to take the appropriate prophylactic pills – at that time paludrine – the problem would be greatly reduced. Peter Stone was shrewd enough to recognize that this was not something that could be achieved by managerial fiat and decided that what was needed was a social anthropologist with a knowledge of India. One of my interviewers was Tom Harris, an imaginative clinical psychologist who, apart from dividing his professional time as a selection consultant between Ludlow and Polaroid, was also, as an illusionist, a star member of the Magic Circle. The other was a London friend of Peter's named Wilfred Brown, who was chief executive of an engineering company. It just so happened that this was the Glacier Metal Company and that Wilfred (later Lord Brown) was the client and collaborator in the Tavistock Institute's first major action research project in industry, recorded in books and papers that I had not only not read but not even heard of. The Tavistock Institute? What and where was that? Wilfred sent me to find out. I met a strange set of people, who seemed to be mixed up with psychoanalysis as well as with 'proper' social science: Tommy Wilson, Eric Trist, Harold Bridger and also Ken Rice who, for me, was the most immediately interesting and relevant. At this time – the winter of 1952–53 – he had begun his seminal experiments on work organization with groups of weavers in an Indian cotton mill. Although he too was slightly 'tainted' (as it seemed to me then) by psychoanalytic thinking, this was the kind of applied social science that I was looking for, and I badly wanted to know more.

First, however, I was to spend some time in the States – initially six months, but this extended to nearly a year – to familiarize myself with industry and with jute processing in particular. 'Applied social anthropologist' turned out to be an identity that I never quite assumed. In more than the obvious sense I found myself in a new world. I had brought with me a pile of Tavistock publications; I was introduced to the American 'human relations school'; met Fritz Roethlisberger – the 'Hawthorne experiment' man – and others at the Harvard Business School; and worked with Tom Harris in developing his already sophisticated battery of psychometric tests, including a version of the Rorschach, to predict the cultural adaptability of expatriates to work in the Indian culture. An additional role as management trainer contributed to my own education. Every week I spent a day in New York with two groups of managers. Out of the whole new literature I was discovering, I gave them articles and chapters to read and we explored implications for their own jobs. At the same time I was learning not only about the technology and organization of the American jute mills but also about their culture – or cultures. In the Massachusetts mill all the notices, such as 'Do not spit in the product', were in Polish and Portuguese as well as in English. In the new mill in Mississippi, the air-conditioning installed for the benefit of the process aroused envy and resentment in the workers' families sweltering at home – a luxury they could never afford. In Pennsylvania, at a works outing for a 'clambake', the clams were much less in evidence than beer and fornication, while in the mill itself women delighted in clipping the wings of a young supervisor by lifting their skirts and exposing their buttocks (the white-bottomed Pennsylvania Dutch?). And, moving from these 'lower castes' to the 'Brahmins', I was, whenever in Boston, the house-guest of my employer, Peter Stone, and discovered that the 'social register' was not just a metaphor: it was a book beside the telephone, with my host's name printed in it, and it admitted me into a circle far removed from Mississippi and Pennsylvania mill-workers. All in all a rich induction for my new role in India.

If this role ever had an official title, it is long forgotten. Perhaps the contract still described it as 'anthropologist'. Nowadays it would probably be called 'internal consultant' or 'change agent', which would have been more appropriate. Nowadays too I would be more specific about authority and accountability; but at that time I was content with a brief from the executive vice-president in Boston, a contract signed by the Calcutta-based managing director of the Indian subsidiary and a working alliance with the manager of the mill itself, where I was based, twenty miles outside Calcutta on the banks of the Hooghly river. My overall task was to help to bring about a cultural change, and for that my client, as I saw it then and would see it today, was the total system, although for different phases I expected to be – and in practice was – working with specific sub-systems.

The cultural change envisaged had two elements. The first was what McGregor (1960) was later to describe as a transition from Theory X to Theory Y. My management training days in New York had been part of this strategy in the US mills; the Indian mill was starting from further back. Bosses gave orders; workers obeyed. Apart from a small nucleus of senior managers, the proposition that workers who were treated as responsible would behave more responsibly was unheard of, and even in this nucleus some were ambivalent. The second element was what we called 'Indianization'. There were still about twenty expatriate managers and engineers at the mill, mainly from the USA and UK, and with the recruitment of more qualified Indians the status hierarchy and the managerial hierarchy were becoming inconsistent. The not-so-long-term objective was a mill managed by Indians with perhaps a handful of expatriates in specialist roles.

On my way to Calcutta I had stopped off for a few days with Ken Rice, who was in Ahmedabad continuing his consultancy to the Calico Mills. This gave me a grasp of what he had been doing there in the development of semi-autonomous working groups in weaving, and I was able to apply his experience in designing the work organization for new, very broad looms for carpet-backing that Ludlow had just acquired. That began to demonstrate that workers actually could become more self-managing. For the rest, my role of change agent was accomplished through consultancy to the senior management group.

Two years later came another shift in my identity: unemployment. I had, with some ambivalence, rejected an offer to become assistant mill manager under an incoming (Indian) manager and had just signed a contract for another two years' consultancy when the holding company in the States was taken over and the new owners decided that they did not need an anthropologist.

Two Indian job offers came my way. One was a route back into applied anthropology: the post of 'rural life analyst' on a big rural development programme in Uttar Pradesh. The other was as an internal consultant in the Calico Mills – a full-time counterpart to Rice's visiting consultancy from the Tavistock Institute. The choice would have been much more difficult but for information that the government of Uttar Pradesh was paying salaries nine months in arrears: even with my golden handshake that would have been a problem. So it was to Ahmedabad that I went and, two years later – almost inevitably it seems – to London to join the staff of the Institute towards the end of 1958.

Those last two years in India were full of learning for me and seemed to benefit the client organization too. Rice described in *The Enterprise and its Environment* (1963) some of the work we did together at that time. Two points must be recorded. First, I learned somewhat painfully the limitations of internal consultancy. On one occasion I was concerned about a management decision which I believed would be detrimental to the form of work organization, in semi-autonomous groups, that Rice had initiated and that was being spread throughout the weaving departments. I protested to the chairman: explaining my reasons, I said, 'I want to dissociate myself from that decision.' His response was: 'Eric, as an employee the only way you can dissociate yourself is by resigning.' I did not resign, but ever since I have valued the greater independence of the external consultant. Even though it is a sanction I have actually exercised only once or twice, the fact that I can withdraw from a client relationship without sacrificing my livelihood enables me to hold on to my authority and integrity.

Second, that period consolidated my hugely valued relationship with Ken Rice: a mentor who became a close colleague and friend. After India, we worked together in a wide range of settings – industry, commerce, the public sector, health and welfare, among others – before his premature death in 1969 at the age of only sixty-one. Eventually I was able to express some of my debt to him in an edited volume of papers building on his work: *Task and Organization* (Miller, 1976a).

And that brings me to this book, which gives a sampling of my own work – some collaborative, some individual – over the last thirty years. It offers a mixture of previously published pieces, including one in collaboration with Rice, and a few examples of what we call in the trade 'working notes'. These are interim papers which put forward preliminary ideas and working hypotheses as a basis for discussion with the client. Among published papers I have, with one exception, excluded those that are reasonably accessible or have been reprinted in other collections. Several, for example, have been reproduced in the *Group Relations Readers* published by the A.K. Rice Institute (Colman and Bexton, 1975; Colman and Geller, 1985). Others have come out in the first two of the three-volume series, *The Social Engagement of Social Science: A Tavistock Anthology* (Trist and Murray, 1990, 1993), or are accepted for the later volumes. The one exception is a paper entitled 'Organizational development and industrial democracy'

(Miller, 1977), from which I include extracts in Chapters 1 and 11; that was reprinted in Colman and Geller (1985).

One consequence of this criterion is that the Institute's Group Relations Programme, which I have been associated with since 1959 and co-directed or directed since 1969, is here referred to only briefly, mainly in Chapter 1. A fairly full account of it is given in a Tavistock Institute Occasional Paper (Miller, 1989), which is reproduced in a slightly abbreviated form in the first Trist–Murray volume (Miller, 1990). As many readers will know, this programme mounts the annual 'Leicester' Conference and other events devoted to the experiential study of group and organizational processes. These have been pivotal in my own personal and professional development and encapsulate much of what I stand for. First, they focus on the interrelatedness of individual, group, organization, community and society, which has been an abiding intellectual and practical interest dating back to my identity as an anthropologist, if not earlier. Second, they convinced me of the relevance of the psychodynamic perspective. That, combined with the systemic perspective, has equipped me with a conceptual framework that has become central in most of my work. The third influence relates to values. The central aim of these conferences is to offer individuals a way of examining and understanding how they get caught up in unconscious processes, so that they can learn to exercise their own authority. That theme, of helping people to gain greater influence over their environment, underlies virtually all of my work in action research and consultancy as well as education and training.

Nowadays some people would call this 'empowerment'. It is a term I avoid because of its ambiguity: between *becoming* more powerful and *making* more powerful. The notion of *giving* power is inherently patronizing – it implies dependency – and hence is of itself *dis*empowering. Power cannot be given, only taken. That having been said, power and dependency are central issues for a consultant working with organizations.

As I wrote at the beginning of the first paper in this collection, organizational consultancy is, among other things, a political process. It inevitably has some influence, small or large, on the distribution of power in the organization. My first inkling of this was in the Indian jute mill, where Indianization of management was beginning to upset the taken-for-granted status and privileges of the white expatriates. It was borne in on me much more strongly in the 1970s and early 1980s, when I was involved with rural development programmes in several Third World countries (see Chapter 10). Even when trying to be the scholarly social anthropologist, I had gradually (albeit reluctantly) begun to learn that the objective social scientist is a myth. What I perceived and failed to perceive in the societies I was working in was influenced by my own predispositions, conscious and unconscious, by the culture I came from and by the inevitably selective nature of the relationships I made in the culture I was visiting. However, when I became a practitioner I still held on to an ideal of being the detached and neutral professional. And indeed a degree of detachment goes with the job. I have to stand back far enough to discover alternative ways of looking at a situation, ways that may be less accessible to those who are caught up in it. I may then help them too to acquire a kind of observing ego. Joining the Tavistock and learning about the transference and countertransference showed me that involvement was not something that one just had to try to minimize: it could be used positively as a means of understanding a situation. The consultant was a measuring instrument and we had to try to develop mechanisms for calibrating ourselves so as to correct for some of the distortions. Like most of my colleagues at that time I went into personal analysis as a means of doing this. However, that still does not fully address the political dimension raised by the examples of Indianization in the jute mill and rural development in peasant societies. There I was plainly taking sides and engaged in a process of redistributing power. In other settings this is much less obvious and too easily goes unrecognized. For example, when colleagues and I were working with industrial clients on the development of new forms of work organization based on 'semi-autonomous work groups', our motivation was to achieve greater effectiveness and greater satisfaction. From my own point of view, at any rate, I did not see myself as promoting 'empowerment'. Indeed, naïve though it may seem in retrospect, I was at times taken aback when innovations foundered partly because they were seen as threats to the established power structure. So I learned the hard way that, like it or not, issues of power are integral to the consultant role and I had better be much more alert to them. I have more to say about this in later chapters.

There is at least some correlation between the power that the consultant exercises, whether knowingly or unknowingly, and the dependence of the client system on the consultant. A degree of dependence is inherent in the nature of the relationship, because the consultant is hired as having some expertise that the client lacks. That I would call a mature dependence. Usually, however, more than that is involved. Investment in the consultant of expectations and hopes that go beyond what can realistically be achieved is an indication of an immature, almost primitive state of dependency. One of the insights I gained from my own analysis is that I have a proclivity to get caught in a collusive relationship of that kind: part of me would love to be the St George who kills the dragon and rescues the damsel in distress. Psychoanalysis did not cure me of that, but nowadays I have an internal early warning system: I become conscious of it much sooner. Some consultants seem to become anxious about such dependency. In my view, it is a necessary part of the relationship. Change, even when intellectually people see it as necessary and desirable, always arouses anxiety. It is part of my task as a consultant to contain some of that anxiety so that members of the client system are not crippled by it. Dependency is therefore not to be avoided but managed during the phase in which they are gaining greater mastery over the situation. My task is then to become redundant. The intervention will be successful if clients have transformed the dependence on me into fuller exercise of their own authority and competence.

Never has so much been owed to so many . . . : colleagues, clients and (an overlapping category) friends, from whom I have spent my life learning and who have provided encouragement and support. Some are named as contributors to pieces in this volume: Wesley Carr, Geraldine Gwynne (now Eynstone), Olya Khaleelee (who is also my wife), Gordon Lawrence, and the late Ken Rice. Others are referred to above or the chapters which follow. The rest, sadly, have to remain unnamed, but not unremembered.

However, in relation to this book, specific thanks are due to Jon Stokes, for advising on selection of papers from a much wider array;

to a publisher's reader – anonymous, but I think I know who he is – for comments that were helpful if not always adulatory; to Edith Crowther, for her patience and care in typing, photocopying and assembling all the material; and to Anita Kermode for doing a quite exceptional job as copy-editor. The responsibility for any flaws and inconsistencies that remain is, of course, mine.

Acknowledgements are due to Van Gorcum & Comp., B.V., for permission to include, in Chapter 1, extracts from 'The open-system approach to organization analysis, with special reference to the work of A.K. Rice', in G. Hofstede and M. Sami Kassem, eds *European Contributions to Organization Theory*, 1976, pp. 43–61; to the Bishop of Chelmsford for permission to publish the material in Chapter 5; to the Northern Ireland Office for permission to publish the material in Chapter 6; to the British Diplomatic Spouses Association for permission to reproduce, in Chapter 7, 'Some reflections on the role of the diplomatic wife', *Diplomatic Service Wives Association Newsletter*, Spring 1978, pp. 13–27; to the Controller of Her Majesty's Stationery Office and Croom Helm Ltd for permission to reproduce, in Chapter 12, an edited version of 'Autonomy, dependency and organizational change', in D. Towell and C. Harries, eds *Innovation in Patient Care: An Action Research Study of Change in a Psychiatric Hospital*, 1979, pp. 172–90 (Crown Copyright); to Routledge for permission to reproduce, in Chapter 13, O. Khaleelee and E.J. Miller, 'Beyond the small group: society as an intelligible field of study', in M. Pines, ed. *Bion and Group Psychotherapy*, 1985, pp. 353–83; to OPUS: an Organization for Promoting Understanding in Society for permission to reproduce, in Chapter 14, extracts from 'OPUS Conference Report: "After 1984: New Directions", September 28–29, 1985', OPUS *Bulletin 20–21*, Part II, 1985; to Jossey-Bass Ltd for permission to reproduce, in Chapter 15, my paper entitled 'Making room for individual autonomy', in S. Srivastva and Associates, *Executive Power*, 1986, pp. 257–88.

PART ONE:
TOWARDS A CONCEPTUAL FRAMEWORK

1   VALUES AND CONCEPTS

This chapter brings together extracts from earlier publications as a statement of the professional values and the concepts that I bring to my research and consultancy at the Tavistock Institute.

ON VALUES

An action research or consultancy intervention cannot but be a political activity, at least insofar as it promotes some values and not others. Professional status, despite the claims often made for it, does not place the practitioner beyond the realm of values. Even in medicine, where the myth of purity and disinterest dies hard, values intrude in crude and subtle ways. The doctor who decides to give one patient better treatment than another is thereby engaging in a political act – regardless of whether his motives are economic or humanitarian. Less obviously, the decision to treat both patients equally, on the premiss that all lives are equally important, is also a political decision, since it implements one particular set of values. If even the treatment of individuals has political connotations, in the 'treatment' of organizations they are patently much more significant. Hence my contention that the responsible professional has to try to make explicit the values that, consciously and perhaps less consciously, bear upon this role. Although we are intellectually

From Miller, 1976c, and Miller, 1977, with slight editorial changes.

aware of the problem, social scientists in general do not pay enough attention to the way in which values enter into the selection of conceptual frameworks and measuring instruments. It is not only the consultant who is in the game of political intervention. Frameworks and instruments that appear to be objective and scientific nevertheless favour certain interpretations of 'reality' and preclude others. The 'pure' research worker too is affecting the organization he is studying simply by being selective – unavoidably so – in the people he addresses and in the assumed roles in which they are addressed: he is not neutral. As Heisenberg pointed out, a sub-atomic physicist can demonstrate that electrons have wave-like properties; but another, taking another perspective and using different measuring instruments, can show that electrons behave as particles. Out of the range of properties of a situation, we see those that we are predisposed to look for. Hence we have an obligation to try to specify our predispositions.

In the 1960s, my colleague Kenneth Rice and I concluded a book with these words: 'Long-term solutions to the problem of maintaining adaptiveness to change cannot . . . depend on manipulative techniques. On the contrary, they must depend on helping the individual to develop greater maturity in controlling the boundary between his own inner world and the realities of his external environment' (Miller and Rice, 1967, p. 269). This theme and the values implied in it have continued to be dominant in my own work and thinking, and also for a number of colleagues in the Tavistock Institute and Clinic and associates outside. If I were rewriting that paragraph now, I would want to reword it in a couple of places. The phrase 'adaptiveness to change' might imply that change is an extraneous – almost suprahuman – process and that all we ordinary mortals can do is to make less or more satisfactory adjustments to it; hence I would prefer now to speak of 'management of change', so as to imply that we ourselves by our decisions and actions create the future: we can be proactive, not merely adaptive. Secondly, 'controlling the boundary . . .' could sound negative, as if the impulses and fantasies of the inner world should be inhibited; whereas my concern is with making the most fruitful use of one's internal resources: some are appropriately held out of one situation and brought forward in another. Consequently, 'understanding and managing the boundary . . .' might be a better formulation. But these are clarifications and refinements: I remain committed to the essence of the earlier statement. A major preoccupation of mine, therefore, as of many colleagues, has been the relationship – indeed the tension – between individual and group, individual and organization: 'An individual has . . . no meaning except in relation to others with whom he interacts. He uses them, and they him, to express views, take action and play roles. The individual is a creature of the group, the group of the individual' (Miller and Rice, 1967, p. 17). At times he is swallowed by the group, at times struggling for separateness.

INFLUENCES OF LEWIN AND BION

This focus has demanded a conceptual framework within which the relationship can be examined. Here Kurt Lewin had a significant influence on my early Tavistock colleagues in the late 1940s. The Tavistock group shared his conviction that conventional modes of scientific analysis would not uncover the 'Gestalt' properties of complex human systems. For example, as Lewin pointed out, whereas in the history of physics the reality of wholes was taken for granted and it was 'the reality of the atom, the electron, or whatever else was considered at that time to be the smallest part of physical material' that tended to be called into question, 'in the social sciences it has usually been not the part but the whole whose existence has been doubted':

> There is no more magic behind the fact that groups have properties of their own, which are different from the properties of their subgroups or individual members, than behind the fact that molecules have properties which are different from the properties of the atoms or ions of which they are composed . . . In the social as in the physical field the structural properties of a dynamic whole are different from the structural properties of subparts. Both sets of properties have to be investigated . . . (Lewin, 1947, p. 8)

And as a way of looking at groups and institutions as 'dynamic wholes', Lewin's field theory (see, for example, Lewin, 1950) was evidently productive. For example, an early Tavistock study of labour turnover (Rice *et al.*, 1950) showed not only that a significant social process could be inferred from numerous individual actions but also that this process attained an equilibrium over time: 'The results are reconcilable with the theory that labour turnover is that resultant of a quasi-stationary process which acts as a self-regulating mechanism . . .' (Wilson, 1951, p. 21). Lewin's application of topology (a branch of geometry) in building models of psychological and social systems (Lewin, 1936) especially attracted Rice and he used topological representations in most of his writings from 1950 onwards.

A second significant influence on Tavistock staff at that time was the work of Wilfred Bion on groups. His series of seven papers was being published in *Human Relations* (Bion, 1948–51) and some staff had been members of Bion-led groups, in which the task was to study the behaviour of the group as a whole. Bion's postulate is that at any one time a group can be analysed as operating at two levels: it is a *sophisticated group* (or *work group*) met to perform an overt task; and it is a *basic group*, acting on one of three covert basic assumptions (fight–flight, dependence and pairing), to which its individual members contribute anonymously and in ways of which they are not consciously aware. Rice applied Bion's concepts in his analysis of an expanding machine-shop (Rice, 1951). He showed how, when a prospective change confronted workers in the department with a severe dilemma, they unconsciously developed leadership at two levels (which Rice called the levels of 'reality' and 'irreality') through which their ambivalence could be contained. Their dilemma was that

> severe competition in the market for their product demanded faster production methods, but this meant a reduction in the number of workers on particular jobs and consequent disruption of working relationships; further, to resist such reorganization would aggravate fears of future lay-off, but to accept reorganization would . . . incur hostility from workers in other departments. (Wilson, 1951, p. 15)

The mechanism used was a small negotiating group, whose ostensible task was to reach settlement of a wage dispute, but whose latent task was to encapsulate workers' sentiments of fight against management. With these feelings deposited in the negotiating group, the workers were free to collaborate with management in the task of expansion and reorganization for the fight against competing firms. Negotiations were unusually protracted over more than a year, until this task was completed, at which point the negotiating group, having fulfilled its latent function, could quickly reach agreement and be disbanded. Brown (1967, p. 40) has argued that such a post factum interpretation may be plausible, but it does not test a theory and is difficult to falsify. However, it does provide an analytical model which can be tested for its effectiveness in illuminating other situations.

Bion's theories were a special case of the strong influence of psychoanalytic thinking on the work of the Tavistock Institute. The Tavistock Clinic, out of which the Institute had developed, was psychoanalytically oriented and Bion, who himself was a practising psychoanalyst, drew heavily on the theories of Melanie Klein. Here I want to concentrate on the extent to which psychoanalysis provided a role-model for Tavistock staff. As I have argued elsewhere (Miller, 1976b), there has been no single Tavistock role-model: for example, Jaques (1951), Sofer (1961), and Rice (1963) all described their positions differently. Commonalities, however, are more important. Nearly all Tavistock research at that time (and most of it since) was, like clinical research in medicine, conducted through a professional relationship, within which the research-worker was usually also a consultant and was always taking professional responsibility for the consequences of his interventions for the client system. There was a shared recognition that both individuals and groups develop mechanisms to give meaning to their existence and to defend themselves from fear and uncertainty; that these defences, often unconscious and deeply rooted, are threatened by change; and that consequently it is an important aspect of the professional role to serve as a container during the 'working through' of change, so as to tackle not only the overt problem but also the underlying difficulties. Additionally – and this comes directly from the psychoanalytic model – there was a shared belief in the importance of the transference and countertransference in such a relationship: that is to say, the consultant's feelings may provide significant evidence about underlying feelings within the client system. Lewin had defined action research as 'a comparative research on the conditions and effects of various form of social action, and research leading to social action' (1946, p. 35). My proposition is that the particular action research role adopted by Tavistock staff, who were professionally involved in experiments in the laboratory of real life, directly influenced the types of theoretical constructs that they generated. For example, their models for understanding organization needed to be communicable to client groups and needed to take account of sources of resistance to change. Research conducted from other roles would tend to generate other types of model (Miller, 1976b).

OPEN SYSTEM THEORY

A further major and continuing influence on Tavistock thinking about organization from the early 1950s onwards was the concept of open systems. Systemic thinking was not, of course, novel: Lewin's use of it has already been mentioned. Already too there had emerged, mainly from the Institute's early studies of coal-mining (Trist and Bamforth, 1951), the concept of the socio-technical system. This provided a way of examining, and possibly reconciling, the relationship between the psycho-social and the techno-economic elements of purposeful organizations. Classical organization theory had subordinated the human element to technological imperatives (a view that still persists in much contemporary 'scientific management'); countering this 'structural universalism' the so-called 'human relations school' had responded by an equivalent 'psychological universalism' (see Lupton, 1976), which sought to demonstrate that organizations could be changed and performance improved by manipulating only the psycho-social variables, such as leadership style (and again this assumption has persisted in the work of such writers as McGregor, Likert and Blake and of many contemporary OD practitioners). The concept of the socio-technical system, therefore, opened up possibilities of jointly optimizing the two types of variables and thus of organizational choice (see Trist *et al.*, 1963; also Rice, 1958, 1963; Miller, 1959, 1975; Emery and Trist, 1960). But its immediate application was at the level of the primary work group rather than the wider organization. The notion of the open system made it possible to look simultaneously both at the relationship between social and technical and also at the relationships between the part and the whole, the whole and the environment. *Inter alia*, it provided a further way of conceptualizing the relationships that especially preoccupy me – between individual and group, individual and enterprise. And, despite the assertion by Lewin quoted above, it showed that 'the structural properties of the whole' might not be so different from 'the structural properties of subparts': both could be seen as having similar systemic characteristics. Consequently, the concept of the open system derived from von Bertalanffy (1950a, 1950b) was eagerly seized. So far as I know, the first published acknowledgement of his influence on Tavistock came two years later in a paper on 'Institutional and sub-institutional determinants of change in labour turnover' (Rice and Trist, 1952). Open system thinking was already implicit in the labour turnover studies, which had essentially identified a process of organizational metabolism; but the clear distinction between closed physical systems and open living systems had not then been recognized. As Rice said later:

> physical closed systems are mechanically self-sufficient, neither importing nor exporting.
> Classical organizational models are for the most part based on closed systems. The implicit assumption is made that the organizational problems of an enterprise can be analysed by reference only to its internal environment . . .
> A major disadvantage of using a closed system as an analogy for the analysis of an enterprise's organization is that, in a physical closed system, final equilibrium is obtained only when maximum entropy is reached, that is, when all energy has been converted into heat and the result is thermo-dynamic equilibrium. In such an equilibrium the system can do no more work. Though maximum entropy is in practice seldom achieved, it is unfortunate that the analogy should have such an ideal, if impractical, outcome . . . (Rice, 1963, p. 183)

Functionalism in the social sciences had been linked to closed system models and consequently, as Merton acknowledged, there had been a tendency 'to focus on the statics of social structure and to neglect the study of structural change' (Merton, 1957, p. 53).

Merton therefore proposed the concept of 'dysfunction', 'which implies the concept of strain, stress and tension on the structural level' as providing 'an analytical approach to the study of dynamics and change' (p. 53). However,

> this concept . . . while it draws attention to sources of imbalance within an organization . . . does not conceptually reflect the mutual permeation of an organization and its environment that is the cause of such imbalance. It still retains the limiting perspective of 'closed system' theorizing. (Emery and Trist, 1960, pp. 84–5)

Open systems, by contrast, 'exist and can only exist by the exchange of materials with their environment'. 'The process of importing, converting, and exporting materials is the work the system has to do to live' (Rice, 1963, pp. 184, 183). To quote Emery and Trist again:

> The . . . conception of 'open systems' carries the logical implications that such systems may spontaneously reorganize towards states of greater heterogeneity and complexity and that they achieve a 'steady state' at a level where they can still do work. Enterprises appear to possess at least these characteristics of 'open systems'. They grow by processes of internal elaboration and manage to achieve a steady state while doing work, i.e. achieve a quasi-stationary equilibrium in which the enterprise as a whole remains constant, with a continuous 'throughput', despite a considerable range of external changes. (1960, p. 85)

Von Bertalanffy (1950a) pointed to one further characteristic of open systems: the principle of equifinality proposes that a given final state may be reached from different initial conditions and by different routes. This is obviously relevant to the analysis of enterprises and to the design of organization.

BOUNDARIES

A key connecting concept, derived from open system thinking, is that of *boundary*. It has become a statement of the obvious to say that an enterprise or institution can survive only through a continuous interchange of materials with its environment. There are the materials that the enterprise distinctively exists to process –

thus a manufacturing company converts raw materials into saleable products (and waste), a college converts freshmen into graduates (and drop-outs) – and there are the other resources that are required to bring about the processing: the production workers, the teachers, the machinery, the supplies, etc. The boundary across which these materials flow in and out both separates the enterprise from and links it with its environment. It marks a discontinuity between the task of the enterprise and the tasks of those other systems in its environment with which it transacts. Because these relationships are never stable and static, because its behaviour and identity are subject to perpetual renegotiation and redefinition, the boundary of the enterprise is best conceived not as a line but as a region. The inner boundary of this region interfaces with the internal sub-systems through which the conversion work of the enterprise – the transformation of intakes into outputs – is conducted, the outer boundary with the related external systems. Thus the boundary region may be seen as the location of those roles and activities which are concerned with mediating relations between outside and inside. For example, the leadership exercised in this region can protect the internal sub-systems from the disruption of fluctuating demands from outside; but it also has to promote those internal changes that will enable the enterprise to be adaptive and indeed proactive in relation to the environment. Survival is therefore contingent on an appropriate degree of insulation and permeability in the boundary region.

This conception is equally applicable to a sub-system within an enterprise, such as a production department. In this case, the rest of the enterprise constitutes a major part of the environment.

Analysis of Production Systems As Open Systems

The paper by Rice and Trist (1952), cited earlier, acknowledged the fruitfulness of von Bertalanffy's concept to their analysis of labour turnover but implied that the authors had not yet grasped the full extent of its relevance to the analysis of enterprises. This had to await publication in 1958 of Rice's *Productivity and Social Organization*, in which he also introduced the concept of primary task.

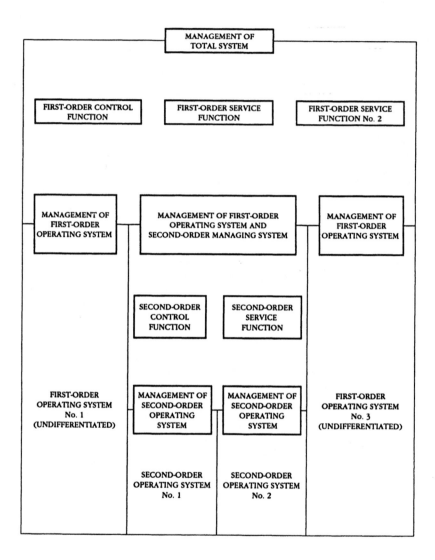

Fig 1.2 Operating and managing systems of the first and second orders of differentiation

From Rice, 1958, p. 44. Reproduced with permission of the Tavistock Institute of Human Relations.

It will be apparent that, along with this open system model, Rice was introducing a conception of management and supervision that was – and to many people still is – unfamiliar. Thus in the experimental loom-sheds it was the shift supervisor's job not to tell individual workers what to do, but to provide the boundary conditions which enabled the work groups within his shift to get on with their task – for example, it was his responsibility to make sure that the necessary resources of trained personnel and materials were available. Managers of the successively higher-order systems – sections, departments, etc. – had a corresponding responsibility for maintaining the boundary conditions for their sub-systems. A follow-up study in 1970 of Rice's weaving experiments showed that the survival of the 'group system' as an effective form of work organization was related to this conception of management and supervision (Miller, 1975). Where work groups retained their autonomy, and supervisors and managers conceived their task as providing the necessary boundary conditions, the results of the original experiments were fully sustained: indeed, productivity was as high and the quality of cloth produced even higher in 1969–70 than it had been in 1954. On the other hand, in locations where supervisors were working on the assumption that poor perfor- mance of a work group was not a phenomenon for which the group, through its leader, could be held accountable, but rather something to be remedied through intensive control over individ- uals, productivity was lower than it had been in 1954 and signs of stress more pronounced.

The Individual as an Open System

If we turn now to the individual, who provides a basic component in the enterprise (a statement on which I shall expand presently), the open system and psychoanalytic conceptions, taken together, allow us to construct a very similar model (Rice, 1969). In the individual, the boundary region may be equated with the ego function. The inner world of the individual includes experiences, emotions, attitudes and skills of which he is largely conscious and which, through the ego function, can be appropriately mobilized or suppressed in the service of whatever goal he is pursuing and role he is taking, at a particular moment of time. The inner world can also be conceived as being populated, as it were, by a set of 'objects' and 'part-objects', which are the residual representations of earlier – including infantile – experiences of relations with others (see Klein, 1959). Thus the individual, when he engages in adult life with, for example, a new boss, will not simply respond in a rational way to what the boss actually says and does, but he will bring forward, from his internal repertoire of objects and part-objects, his experience of earlier authority figures, including mother and father. These will underlie the new relationship and so affect his perceptions.

Both enterprise and individual, therefore, can be conceived as open systems, engaged in continuing transactions with an environment; each has a boundary region exercising a regulatory function mediating between the inner world and the environmental systems with which it interacts. (A group, of course, may also be thought of in similar terms.) I shall return to the relationship between individual and enterprise.

THE CONCEPT OF THE PRIMARY TASK

Rice's 1958 book also introduced the concept of primary task. Rice pointed out that a production system will perform many tasks, including, for example, making profits, manufacturing and selling goods, providing employment and also, at both conscious and unconscious levels, providing 'mechanisms for the satisfaction of social and psychological needs and for defence against anxiety'. Each part of the system has its own sub-set of tasks, and tasks also vary over time.

> Each system or sub-system has, however, at any given time, one task which may be defined as its *primary task – the task which it is created to perform* . . . In making judgements about any organization two questions have priority over all others: What is the primary task? How well is it performed? (Rice, 1958, pp. 32–3; author's italics)

Rice compared his definition of 'primary task' with Bion's definition of 'sophisticated task' as 'the specific task for which a work-group meets' (Rice, 1958, p. 229, citing Bion, 1948–51), and said that the primary task included the sophisticated task, but might also include other tasks undertaken by a group, of which its members might or might not be completely aware. Thus, going back to the machine-shop case, 'although the apparent task of [the] negotiating group was to settle a wage dispute, its primary task was to encapsulate a conflict between management and workers about a programme of expansion' (1958, p. 229). There was obviously room for confusion here, and subsequently Rice redefined primary task as the task that an institution or part-institution at any given time 'must perform to survive' (Rice, 1963, p. 17; Miller and Rice, 1967, p. 25). Miller and Rice go on to say:

> The primary task is essentially a heuristic concept, which allows us to explore the ordering of multiple activities (and of constituent systems of activity where these exist). It makes it possible to construct and compare different organizational models of an enterprise based on different definitions of its primary task; and to compare the organizations of different enterprises with the same or different primary tasks. The definition of the primary task determines the dominant import–conversion–export system . . . (1967, p. 25)

But the concept was still subject to criticism. Fox (1968) pointed out that the same term was being used to refer to what was objectively necessary for survival of an enterprise and to what, subjectively, its members believed was necessary; while Silverman (1968) objected to reifying organizations by attributing to them 'goals' or 'needs'. Lawrence (Lawrence and Robinson, 1975) has offered a helpful clarification by making explicit the hitherto partly implicit distinction between:

1 the *normative* primary task as the task that people in an organization *ought* to pursue (usually according to the definition of a superordinate authority),
2 the *existential* primary task as that which they believe they are carrying out, and
3 the *phenomenal* primary task which it is hypothesized that they are engaged in and of which they may not be consciously aware.

Indeed, I would look upon 'primary task' not as a property of an organization but as an exploratory tool of the consultant–client relationship (Miller, 1976b). As Rice said earlier, it is 'a starting-point for making decisions about change' (Rice, 1963, p. 185). Alternative organizational models can be constructed for different definitions of the primary task. Various groupings in the enterprise can then work with the consultant and with each other in considering the alternatives and comparing them with the existing organization. These dialogues generate hypotheses to explain divergences between the phenomenal, existential and normative definitions of primary task, and out of this process a more explicit understanding of task and constraints may emerge. In particular, it may become possible to identify ways in which a given form of organization provides defensive mechanisms for its members. I emphasize that this is a dialectical process, because criticisms levelled against the work of Rice, myself, and others using systemic models include charges of 'a failure to distinguish "is" and "ought" propositions' and 'a commitment to a primary prescriptive frame of reference' (Silverman, 1970, p. 120). The approach is not prescriptive in the sense of telling people what they ought to do; but it does involve drawing attention to factors that members of a group need to take into account if they desire to pursue its stated task more effectively.

INDIVIDUAL AND ORGANIZATION

Now what the normative primary task requires from people is only their contribution of activities, their roles. The roles that individuals bring to the task belong inside the boundary of the enterprise; the individuals who provide the roles belong outside: they are among the more important elements in the environment with which the enterprise has to interact. This implies, therefore, that the appropriate perspective for examining the relationship between the enterprise and the individuals who supply roles within it – and, indeed, whose role-taking gives the enterprise its existence – is an inter-systemic perspective: it is a relationship between the enterprise as a system and individuals (and groupings of individuals) as systems.

This perspective is difficult to hold on to. As Goffman puts it succinctly: 'every institution has encompassing tendencies' (Goffman, 1961, p. 15). The group or the enterprise draws upon, and the individual colludes in supplying, more than the requisite role. The individual requires group membership to give meaning, to confer status, to confirm his picture of himself, his identity; and also, as Bion demonstrated, he uses the group to express what appear to be quite primitive feelings in the areas of dependency, aggression and hope. The individual is usually unaware of this process: these basic emotions slip under the guard, as it were, of his ego function. He thus finds his supports and defences in what have been called sentient groups, which may or may not correspond to the boundaries of the task groups – the socio-technical sub-systems – in which he exercises his work-role (Miller and Rice, 1967). Although his role in the enterprise does not predetermine the relative sentience for him of the various groups to which he belongs, which will be located both outside and inside the enterprise, these memberships are nevertheless relevant to the effectiveness of task performance, supporting or opposing it.

As a consequence, the relationship between individual and enterprise is usually not seen, by either part, as a relationship between two systems, one of which supplies a role for the other; much more commonly it is seen from both perspectives as a relationship between part and whole – as if the individual were a sub-system of the enterprise as a supra-system. For the interdependence of the inter-systemic relationship there tends to be substituted the dependence of the subordinate–superior relationship. It is a necessary condition for the survival of the enterprise that the leadership function – the regulation of the boundary between outside and inside – should be credible to those who contribute roles to it (as well as to the external systems). Indeed, an enterprise as such is no more than the product of the shared beliefs of those outside and inside that it exists and that the organizational boundaries of the enterprise as a whole and of its parts are located in particular places. Its survival is therefore contingent on the sanctioning of the role-holders on these boundaries by the role-holders inside them. Consequently, some degree of dependence is realistic. But the encompassing tendency of institutions exaggerates this dependency. Those on the boundary tend to receive and assume power and prestige that go beyond the sanctioned authority for the boundary role. Correspondingly, those inside are surrendering power and prestige to those in the boundary positions. The reciprocal dependence of the boundary role-holders on the role-holders inside goes unrecognized; it gets forgotten that there can be no leaders without followers.

Following Bion's formulation, we may ask what happens in this situation to emotions associated with 'fight'. Often they are deposited in the trade union. The employee can use his union to express his aggression and hostility by contesting with an undifferentiated 'management', and this preserves the dependency of the individual superior–subordinate relationship. 'Unofficial' actions, such as wild-cat strikes, evoke considerable anxiety because they threaten to impinge on and to question the unassailability of the dependent relationship.

CONFERENCES FOR THE STUDY OF GROUP RELATIONS

The set of values, concepts and methods discussed here is expressed in a particular approach to group relations training with which I have been closely involved. This approach derives much from the pioneering work of Rice and Turquet at the Tavistock Institute in the early 1960s (see especially Rice, 1965) and has been carried on by Turquet, myself and other colleagues in recent years both at the Tavistock and in other institutions (including, in the United States, what is now the A.K. Rice Institute). Bion (1948–51) had established a mode of working with groups in which individual behaviour was explained in the context not of personality variables but of processes occurring in the group as a whole. The interpretative focus, by analogy with psychoanalysis, was the relationship between the group and Bion as consultant. This method was established as having not only therapeutic but educational relevance. Early group relations training conferences organized by the Tavistock Institute in the 1950s were primarily devoted to using the method to give participants experience of the behaviour of small groups (of ten to twelve members) and to reflect on its applications to their own roles (Trist and Sofer, 1959). In

1959, Bridger extended the method to the study of inter-group behaviour (Higgin and Bridger, 1964). Subsequently, other events were added to the conferences. These included the 'Large Group', which explores the processes that occur in a group of between forty and eighty members with perhaps four consultants. This is not an unstructured group, since there is at least the role differentiation between members and consultants, but it is a good deal less structured than most groups of this size, which in a work organization, for example, might include several different sections and hierarchical levels. Hence it probably displays dynamics that underlie formally structured groups, including anxieties against which structures provide some form of defence (see Turquet, 1975). (At the other end of the scale, some conferences now also provide for study of the potentially intimate relations within a 'Very Small Group' of five or six members.) A further extension from the 1960s onwards has been to provide opportunities to experience and study organizational relationships of a more complex kind: the focus in certain events is the 'here and now' relationship between the total membership and the total staff group within the conference as a whole, which is conceived as a temporary institution.

The conferences as they are operated today therefore offer a variety of settings within which to explore the interplay – or, as I called it earlier, tension – between individual and group, individual and organization. Except for some sessions set aside for review and application work, all the events are devoted to experiential learning from behaviour as it occurs. In contrast to certain other group methods (and there are many of them), the consultant in these conferences does not purport to be an uninvolved commentator on individual and interpersonal behaviour. On the contrary, what the members make of the role, authority and person of the consultant, and what he in turn experiences of their projections on to him, constitute primary data for the elucidation of group processes.

Correspondingly, the member has a chance to explore the part he plays in different kinds of authority relationships – for example, how far he is responding to what the other person is actually saying and doing, and how far he intrudes into the relationship primitive images of a benign or punitive authority that belong to his own

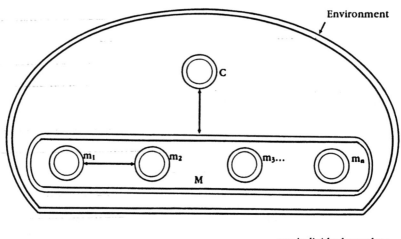

m = individual member
M = member group
C = consultant

Fig. 1.3 The consultant and the group: a systemic perspective

internal world. What he learns, therefore, is unique to him. He cannot be told what he 'ought to have learned': indeed, that phrase itself is an expression of dependence on authority. Other people, including the consultant, may offer their views of a situation, but only the individual member is in a position to understand, in light of the role he has, the relationship between what is happening around him and what is happening inside him; hence it is on his own authority that he accepts what is valid for him and rejects what is not.

Figure 1.3 illustrates the kind of systemic framework that I have in mind when I take a consultant role in such a conference. (The double line around individuals and groups depicts the boundary region, described earlier, between the inner world and the environment.) Transactions between individual members $m_1 \leftrightarrow m_2$ are to be understood in terms of a hypothesis about the relationship between the member group and the consultant, $M \leftrightarrow C$. The relationship M↔C in turn implies some image or fantasy of the wider system that includes both – the group or institution – and its relation to its environments. The same basic model can be extended to include the more complex situation, in which, for example, m may itself be a sub-group of members, M the total membership group, and C the staff of a conference, and thus the outer boundary is that of total conference as an institution. Application of this method to 'in-house' conferences – that is, where the members are all drawn from the same institution – has demonstrated repeatedly that assumptions about M↔C and about the containing system reflect significant, though often not overtly recognized, aspects of the culture of the institution from which the members are drawn.

These group relations training conferences, therefore, epitomize the main concepts, methods and values that I have attempted to describe. Conceptually, they use an open systems framework, together with propositions derived from psychoanalysis, to explore the relatedness between individual, group and organization. They suggest that important elements of the intakes and outputs of these systems are not merely material objects but images, fantasies and projections. The method too is derivative from psychoanalysis, in that it makes use of the various forms of transference in the client–consultant relationship as a means of illuminating dynamics within the client system. Finally, in terms of values, I see the conferences as vitally concerned with 'helping the individual to develop greater maturity in understanding and managing the boundary between his own inner world and the realities of his external environment' (Miller and Rice, 1967, p. 269). It is on his own authority that he decides what to do with this understanding in his roles in other institutions, whether as manager or managed. However, I acknowledge that I personally hope that he will acquire greater potency to question and perhaps change his relationship with his working environment.

PART TWO:
THREE STUDIES OF 'PEOPLE-PROCESSING' INSTITUTIONS

INTRODUCTION

The first and longest paper in this trio is a slightly shortened version of four chapters on airline organization taken from *Systems of Organization* (Miller and Rice, 1967). This is long out of print; but I have several other reasons for wanting to include it.

First and foremost, the airline research had sparked off a new way of conceptualizing organization, and it was to present this that we wrote the book. The key concept of the *socio-technical system*, formulated fifteen years previously by Trist and Bamforth (1951), had led to effective forms of group working – semi-autonomous groups – which optimized the psycho-social needs of the workers and the demands of the technical system. The versions that Rice himself developed in textiles (Rice 1958, 1963; Miller 1975) were an outstanding example. As we gained experience of consulting in a range of organizations, we found that whereas the model seemed to fit well in various manufacturing activities, there were other settings in which it was difficult to apply: for instance, in working with the management of companies undergoing rapid change; or in selling, where the essential task system is the transaction between salesperson and customer, which crosses the boundaries of two organizations. The airline offered another example. There the essential socio-technical system was a flight, which comprised a set of flying and cabin crew and an aircraft. We found, however, that it was rare for the same crew to stay together for more than one or two flights. This was partly due to the complexities of staff and aircraft scheduling and partly it was a deliberate policy: if the same group stayed together it was likely to develop idiosyncratic deviations from the strict standard procedures, a situation which might not be dangerous in itself but could become so when crew moved between groups with different practices and procedures. Arising from this, Rice and I drew a distinction between a *task system* – the set of activities, whether human or mechanical, through which a task is performed – and a *sentient system*, which meets people's needs for groupings to belong to. We argued there that 'any enterprise requires three forms of organization – the first, to control task performance; the second, to ensure the commitment of its members to enterprise objectives; and the third, to regulate relations between task and sentient systems' (Miller and Rice, 1967, p. xiii).

In the airline, the flights were temporary task systems; the sentient systems with which staff were identified were their 'professional' units or pools of flying crews and cabin staff. We called this a form of 'project' organization. Within this framework, the semi-autonomous work group, in which the boundaries of the task and sentient systems coincide, could be seen not as the universal elegant solution – an assumption that was becoming prevalent – but a special case. It was particularly appropriate to production systems in which the technology remained stable over fairly long periods, but the socio-psychological investment in the task system boundary was plainly a built-in obstruction to change.

The fact that the airline study stimulated real advances in our conceptualization of organization is a major reason for including the paper here, but it is not the only one. A second reason is that the model presented in the paper led to a significant shift in the thinking of the management of the airline concerned – British European Airways (BEA) – and to important organizational changes, which largely survived its merger three to four years later with the British Overseas Airways Corporation (BOAC). And despite technological advances over the last twenty-five years, there is little in the analysis that I would want to modify if I were writing today.

Third, the paper offers a fairly full example of the approach to the analysis and design of organizations outlined in Chapter 1, an approach I have continued to find useful and relevant in a whole range of other settings.

Finally, it presents an example of a 'people-processing' organization. Most of our previous studies had been in manufacturing systems such as textiles, where the input is an inanimate raw material (for example, raw cotton) which is converted through various processes into a finished product (woven cloth). In the textile mill, the plant – spinning frames and looms – is fixed and the material passes through it. In the airline the 'plant' – that is, the fleet of planes – is mobile and the throughput is human.

These were the characteristics that made the airline study attractive. The Tavistock Institute's first major piece of research into a people-processing organization had been by Isabel Menzies and led to her seminal paper on a hospital nursing service (Menzies, 1960). This had shown how the anxieties generated in nurses by interaction with the 'human throughput' of patients led to shared social defence mechanisms, which were embedded in the structure and culture of the hospital and in its mode of functioning. We postulated that an airline might display similar defences. And there was another complication: in the airline, profit was the ultimate criterion of performance.

Before the work with BEA was finished, I found myself involved with another type of people-processing organization: a residential establishment for people with severe physical disabilities. An appeal had come from the residents of a Cheshire Home, who felt they were suffering from a restrictive régime that failed to acknowledge their needs and capabilities as adult human beings. Could we at the Tavistock Institute help to make their home more of a therapeutic community? The then Ministry of Health funded an action research project, which I carried out with a colleague, Geraldine Gwynne (later Eynstone). We visited many institutions, studied half a dozen in some depth, and worked intensively with the original Cheshire Home, Le Court in Hampshire, which evolved a set of structures and a culture which allowed the residents to take more control over their own lives.

The paper reprinted here as Chapter 3 is based on parts of our book, A Life Apart (Miller and Gwynne, 1972). This turned out to have a significant influence in the whole field of residential care. It was reprinted several times, was the set book for an Open University course on 'The Handicapped in the Community', and still seems to be used in some courses on residential social work. (It also conferred on me an unwarranted identity as an expert on physical handicap.)

The book nevertheless offended some readers. During our study we were constantly struck by society's ambivalence towards its physically disabled members and by the hidden hypocrisy that went with it. Too often the language – of 'people just like us but with a disability', who were 'residents' in happy 'homes' – was empty rhetoric; the observable reality was that these people were set apart as cripples, extruded from their families and communities, to become inmates in institutions. To confront the hypocrisy, we purposely (though not without trepidation) chose to use that blunt terminology. Feedback indicated that the shock tactics, though offensive to some, prompted quite a lot of others to face the painful discrepancies between their words and their behaviour.

In a follow-up ten years later, Tim Dartington joined Geraldine Gwynne and me in a further piece of research on attitudes, drawing on studies of the relatedness between disabled and non-disabled people in, mainly, community care settings. We wanted to call our book *A Part of Life*, but settled for the publisher's choice, *A Life Together* (Dartington, Miller and Gwynne, 1981). Over the period there had been positive signs of change: the Chronically Sick and Disabled Persons Act of 1970; appointment of a Minister for the Disabled; an upsurge of pressure group activity; and much more media attention to disability. Actual improvements in provision were also visible: the new mobility allowance; wheelchair access to more public buildings; adaptations to some dwellings; the emergence of the Crossroads care attendant schemes (the outcome of a television series) – all these were beginning to create a less handicapping environment. The régimes in some residential establishments were also becoming a little more enlightened. But our study showed that the gap between professed attitudes and actual behaviour was as wide as ever.

In our society we also have difficulty – more than in many less 'advanced' societies – in relating to our elderly and dying members. This is evident in the third paper in this section, which is based on research in two geriatric hospitals between 1969 and 1973. Tim Dartington worked with me on both studies, together with Geraldine Gwynne on the first and another colleague, Penny Jones, on the second. Sheila Scott undertook all the analysis of records. Regrettably, our report never got published. I drafted this paper as a chapter for a book that also never happened, on the work of the Tavistock Institute in the health sector.

Once again, looking back after some twenty years, I am reasonably satisfied with the analysis of the issues but depressed by the lack of any real change. So long as we as a society continue to devalue our elderly and infirm members, responsibility for their care and they themselves will continue to be tossed between their families and an array of health and welfare agencies, while the minority of individuals who are personally committed to caring, whether as spouses, offspring, nurses or others paid for the task, will carry the emotional and often physical burden on behalf of everyone else.

2 TASK AND ORGANIZATION IN AN AIRLINE

AIRLINE OPERATIONS: TASK AND CONSTRAINTS

PRIMARY TASK, THROUGHPUT, AND BASIC ACTIVITIES REQUIRED

The primary task of any commercial airline may be defined in general terms as the transport of passengers and/or cargo by air at a profit – 'at a profit' being used as shorthand for 'in such a way as to secure the survival of the enterprise over the long term'. Financially, this means ensuring that revenue (for some airlines, of course, revenue plus subsidy) exceeds expenditure so that there is, in the long term, sufficient capital and credit for growth, development, and the replacement of equipment; and, in the short term, adequate working capital to run the services provided.

The process by which the airline performs its primary task is the transport of passengers and cargo from departure points to arrival points. The dominant intakes are therefore passengers and cargo; the conversion process turns them from departures into arrivals; and the outputs are the same passengers and cargo when they arrive.

The basic activities required to process passengers through this system are shown in Figure 2.1. A similar diagram, with rather

---

From Miller and Rice, 1967, pp. 184–221.

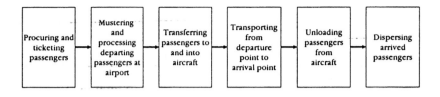

Fig. 2.1 The basic import-conversion-export activities for a
passenger throughput

different activities, could be drawn to show the process for cargo. Because a high proportion of airline revenue is derived from passenger-carrying, it is on this aspect of airline activities that we propose to concentrate.

Each of these activities is obviously susceptible to considerable elaboration. Procurement of passengers may require more active marketing – advertising, promotion, and selling – than mere publication of timetables. Mustering departing passengers may call for city terminals and transport between city and airport. Transferring passengers from check-in points in airport buildings to aircraft may involve shepherding them through customs and waiting rooms, making separate arrangements for their baggage, and supplying ground transport from building to aircraft. In the aircraft both passengers and crew may have to be fed and provided with other services during the flight.

PROFITABILITY, SAFETY, AND SERVICE

Safety is a costly preoccupation for every airline. Flying is, or, more importantly, is widely believed to be, inherently dangerous. Civil airlines throughout the world are accordingly governed by law to protect not only the passengers they carry but the people and property over whom and which they fly. Aircraft, aircrew, and engineers all have to be licensed by government agencies; flying height and direction, take-off and landing are subject to govern-ment-appointed traffic controls; and the kind of equipment for flying and landing that aircraft must carry is laid down by government orders. All reputable airlines not only obey both the letter and the spirit of the law but, in addition, take their own precautions and lay down strict rules to regulate conditions – regarding the weather and the state of the aircraft – under which flying is, and is not, permitted. As little as possible is left to chance.

It remains true, however, that just as the only 'safe' motor car is one that never leaves a garage, so the only 'safe' airline is one whose planes never leave the ground. Absolute safety – not only in airlines but in any other human activity – is an ideal that can never be achieved. To this extent, airline management has to accept that, for all the statutory regulations, and for all the additional precautions it may take, there is a limit beyond which the multiplication of safety devices and the addition of safety regulations cannot be justified in terms of risk reduction; indeed, they may increase risk. This is because in any human activity there must come a point at which the requirement to utilize yet another device or to observe still another regulation actually adds to danger by distracting those responsible for the activity from what they have to do. Operation of the device or compliance with the regulation occupies their attention and energy, and hence confuses rather than helps them in their task.

Airline management also has to steer an optimal course between safety and profitability. At some point a decision has to be made, explicitly or implicitly, that the reduction of risk likely to be achieved by installing new equipment or issuing new regulations is too small or uncertain to justify the expenditure involved; or alternatively that, because of improvements in technology, operating standards can be relaxed to increase revenue or reduce costs, on the grounds that any added risk is minute. For example, because of improved landing devices certain types of aeroplane may be allowed to land with lower cloud-ceilings than others, or because of built-in reliability some makes and types of engine may be permitted to fly for longer periods without overhaul.

The making of such decisions is likely to pose fewer problems for a subsidized airline, which could presumably, in the extreme, define its primary task as 'to run as safe an airline as is consistent with flying at all'. Such an airline need worry less about the effect on its competitive position of delays and cancellations because of weather conditions or 'technical faults'. Again, decisions of this order may be less critical for a scheduled airline than for a charter company. For such a company, which has to maintain a profit rate in the short term, safety can be a very costly constraint.

In the long term, however, airline safety is essential for profitability: an airline with an unacceptably high accident-rate loses passengers and therefore revenue. Thus, at the strategic level, there can be no major conflict between safety and reliability on the one hand, and profitability on the other. In day-to-day operations, in contrast, as we shall see later, safety and profitability – or, more strictly, safety and the maximization of revenue – are always in potential conflict. Take-off, for example, is governed by the weight that has to be lifted under varying weather conditions. Poor conditions limit pay-load: the greater the quantity of fuel that has to be carried, the fewer the passengers and the smaller the cargo that can be lifted. The amount of fuel taken depends on flying conditions and on the expected weather at the scheduled destination and at alternative landing-points. A 'superfluous' safety margin of 250 gallons of fuel might mean disembarking ten passengers, or the equivalent in freight, and incurring a corresponding loss of revenue.

In the case of any national airline, whether nationalized or not, the public definition of its primary task is commonly in terms of providing a service rather than making a profit. Public demand, often reinforced by government pressure, is for cheap, comfortable, frequent services, with seats available whenever required. But ready availability of seats means lower occupancy, which in turn means either lower revenue per flight or a higher fare per passenger. Similarly, the use of smaller aircraft to carry the same traffic by operating at greater frequencies involves higher capital costs and higher operating costs per seat. Profitability can be reduced if the airline yields either too little to such pressures or too much: a nice judgement is required.

OTHER ENVIRONMENTAL CONSTRAINTS

Operations of all airlines are controlled by national laws, international regulation, and intergovernmental agreements (bilateral and multilateral), which limit their freedom to operate services and to determine fares. For most airlines such freedoms are also further constrained by membership of IATA (International Air Transport Association) and by specific commercial agreements with other airlines. Such pool and consortium agreements may give an airline the protection that a cartel affords; but the accompanying restrictions may be the price that has to be paid for securing traffic rights.

We have already referred to the external traffic controls to which aircraft are partly or wholly subject between taxiing out at the beginning of a flight and taxiing in after landing. An additional constraint for most airlines is that airports and terminal buildings are usually owned, designed, built, and managed by other and different authorities, each of which has its own ideas of design and management. It is as though railway companies had to operate from stations none of which they owned and most of which were under different managements, and whose staff had different customs and spoke different languages.

The other major external constraint on airline operations, as all passengers know, is weather. Technical advances are combating this constraint – June 1965, for example, saw the first automatic landing of a scheduled passenger flight – but many years must elapse before all or even most of the disruptions to services caused by weather will be overcome.

A delay due to weather conditions inevitably affects the customer's attitudes towards flying generally and towards the airline concerned; and there is the added difficulty that the conditions causing the delay may not be at his departure point, but at the arrival point or *en route*, or even at the aircraft's earlier departure points. This would matter less if in the meantime the passenger did not see other aircraft, coming from or going to different places and flying different routes, arriving and taking off on time. Rationally, an explanation of the delay is readily comprehensible, but even rational comprehension is made more difficult for the layman if, because of different performances on take-off and landing, operating standards vary for different types of aircraft and for the same types on different airlines. It is particularly confusing when the standards are more stringent for the newer types than for the old, or when, because of greater familiarity with route or airport, one captain will fly when another will not.

Constraints Inherent in the Task

Delays, whether attributable to weather or to other causes, have the effect of marginally prolonging the 'shelf-life' of a product which, as someone has remarked, is more perishable than strawberries. For a transport undertaking or for a hotel, a seat or room not occupied is wasted. And, unlike a railway train, an aircraft cannot accommodate standing passengers who might make up for wasted seats on other services. It is a matter of semantics whether one defines the products of an airline as passenger seat miles and cargo ton miles or as arrived passengers and delivered cargo – we would favour the latter definition – but whether one treats the empty seats as unsold products or as superfluous resources they are part of the costs of scheduled airline operations. In a large airline a rise or fall of 1 per cent in load factor (the proportion of space occupied to space available) can represent £1 million [1965 prices] in revenue over the year and the difference between a profit and a loss. And because, in contrast to that in a manufacturing enterprise, the 'plant' – the physical resources required for the conversion process – in a transport undertaking is mobile, each arrival point is also a departure point. Consequently, even a full aircraft that has to return empty achieves only a 50 per cent pay-load. More generally, for an airline as for any transport undertaking, the market is forever shifting; its potential is a function of aircraft location and flight schedules.

'Mobile plant' creates another constraint: this is the need to standardize operations at the departure/arrival points that it connects. In an airline, where the points are numerous and widely scattered, local differences in law, custom, language, and even climate have to be surmounted in order to achieve the necessary standardization of procedure and adequate communications between the many parts of the enterprise. Administration of the stations by other authorities thus further complicates an inherent airline problem.

But of the constraints intrinsic to the task of a passenger airline perhaps the most significant are those that derive from the fact that the throughput of the process consists of human beings. We consider these constraints here in some detail and will be returning to them later.

CONSTRAINTS IMPOSED BY THE HUMAN THROUGHPUT

The problems arising from the nature of the throughput can, at least in theory, be considered as falling into three categories.

First, there are problems connected with the requirement that passengers surrender some of their individuality and exchange it for dependence on the airline. The apparently simple, reality-based, demand that the customer makes of a service enterprise is often complicated by less rational and less conscious demands; moreover, dependent relationships in themselves inevitably arouse anxiety and provoke hostility.

Second, there are problems associated with travelling away from home. It would appear that this is an experience that is dynamically similar to temporary separation from the mother in infancy, and that the frustration and anxiety associated with that early experience are, so to speak, 'stored' in the inner world of the individual. These infantile fantasies attach themselves to and suffuse comparable situations in adult life. Travelling therefore tends to induce anxiety, not necessarily conscious, which is greater than realities might warrant.

The third type of problem is related to flying itself. As a means of transport the aeroplane is relatively new. It is also 'unnatural', in the sense that whereas human beings can, without mechanical aids, propel themselves on land and in water, they cannot fly. And both these factors combine with dramatic reports of accidents, which may kill many people, to evoke a belief that flying is inherently more dangerous than other modes of travel. It is seen as glamorous and adventurous, and frightening as well.

Thus an airline has to contend with the problems of dependence common to all service industries, with the anxieties that people have about travel away from home, and with the still more specific anxieties provoked by flying itself. These last anxieties are probably the strongest and they subsume the others.

It is possible, of course, that the level of anxiety will diminish as flying, like motoring, loses its novelty and becomes more mundane. This is probably happening already: the reduction in the incidence of air-sickness, for example, may not be entirely attributable to the smoother and more comfortable flying conditions in modern pressurized planes, but in part to a wider acceptance of flying as a normal form of transport. On the other hand, a recent study suggests that even among motorists there is a high level of unconscious anxiety, which seriously affects their judgement of reality (Menzies, 1965). It is to be expected, therefore, that in flying as in motoring a number of mechanisms will be used to cope with the fear that it engenders. Moreover, many of the mechanisms, like the anxieties they are created to allay, will be unrecognized and unconscious.

When we postulate unconscious factors we are, of course, exposed to the retort: 'But if anxiety is unconscious, how do you know it exists? And even if it exists, is it relevant?' We derive our postulates from two sources. First, there is the accumulated body of knowledge about human personality; second, there is observable behaviour. Paradoxically, a denial of anxiety is often an expression of anxiety, especially if it is an unsolicited denial. The anxiety that is denied has come from within oneself. More generally, behaviour that is inadequately related to reality, and that the people concerned would themselves acknowledge in other circumstances to be irrational or abnormal, is *prima facie* evidence of the presence of anxiety.

Under normal conditions, passengers' anxieties are to a large extent contained. It is true that passengers can fail to turn up, can get lost between check-in and aircraft, can mishear announcements (not always their fault), and can misread directions; but perhaps this is characteristic of the unpredictability of any human throughput and it is difficult to be sure about attributing such withdrawal to anxiety. Simple manifestations are nevertheless familiar enough: on any flight it is possible to observe some passengers making the sign of the cross when entering the plane or crossing their fingers before take-off.

When a delay occurs for any reason, however, anxiety becomes much more overt. What was an orderly 'package' of passengers awaiting embarkation can disintegrate in minutes into a disorderly rabble: some angrily demanding an immediate alternative, some making their own arrangements, others deciding not to fly but not telling anybody about their decision, and still others sinking into an apathetic, passive withdrawal in which they neither hear announcements nor see messages put on screens right in front of them.

Observations of this kind suggest that the containment of anxiety is brittle. It is as if passengers have geared themselves to accept that for a limited period they will surrender their independence and tolerate the anxieties of travelling away from home and of flying. But once this time-boundary is breached by a delay, the pent-up anxiety is unleashed and expressed in irrational and abnormal behaviour.

Behaviourally, of course, the different kinds of anxiety are inseparable: they interact with each other. *In toto*, however, passenger anxiety is a major problem for airline management. As we shall try to show, it interacts with and mobilizes the anxiety of airline employees and ramifies through the organization in unexpected and undetected ways.

Changes in the Primary Task

With the increased speed and lower cost of air travel, airline operations, particularly those of the short-haul carrier, are becoming far more akin to local rail travel in terms of duration (as distinct from distance) of journey, frequency of service, and complexity of connections. In the meantime, however, the present generation of air travellers has been brought up to expect far more in the way of comfort and service than the rail traveller. In sharp contrast to the latter, air travellers, even though going on what in terms of railway timing would be only a suburban journey, expect to be relieved of baggage-handling, to be fetched and escorted about airports, and to be fed and generally looked after *en route*. Moreover, if any delay occurs for whatever reason, they expect to be provided with free meals and if necessary free alternative transport or overnight accommodation.

Such expectations descend in part from the early days of

commercial aviation when it had two quite distinct markets: it provided long-distance services for the very wealthy (and adventurous), and extremely short-distance services (e.g. between Portsmouth and the Isle of Wight) for the man in the street. It has been the objective of airlines during the post-war years to bridge the gap between these two markets – in other words, to get flying accepted as a normal means of transportation available to a majority of the population. The emphasis has been on building up an image of regular, reliable services with few luxuries. There has been a process of scaling down passenger's expectations – of an exotic, exciting experience – and of bringing them into closer conformity with what an airline endeavours to purvey – a quick, reliable service from A to B. This process has, however, been made hesitant by competition between different airlines. When fares and frequencies are limited by statutory bodies and international agreement, then aircraft type, comfort, and other passenger benefits are the only competitive variables left. A reduction in comfort and benefits offered that is not agreed by all can adversely affect competitive status. Initiative by any one airline has thus been curtailed. The only alternative to generally agreed standards would appear to be the introduction of aircraft so superior to competitors' that chances could be taken on a relative reduction in the comfort and benefits offered. At the present stage of aeronautical development no one airline is likely to be able to introduce markedly superior aircraft; and slightly superior aircraft could be expected to give only a temporary advantage.

But competition draws airlines in the opposite direction in other ways as well: for example, to sell more than a service from A to B. By 'selling' destinations (in conjunction with travel agents) airlines have tended to reopen and widen the gap between the expectations of their newer customers and the service they purvey. For customers who have bought an all-in holiday, a punctual efficient service *en route* may be a relatively unimportant criterion of the airline's performance compared with the weather, the hotel, the food, the service, and the beach on arrival. (It is also possible that by selling exotic destinations an airline is selling a feeling of adventure and excitement as well, and is thus raising, by other means, the unconscious anxieties of passengers about the journey.)

In other words, although the activities of most commercial airlines can still be embraced by the definition of the primary task given earlier – 'the transport of passengers and/or cargo by air at a profit' – an increasing range of activities may call for a redefinition of the strategic task. This would have the effect of turning the airline company as a whole into the equivalent of a holding company with the primary task of making a profit through investment in transport, hotel, tour, car-hire, and holiday activities. Air transport as such would then become the primary task of one of the subsidiaries.

BOUNDARY CONTROLS IN AN AIRLINE

OPERATING AND MANAGING SYSTEMS OF AIRLINE ORGANIZATION

Figure 2.1 above (p. 33) depicted the basic import-conversion-export activities of a passenger-carrying airline. These passenger-processing activities are the airline's transport operating activities and are carried out in operating systems. The organizational boundaries between the operating systems of the airline must therefore occur at points in this process. Moreover, if the organization is to fit primary task performance these boundaries will be drawn at those points, and only at those points, at which there are discontinuities in the process; whether in terms of the technology used, the territory where the process occurs, the time at which it happens, or some combination of these dimensions. At these points boundary controls will be required.

The major discontinuities of the total transport system lie, obviously enough, at each end of the actual flying operation. Flying has its own technology, which differentiates it from anything that happens on the ground.(In a sense it has its own 'territory', too – the air – which also differentiates it from ground activities.) On the ground, the activities concerned with mustering departing passengers and transferring them to aircraft, on the one hand, and with unloading arrived passengers and dispersing them, on the other, have much in common. Departure points for outgoing flights are arrival points for incoming flights; and shepherding and transporting arrivals are much the same as shepherding and

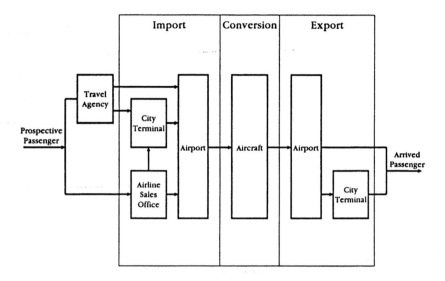

Fig. 2.2 The import-conversion-export systems of an airline

transporting departures. Procuring and ticketing passengers may or may not be grouped organizationally with mustering and loading, depending on the extent of marketing activities and on the congruence or incongruence of marketing areas and arrival/departure points.

It follows that, in a simple airline, the basic organizational model would differentiate two major operating systems: a ground system committed to 'import' and 'export'; and a flying system, committed to 'conversion'. The basic activities of the throughput process differentiated in this way are shown in Figure 2.2.

Until air transport operations become pure bus services, and passenger-handling at departure and arrival points is therefore not required, the essential operating units within the ground system will consist of a number of territorially differentiated departure and arrival stations. There may be, in addition, a number of selling-points, and still further units which combine selling-points and departure/arrival stations. Seats on any one flight may, of course, be sold at a number of different selling-points; the managing system of the ground organization will therefore have to control and coordinate reservations. It will also have to provide services for passengers being mustered and awaiting take-off.

In contrast, within the flying system the basic operating unit is a serviceable aircraft, properly loaded and crewed for a flight. Until flying becomes entirely automatic and the flight deck uninhabited, the management of this unit is vested in the captain of the aircraft. As soon as he starts his engines on the apron he comes under the direction of an authority outside his own company – the air traffic control system. It is this system that gives him instructions about which runway he may use, at what height he may fly, and by what route he must travel while in its area. From the time he starts his take-off, therefore, his own superior management must have delegated to him full authority and responsibility to make his own decisions about the conduct of the operation. But as soon as the flight has been completed, the particular operating unit – aircraft, flight crew, and cabin crew – has fulfilled its purpose. Although in some small airlines, with few flights, the same flying and cabin crews and the same plane may stay together for some time, even in this very simple case constraints (more fully discussed below) of aircraft cost and maintenance and the limitation of crew flying hours mean that such operating units are constantly being broken up and re-formed. More commonly, in large airlines the same crew members and the same planes seldom stay together for more than one outward and return flight. Indeed, on longer flights, because of limits on crew flying hours, either flight crew or cabin crew, or both, may be replaced, and the flight completed with others.

The model appropriate to this task is therefore a form of project organization. In this terminology, the flight or sector using the same aircraft and crew would be a 'project', and small self-contained networks, with their own flying system, staff, and aeroplanes, would be regarded as 'programmes'.

The major control and service functions of the managing system of the flying organization are thus the provision of pools of flying crew, cabin staff, and aircraft. There may be, in addition, a differentiated supplies function providing catering and other requirements of the temporary project operating units. The aircraft pool must obviously be backed by an engineering maintenance function, and the pools of flying crew and cabin staff, similarly, by training functions.

Using this organizational model as a basis, we now examine the boundary controls required in an airline in the light of the nature of its task and the constraints upon it. We consider first the control of the boundary between the enterprise and its environment, and subsequently the control of internal boundaries.

STRATEGIC BOUNDARY CONTROLS

The glamour and the hint of danger, the publicity accorded to airline operations, the long time-span of the strategic decisions that have to be made, government and international control of aircraft, airways, and air traffic, the constantly advancing technology of flying, and the continuous attention that needs to be paid to the definition of the primary task that determines the nature of the transactions between the airline and its environment, all mean that a senior member of overall management – usually the chairman, president, or whatever title he carries – cannot avoid being a public figure. His task is so to present the airline to its environment that he can protect the operating systems and their relevant control and service functions from the kind of interference that jeopardizes the performance of their sub-tasks. He has to be perceived as reliable and well informed. To fill this role he has to be, in reality, reliable and well informed. Hence the organization of which he is the head has to be one that avoids long lines of communication. In other words, traditional hierarchies, which, in a large enterprise, might have ten or more levels, are inappropriate for airline management, or alternatively, there has to be a rapid bypassing communication channel built into the organization.

In practice, top management contains three roles: the public role – to mediate relationships between the airline, government, and the public as a whole; the long-term planning role – to formulate, implement, and monitor airline strategy in the light of traffic development, on the one hand, and technical advance, on the other; and the executive role – to run the airline's day-to-day and week-to-week operations. The extent to which the roles can be taken by different individuals depends on the extent of the airline's operation and, of course, on the experience, qualifications, and personalities of those who fill top-management posts. In a small airline all three roles may be filled by one experienced and versatile individual; but overall management of a large airline is likely to require three people or even more.

In the same way, the functions differentiated in the first-order managing system depend on the extent to which overall management requires specialist help in market forecasting and planning, aircraft procurement, economic forecasting and financial control, personnel management, public relations, and other parts of its overall task of controlling transactions between the airline and its total environment.

Major Operating Controls

By major operating controls we refer to the management controls that are exercised over the throughput at the major discontinuities in the import-conversion-export processes. In an airline, the controls may be judged effective in so far as the throughput, whether passenger or cargo, is processed through the system and exported at the required destination without being subjected to any change other than in location.

Strictly speaking, a passenger enters the system when he makes an enquiry about a flight and makes, or does not make, a booking. We shall restrict our discussion here, however, to the ticketed passenger who presents himself, at city terminal or airport, for his correct flight. From that time to the time he climbs aboard his aircraft he is, from the airline's point of view, the responsibility of the passenger-handling staff on the ground; in the aircraft, both on the ground and in the air, he is the responsibility of the staff of the flying system; and on disembarkation he once more becomes the responsibility of ground staff, but at a different station.

It follows that, at the day-to-day operating level, four major regulatory activities are required: the first in the import system, concerned with converting individuals arriving at check-in into orderly loads at the aircraft's side; the second at the boundary between the ground and flying systems, to relate loads to seats; the third in the flying system, at take-off, during flight and landing, to ensure 'safe' behaviour; and the fourth in the export system where, flying finished, passengers have to be disposed of promptly and with a minimum of negative reactions.

In a great many respects, of course, the nature of the controls follows rationally from the nature of the process. Basically, controls over quantity, quality, and cost in an airline are comparable to those in a manufacturing enterprise. Our concern here, however, is with factors specific to airline operations and the extent to which these complicate and interfere with control mechanisms and with organizational functioning generally. We have in mind particularly the characteristic that airlines 'produce' their 'products' under the eyes of their customers, and the responsibility and associated anxiety of flying.

RESPONSIBILITY AND ANXIETY

An airline management cannot but respond to passenger anxieties. To quote one authority:

> Management must plan to allay individual fears, and to control group fear. They must plan to encourage the nervous, and comfort the fear-stricken and stop panics. Employees must be trained to avoid giving rise to unnecessary fears. They must be trained to recognise signs of individual fear so that they can behave sympathetically, and ease it. Above all they must be trained to sense the beginnings of group fear so that it can be dealt with before it gets out of hand. Sensible precautions taken openly and in a matter of fact way cause far less fright than strained and covert moves. (Barry, 1965, p. 40)

As the same writer emphasizes, 'however ill-founded his (the passenger's) fears are, the airline must deal with them' (ibid., p. 40); but not all the anxieties are unrealistic: 'Of course, air transport is inherently dangerous, and that fact must never be forgotten' (ibid., p. 317). Therefore, airline employees must find ways of coping not only with passenger anxieties but also with also with their own anxieties, which arise from their responsibilities for passengers in their care. These coping mechanisms should be based on reality:

> The dramatic nature of an airline crash tends to cast an unhealthy spell over the minds of airline officials . . . Having emphasised safety airline managers must then put it into perspective. Thinking about safety does

not preclude them from thinking about profitability. Safety and profitability are just as compatible objectives in airlines as they are in any other business. (ibid., p. 317)

This is a valid point. Activities directed towards raising safety standards can be a satisfying means of discharging anxieties. Accordingly, there is a risk that safety precautions may be elaborated to the point at which they become not only uneconomic but also, as we suggested earlier, even dangerous in their multiple application.

In general, if anxiety can be acknowledged it is less likely to distort judgements of reality. The advice that managers should never forget the dangers of air transport is therefore sound. Many managers are able to articulate their anxiety. One senior executive said in conversation, for example, 'My telephone rang at two in the morning, and when that kind of thing happens, I always fear the worst' – 'the worst', of course, being an accident. Or, to quote another: 'The one thing I dreaded when I took this job was becoming involved in dealing with an accident.' Capacity to acknowledge anxiety does not, of course, mean that it need 'cast an unhealthy spell': 'You keep it at the subconscious level: it's always there, but you mustn't let it worry you.'

To the extent that their membership of the airline organization involves any emotional investment, all its employees must carry a share of the responsibility and concomitant anxiety. We would postulate that anxiety is a function of commitment to the organization rather than of delegated accountability as shown on an organization chart. Indeed, the less the actual accountability for safety and the less the personal exposure to danger, the more difficult it is to find activities that provide a rational and realistic way of discharging anxiety, and the more difficult it is, too, to acknowledge and to articulate it. It follows, therefore, paradoxical though it may seem, that those who are overtly least accountable and personally least at risk may be most subject to unconscious anxiety. Lacking rational outlets, this may express itself in dysfunctional ways and in unexpected places. Some of these are explored below.

TASK AND SENTIENT GROUPS IN THE FLYING SYSTEM

The jobs of aircrew – of captains in particular – are manifestly the most stressful. They are central to the task of the airline; they carry the immediate risk of flying and immediate responsibility for passengers' safety. It is important therefore to consider by what mechanisms – some deliberately created, others not so and perhaps less obvious – their anxieties are dealt with, how effective these mechanisms are, and to what extent the stress is contained within the flying system or spills over into other parts of the organization.

THE PILOT

The high standard to which aircrew are selected and trained is itself a discharge mechanism. Both flying skills and medical fitness are regularly and frequently checked. Intensive retraining is accepted as standard practice whenever there are changes in equipment or flying procedures. So far as his training or skill is concerned, the individual never gets the benefit of the doubt. Either he satisfies the high standards of competence or he ceases to be a pilot. The risk of losing one's licence is a lurking fear; but, correspondingly, retention of the licence is a substantial vote of confidence.

Sophisticated managers of pilots are very much aware of the stress of flying and of the dangers to which this can lead. Research in aviation medicine and practical experience confirm that

> when anxiety is felt, mental activity . . . is disorganised in greater or lesser degree. This disorder and the disorder of skill should be regarded not as cause and effect, but as complementary aspects of a disorder of the reaction to complex psychological dangers, which the individual perceives to be present in his environment, and which he cannot immediately remove. (Davis, 1964, p. 13)

Or again:

> In certain marginal circumstances – marginal in weather, or workload, or both – it can be shown that any pilot concentrates on the primary task in hand, resulting in a diminishing field of consideration. Thus, at a critical phase of the flight, the commander is narrowing the scope of his thinking to a point where the wider 'commander view' ceases to

exist – just at the time when the exercise of the widest degree of responsibility is of paramount importance. It is at this point too that if any emotional stress is placed upon the pilot, mistakes are more likely to happen. (Baillie, 1964, p. 20)

Over and over again, reports of aircraft accidents – and in 50–60 per cent of these human error is at least a contributory factor – point to situations in which stress has interfered with a captain's judgement. One such report of an accident arising from an abandoned take-off identifies eleven environmental conditions and concludes:

> Such factors individually are not abnormal in winter operations; cumulatively they may cause a high degree of stress, the effect of which will depend upon the sensitivity of the individual. In this case they may well have contributed to a build-up of tension in the mind of the captain, but the extent, if any, to which this influenced his actions cannot be determined.*

The rate of technical change is rapid. As aircraft become faster, instrumentation and other aircraft systems become more complex, and traffic control procedures in the air become more stringent in regulating aircraft movements, there is a proportionate increase in the probability of pilots' becoming overloaded and making mistakes. To combat this, more rigorous training is not sufficient; nor is

> exhortation to 'fly safely' . . . sufficient. Pilots do not like thinking about accidents. If forced to do so they will invariably project their fears and anxieties on to other people and other things by attributing the most likely cause of any accident in which they may be involved to deficiencies in the aircraft, its performance, its equipment, radio aids or other facilities and services associated with the operation. Only very reluctantly indeed would they ever willingly consider the possibility of accident due to their own mistake, error or misjudgement. After all, this is not very surprising because it is surely going against human nature,

---

* Ministry of Aviation Civil Aircraft Accident Report (C.A.P. 223, 1965), quoted in *Flight International*, 4 March 1965.

and certainly the nature of most pilots, to ask them to adopt a defeatist attitude of this sort. (Baillie, 1964, p. 21)

(This closely corresponds to motorists' attitudes and behaviour as described by Menzies (1965).)

Accordingly, progressive airlines have introduced control cabin procedures which redistribute the work-load in such a way as to provide for double-checking and at the same time leave the captain freer to act as 'the supervisor or manager of his aircraft to the greatest possible extent' (Baillie, p. 24).

Detailed specification of the activities and interaction of aircrew is the more necessary because they constitute such a transient group. Not only are the 'project units', consisting of the aircraft, the aircrew sub-group, and the cabin crew sub-group being repeatedly broken up and re-formed; but membership of the sub-groups too is transitory. In short-haul airlines in particular, it is infrequent for the same crew of captain and co-pilots to be rostered together for more than a few days at a time; often it is only for a few hours. Some airlines avoid keeping the same group together as a matter of principle, on the ground that they are likely to develop short-cuts and other deviations from standard procedures, which could cause difficulty or even danger when individuals did have to be transferred to other crews. All pilots on a particular type of aircraft should therefore be completely interchangeable. Frequent reshuffling is in any case necessary for economic reasons. Statutory regulations, airline policies, and union agreements closely prescribe the individual's flying hours and minimum rest-periods; leave, sickness, and training events intervene; so that if maximum utilization of expensive pilot time is to be secured, rostering has to be on an individual rather than on a group basis. To roster the same plane, aircrew, and cabin crew together continually would be prohibitive.

This does mean, however, that the sentience of the flying group is temporary and limited. The pilot's commitment is not to the task group. The kind of emotional support that an enduring small group can provide, especially in stressful conditions (for example, coal-mining), is thus denied to aircrew.

The significant sentient grouping within the organization is, then, the pool of flying crew. In a smaller airline this may constitute the whole body of pilots; in a larger airline there will be sub-pools associated with particular aircraft types. For many pilots, however, 'pool' membership is less significant as a defence against stress than are identification with flying as such and a professional commitment to those who fly rather than to the employing organization.

Towards the employing organization pilots are inevitably ambivalent. They cannot afford to display hostility towards their own immediate flying management, because this is the management that supports the values of safety on which they themselves depend; and most managers are fellow fliers themselves. Union activity, on the other hand, is a less risky outlet for aggression that cannot be expressed in the subordinate–superior relationship. Moreover, in so far as management's formal negotiators are representatives of overall management, rather than of flying management, it is all the easier for fliers' representatives to behave toughly and to cast themselves in the role of defenders of safety in the face of rapacious, profit-seeking commercial managers. One suspects, nevertheless, that pilots are sometimes ashamed of their threats of industrial action; that they do not always respect their shop stewards and would disown them if union activity were not so important as a stress-reducing mechanism.

More generally, we can suggest that the anxieties of aircrew appear to be characteristically dealt with by processes of insulation. The glamour that surrounds the flier in our society – a glamour that in itself provides some defence against occupational stress* – is institutionalized within the organization. Pilots are accorded high status and receive salaries that put them on a par with, or above, relatively senior managers on the ground. They are equipped with comprehensive, written regulations that dictate the operating and

---

* It may be speculated that in a similar way in medicine glamour has helped to defend doctors against stress. Moreover, the profession and the public have increasingly glamorized and raised the relative status of the specialist, to the point where the work of the general practitioner is relatively denigrated. The parallel with aircrew and ground staff is suggestive.

safety standards to which they must conform. In operational flying they have complete responsibility and authority to decide whether to fly or not to fly, and, if they do fly, how much load they will carry. A captain's right to say 'no go' is respected and usually unquestioned by ground staff. In any dispute with ground staff the captain automatically receives his own management backing. He is encouraged to use his authority to cut through inefficiency and delay in ground handling, and even the passengers the captain meets are in a sense different people. However truculently they may complain to a member of the ground staff about a delay, they invariably accept attentively and submissively a captain's explanation. Passenger-handling staff are inferior in rank, and are not flying. The captain is the man on whom the passengers will have to depend, literally for their lives, within the near future. Unless they believe in his competence and authority, they can only decide not to fly.

The Cabin Crew

The apparent task of the cabin crew is to look after the passengers during the flight: to provide them with food and drink, take care of special passengers – children travelling on their own, invalids, and so on. In practice, they spend most of their time as waiters and waitresses. The status they are accorded derives, however, from their less obvious but nevertheless very real tasks. Safety regulations demand the employment of cabin staff, trained in emergency procedures, in a fixed ratio to the number of passengers. Thus they would have to be carried even if they had no other function to perform. Their other, covert, task is to reassure the passengers that all is well and there is no need to be afraid of flying. While they have to be skilful at their jobs, their primary qualifications are a capacity to remain pleasant and helpful whatever the conditions, and the ability, in the fortunately rare moments of crisis, to give passengers precise instructions for their safety. Because they are more 'on view' than flying crew, their behaviour has to be such as to confirm in the minds of the passengers an image of competence and reliability – of the airline in general, and of the particular captain and aircrew on whom they, like the passengers, depend for their safety.

Cabin crew share in the glamour, excitement, and anxiety of flying; but they have far less responsibility for safety than have the crew on the flight deck. The glamour defends them to some extent from the anxiety. As with aircrew too, the cabin crew sub-groups are constantly dissolved and reconstituted so that the relevant task-oriented sentient group to which they commit themselves, and which affords them protection, is the total cabin-staff pool. Unlike aircrew pools, however, the cabin-staff pool is not always divided into sub-pools that are technically differentiated from each other by aircraft type. Sub-pools that have no technical basis for differentiation are arbitrarily defined and are therefore likely to attract less commitment. Barry notes: 'One airline has adopted the device of breaking-up 100-strong "flights" of cabin staff by appointing a number of "aunts" and "uncles", without organizational status, who are expected to work informally among groups of 25 cabin staff' (1965, p. 155). Partly because such arbitrary groups provide less support and partly, too, because cabin crew do not depend on their own management to support the values of safety to the same extent as aircrew do, cabin crew can afford to be more truculent in direct negotiations.

ENGINEERING

The second major function of the flying system is to provide serviceable and properly loaded aircraft. Service and loading take place on the ground, and, because of the need to refuel, unload, reload, and service at every stop, these functions have to be geographically differentiated. Nevertheless, in terms of technology they belong to the flying system, since without them it could not operate.

The status of the engineering function is determined to a considerable extent by law. A station engineer, responsible for fault eradication and routine checks, has to be licensed, as do those members of his staff who sign the clearance certificates without which the aircraft cannot take off. As a final sanction, the licensed engineer, like the captain, can be prosecuted in the criminal courts if he fails to carry out statutory regulations. (In practice this rarely, if ever, occurs. Engineers have, however, had their licences withdrawn.)

For engineers, as for flying crew, there is a precise and written procedure that must be gone through before every take-off. In addition, specified checks have to be made daily and after specified numbers of flying hours.

Organizationally, engineers on stations always have the right of direct contact with their home base for any advice and help they may need. Indeed, whatever the apparent local organization may lay down, out-station engineers invariably regard themselves as directly responsible to the headquarters engineering department. But because they share with aircrew in a complex technology to which each makes a specific contribution, there is considerable mutual respect between them. Engineers, too, have the authority and the responsibility to say 'no go' if they are unsatisfied with the serviceability of the aircraft. Thus problems stemming from the imbalance between the flying group and the rest of the organization do not emerge as conflicts between aircrew and station engineers: this would be much too dangerous.

On an engineering base, however, where major overhauls are undertaken, the problems are more acute. The level of responsibility, as measured by the consequences of a mistake, is high; but by the very nature of the task the base is organized more like a traditional factory and hence has little of the glamour attached to station engineering, and none of that attached to aircrew. On an engineering base there is never a dependent, trusting, and admiring audience of passengers – or even of other ground staff. Nor do the engineers have much, if any, contact with aircrews. To the stress inherent in their task is added the 'overspill' or the residue of conflict between fliers and others that is not worked out elsewhere. It is to be expected that negotiations between engineers on the base and their management, and between management and trade unions, will always, in consequence, tend to be characterized by what on the surface appear as irrational and unreasonable demands. Exchange of staff between base workshops and stations can help, but until means are found of neutralizing the effects of the special position of aircrew, the management control of any engineering base will always be more difficult than the actual problems warrant.

Thus the flying system, and within it the aircrew, represents a powerful and dominating elite within any airline. This creates an imbalance between the flying system and other systems. We consider below some of the consequences of this imbalance and, in so doing, the particular position of passenger-handling staff on the ground.

THE FLYING SYSTEM/GROUND SYSTEM BOUNDARY

THE CULTURES OF THE FLYING AND GROUND SYSTEMS

Before taking up the problem of imbalance between flying and ground systems, however, one other phenomenon that arises from the nature of the primary task of an airline and from the special position of aircrew should be mentioned: danger creates a culture that encourages personal leadership. Just as a nation at war requires its Churchill, so a ship or an aircraft requires its captain who is expected to rise to moments of crisis – to go beyond technical competence and to produce the extra touch of genius that will convert a near-disaster into a brilliant coup. One would expect a higher premium to be set on personal leadership in an airline, therefore, than in less hazardous industries, and one would expect, too, that this attitude would extend beyond the actual task of flying, where it is most relevant.

On the other hand, a culture that encourages personal leadership also expects that the leader will at times break – or rise above – the rules. This may well be functional on the flight deck and in a chief executive's office. But there are other aspects of airline operations in respect of which personal leadership in this sense is positively dysfunctional and for which bureaucratic forms of organization are much more appropriate. In ticketing, for example, and in accounting activities generally, meticulous attention to detail is required. Standardized procedures are needed throughout the airline and any improvisations resulting from local exercise of 'personal leadership' could be, from the commercial point of view, 'dangerous'. One would expect, therefore, that just as those concerned with flying realistically need mechanisms to insulate themselves from commercial pressure, so also, equally realistically, would those concerned with maintaining bureaucratic procedures require corresponding protection from the 'dangers' of personal leadership.

It follows that any airline may be faced with the organizational problems of containing and reconciling what are, in effect, two cultures. Such problems are especially likely to emerge where the two cultures collide; but if this boundary is 'protected' from the possibility of conflict, overspill is probable elsewhere in the organization – overspill into the engineering base has already been mentioned. In effect, if the resolution of conflict does not occur in the control region between the boundaries of the conflicting cultures, it is likely to be projected into other regions. But, without very special provisions, it is unlikely that other control regions will be equipped, organizationally or culturally, to deal with the projected conflicts and hence controls will break down more frequently than might otherwise be expected.

The Boundary Between Flying System and Ground System

Overspill into the engineering base would be less if the boundary between the ground system and the flying system was itself not so heavily guarded against expression of the hostility that the powerful and superior position of aircrew must inevitably provoke. The operating boundary is crossed at the aircraft side when the throughput is transferred from one operating system to the other. A number of mechanisms are used to protect this boundary. The most obvious, of course, are the reservations and load-control systems.

Unless aircraft capacity were unlimited, the absence of a reservations system would result in frequent negotiations between passenger-handling staff trying to dispose of their throughput and captains resisting the overloading of their aircraft.

Load control, on the other hand, is a function that guards the boundary by blurring it. Strictly speaking, it is the captain of the aircraft who is responsible for load control – for ensuring that the total weight is within the prescribed limits for the aircraft, that the load is properly distributed around the centre of gravity, and that the fuel carried is appropriate to the weight, to the distance to be covered (including alternative landing-points), and to the prevailing weather conditions (for example, head winds). But what is commonly called the load-control function is the detailed calculation of the load and fuel data for each flight. Much of the activity is routine arithmetic, and discretion is severely limited, but whoever is responsible for the calculations shares with aircrew and engineers anxiety about the consequences of a mistake. He has to face the likelihood that the captain will often rely on the figures and sign the load-sheet without any but the most perfunctory checking. Thus a mistake in the working could literally be a fatal mistake. But the one who made it would survive. Located, as he often is, within the ground organization, the person (or, at a large station, the whole section) responsible for these calculations can provide an intolerable focus for the anxiety of those passenger-handling staff who want to put the maximum load onto a given aircraft. His sentient groupings are within the ground system; but the values he is called upon to uphold are the flying values of aircraft safety rather than the ground values of maximizing traffic.

Performance of the primary task of an airline requires the assembly of 'packages' of passengers and their baggage at a departure point. It then requires that these be correctly loaded into a serviceable and adequately crewed aircraft before take-off. If providing the aircraft and the crew forms a technologically differentiated system from procuring and mustering passengers, then the amalgamation of packages and aircraft – loading, and its control – would more logically be located within the flying system. This would certainly be a 'safer' organizational position from which to resist commercial pressures, which is to a large extent what the load calculator on the ground is required to do. A load controller located within the ground system has to be protected by very high status indeed if he is to be in the position to uphold commercial values and to confront the captain with them.

Yet another theoretically possible solution would be to locate this function within a separate operating system, interposed between what we have called ground and flying operations. The load controller would then take over the throughput from the ground system, dispatch a correct load, and return the remainder, if any, to the ground system. To be able to do this his status would, again, have to be very high.

At all events we can say that this function, especially if located within the ground system, has the effect of blurring the boundary and blunting the confrontation between the ground and flying systems.

Confrontations are therefore relatively rare. This does not mean that captains are not subject to some pressures from passenger-handling staff. The latter may suggest that the captain should change his route and, by making an additional stop, take more passengers and less fuel; or they may point out that another captain has taken off under identical conditions with a heavier load. Captains, however, have the power to make the decisions and if they wish to veto such suggestions they can always adduce justifications in extraneous factors (meteorological reports, air-traffic control, statutory restrictions on flying hours) or in technological mystique. Thus although captains may yield to suggestions of this kind, the amount of 'give' is usually negligible.

In effect, such transactions across the boundary of the ground and flying systems are not genuine bargains. They have the function of exposing aircrew to a glimpse of the pressure under which the passenger-handling system operates. They are a reminder that pilots are members of a commercial enterprise* and not just fliers; but it is a reminder under such protected conditions that safety is unaffected. On the other hand, an occasional 'victory' for passenger-handling staff provides some measure of compensation

---

* Not that the pressures are solely commercial: ground staff are likely to be more concerned with the immediate problem of dealing with superfluous passengers than with loss of revenue.

for their constant occupation of the inferior status. It makes an unequal relationship slightly less unequal.

On the ground, staff may tend to magnify their victories. They attribute any change of flight plan to their own influence, and in this way deal with some of the hostility that the unequal status inevitably generates. Too large a victory, however, can raise their unconscious anxiety unbearably, or make them consciously anxious: safety margins may have been eroded. On one occasion a number of passengers were waiting for the only aircraft of the day due to call at a particular airport. The weather was bad. The captain of the aircraft before leaving his previous destination asked for a local weather report. His message was overheard by a member of the ground staff responsible for mustering and loading the passengers. Anxious to get his passengers away, he informed the station of departure that the weather would be clear by the time the aircraft arrived. He next heard that the aircraft had taken off. As the time of its arrival approached and the weather did not clear, he became more and more worried, until all he could do was to lock himself in a lavatory and pray. The weather cleared with ten minutes to spare. Even though it was not his responsibility to give weather reports, and the captain had in fact obtained his report through the meteorological office, he declared: 'I'll never do that again – I wouldn't go through what I went through for anything.' Thus though a captain's decision may make life extremely difficult for passenger-handling staff, they can seldom retaliate without restraint, because they dare not win too well.

In general, therefore, the boundary between ground and flight operations is strongly defended by various mechanisms. The safety/profitability conflict is not fought out there; it is replaced by a pseudo-bargaining procedure. This has the positive effect of preserving safety standards from erosion. On the other hand, it leaves the conflict unresolved. Before we examine the consequences for passenger-handling staff of the lack of conflict resolution at this point, we must turn briefly to the export boundary – the flight is over, the passengers have arrived and have to be disposed of.

Once the flight is completed and passengers have been delivered to the destination to which they have booked, the airline – regarded only as a transport undertaking – has finished its job. The sooner, therefore, the passengers are removed from the system, the better. Anything further that has to be done for them incurs more cost and reduces profit. But it often takes passengers some time to readjust to their different status. They have been wooed by advertising and other devices to book on a particular airline; they have had their baggage taken from them with the assurance that it will accompany them; and on the flight they have been offered food, drink, papers, and other services. At the end of the flight they have been told by a charming stewardess how much their custom has been appreciated and hopes have been expressed that they will travel by the same airline again. Suddenly they are left on their own. Cold impersonal notices tell them where to collect their baggage, ruthless customs officials rifle through their old and new possessions, and, if they are lucky, a notice or another official tells them where to get a bus to the city. Small wonder if sometimes they feel let down or squeezed dry. If, at the same time, the journey from A to B has converted them from citizens into unfamiliar aliens, and as such they are subject to special regulations, the sense of loss and let-down can be severe, depriving them even of their normal common sense. It can react against the airline that has carried them. In many airports, particularly the large ones, in which disposal of arrived passengers is the business of the airport authority, the airline may be unable to control the boundary adequately and have to tolerate the undeserved odium that results.

The situation can be exacerbated if the airline is one that sells inclusive holiday tours, including hotel accommodation and sightseeing visits. If there is a discrepancy between the 'safe, reliable service' from A to B that the flying system purveys and the expectations that the customer is buying, it usually falls to the passenger-handling staff to straddle the gap. If the customer buys a blue sky, bright sunshine, palm trees, golden sands, and blondes in skimpy bikinis, he is likely to complain not only about delays and uncomfortable journeys but about dull skies, stony beaches, and well-covered bodies. Whoever is nearest will catch it. This is never the flying staff and seldom the office from which the original ticket was bought.

PASSENGER-HANDLING ORGANIZATION WITHIN THE GROUND SYSTEM

The activities that make up the task of the passenger-handling staff are mustering passengers and their baggage in aircraft-sized loads; and getting them from the point or points of assembly to the aircraft. The task is inherently centred on departure/arrival points – airports and their ancillary town terminals. Although, even when the weather is fine, passenger-handling staff can never insist on a captain's taking a full complement, they are nevertheless subject to strong pressure from the commercial side of their own ground system to dispose of the maximum number of passengers; and, in the event of passengers' being unable to get into the plane for which they have booked, to pressure from passengers to make alternative arrangements for them. In addition, they are far more exposed to passengers' pre-flight behaviour than are any other airline employees, and passengers' anxiety is likely to interact with and to exacerbate their own.

They work for the most part in buildings provided by other organizations, with all the additional problems that this entails. Abroad, the buildings are frequently owned by competitors, who, however co-operative they might be, are unlikely to be so co-operative as to weaken their own competitive position. And passenger-handling staff have to contend with passengers' irritations over things that have nothing to do with air traffic as such – delays at customs, or even in road traffic before arrival at the airport; inadequate airport buildings or catering; and a host of other, often trivial, but cumulatively annoying disappointments. Between arrival at the airport and boarding the plane, passengers move across a number of boundaries – typically from check-in to boarding-card check, to passport control, to departure lounge, to bus or directly to aircraft. City-centre check-in adds to the boundaries. At each movement across a boundary there is a chance of passengers' straying – and stray they do. Even if there are no delays, these discontinuities can themselves rupture passengers' brittle control over their anxieties.

In short, the efficient and profitable operation of an airline ideally requires passengers to be predictable, uniform, interchangeable units, who will check-in in the appropriate numbers at the appropriate time and will be amenable to being counted, packaged, stored, and transferred to the aircraft in an orderly way. Yet while the pressures for efficiency and profitability are strong, what passenger-handling staff are dealing with is an unpredictable throughput of idiosyncratic individuals over whom they have only intermittent control in an uncertain and anxiety-provoking situation over which they have no control. The very unpredictability of the throughput with which they have to deal makes it impossible to lay down routines to cover every possibility. Passenger-handling staff have to be given authority to exercise judgement and discretion in how they deal with disappointed and anxious passengers – and far more of them are anxious than would ever admit it. But the exercise of judgement and discretion, which can be very satisfying, is usually required only when something has gone wrong: over-booking of the aeroplane, delay, lost baggage, or other major or minor catastrophe. They also have to deal with the effects of changes in policy and procedure which, whether good or bad, are more likely than not to evoke negative responses from passengers, simply because they are changes. Apart from the exasperation that such events can cause, passenger-handling staff can hardly but feel that if other people only did their jobs more efficiently they would have an easier time. They cannot 'get at' flying crews; they should not act out their exasperation and annoyance on the passengers; their only outlets are their own management and other passenger-handling and booking units within the commercial sub-system of their own company. At the same time, those members of commercial sub-systems who never come face-to-face with passengers and for whom the airline is just a commercial operation are not likely to sympathize with expressions of anxiety of which passenger-handling staff themselves are unaware. They realistically need organizational protection from kinds of behaviour, and especially kinds of leadership, that would upset their routines.

On stations where there is comparatively little of a particular airline's traffic, the small working group of passenger-handling staff can provide mutual support, and the group can reinforce allegiance to the airline. On those stations in which selling and traffic boundaries coincide, it is also even possible for sales staff in a city office and passenger-handling staff at the airport to be interchangeable, and the reinforcement can then be maximized by the insight that each is given into the other's problems.

But larger stations have to be manned for twenty-four hours every day of the week; they require large numbers of staff who are generally divided, for economic reasons, into different sections for each of the processes shown in Figure 2.1, and interchange with city sales staff is usually a practical impossibility. Naturally, the duty officers in charge on any given shift have to exercise their judgement and discretion in the handling of day-to-day contretemps of the task; and inevitably, because they are different people, they do so in different ways, emphasizing different aspects of the situation.

In effect, the task group for passenger-handling activities has to be of the project type, groups being formed, disbanded, and re-formed with each change of shift, season, and kind and density of traffic. Furthermore, in a large airport the members of a shift group are widely dispersed. Accordingly, it is difficult to integrate, for example, check-in staff on the import boundary with escort and dispatch staff on the apron; and still more difficult to integrate both of these with staff at the city terminal. Thus the task group on each shift is unwieldy and incoherent, so that members cannot readily experience the satisfaction of a unitary task well done, and at the same time the sections to which individuals belong – check-in, departure lounge, escort, and others – are insufficiently distinctive in their expertise to form quasi-professional bases which could attract commitment and provide support.

The problems encountered in this area, though greater at the large busy airports, seem to be intrinsic to passenger-handling in today's conditions and, until a more sophisticated organization is invented, or the technology of checking-in more advanced – by the use of automation and computers and the redesign of airports – it seems inevitable that maladaptive mechanisms must continue. Three are observable:

1   Passenger-handling staff behave *as if* their technology were more complex than it is – and thus more comparable to that

of flying. This applies, for example, to communication. In aircraft, reserve radios are required and are usually available; but procedures determine which crew member will send or receive specific types of communication on air-traffic control or on company frequencies. On the ground, on the other hand, it is not uncommon to find many alternative types of communication (such as telephone, teleprinter, walkie-talkie, and lamsen tube) being used simultaneously and independently for the same purpose, resulting in a total of information that the organization fails to digest and reconcile.

2   Passenger-handling staff behave *as if* they had more power than they actually do have – and are thus more comparable with air-crews. Therefore negotiations about changes of route or of fuel-load are treated as though they were bargains between equals.

3   Passenger-handling management models its organization on that of flying. Thus whereas the organization of traffic activities tends to be based on seniority and rank as on the flight deck, the task, with its unpredictable throughput in dispersed points – check-in, customs, lounge, and apron – demands a far more egalitarian system with widely dispersed responsibilities and authorities.

Some of the bustle and activity at an airport when flights are delayed undoubtedly represents action for its own sake rather than action directed towards a positive goal – it is better to do something, anything, than to do nothing. In other words, the action itself serves as a discharge mechanism for the anxiety, both conscious and unconscious, that is inherent in the job.

THE ELIMINATION OF DISCHARGE MECHANISMS

We have shown that the ground/flying systems boundary is heavily protected in that, in reality, all the power and authority are vested in the flying system, and the flying staff are to some extent insulated against the anxiety inherent in the nature of the airline task. The protection of the ground/flying systems boundary precludes the possibility of working out the hostility that inevitably arises or the unequal conflicts across it. This is likely to 'overflow' into other parts of the airline. One would therefore expect airlines to be particularly prone to types of conflict – whether between departmental groupings or between employees and management – that appear to be largely irrational. It is also possible to suspect that some of the let-down experienced by passengers on arrival is the result of an indirect expression of the resentment felt by passenger-handling staff against both passengers and flying staff.

Some of these problems will disappear as procedures are simplified and technology improves, as check-in becomes automatic and loading computer-controlled. But as the problems disappear, so will the mechanisms they provide for the discharge of stress. There will be fewer boundary relationships into which the unresolved conflict at the ground/flying boundary can overspill. We can therefore expect that difficulties in those that remain – between selling and passenger-handling; between cabin staff and their management; between engineering base and management; between personnel management and other management control and service functions – will be intensified. And as flying becomes more and more automatic, and the flight deck eventually even uninhabited, it is not difficult to predict that very special steps will have to be taken to protect those on the ground who will be responsible for programming and monitoring take-off, flight, and landing.

3 DEPENDENCE, INDEPENDENCE, AND COUNTER-DEPENDENCE IN RESIDENTIAL INSTITUTIONS FOR INCURABLES

This paper is based on a three-year pilot study, carried out between 1966 and 1969, of residential institutions for the physically handicapped and chronic sick. The study, which was financed by the then Ministry of Health, had a two-fold purpose: first, to explore the characteristics of systems of organization that tend either to foster or to mitigate the well-known problems of institutionalization; second, to take an action research role in one such establishment to discover whether and how it was possible to create a more benign psycho-social environment. Out of a much larger number of institutions which we visited, we concentrated on five – two voluntary homes, two Regional Hospital Board units and a local authority establishment. All of them had been set up specifically to cater for the younger disabled ('younger' in Ministry parlance meaning pre-geriatric). In each of them we interviewed the majority of inmates and staff and observed them in their daily activities; and we collaborated with one of the voluntary homes in action research.

One of the RHB units was located within a geriatric hospital, while the other four occupied independent premises, two being purpose-built and the other two being converted houses. The smallest had sixteen inmates, the largest forty-seven. Except for the unit in the hospital, which was all-male, they housed both sexes,

Miller and Gwynne, 1973.

and the age range was between sixteen and sixty plus, with the majority between thirty-six and fifty. Of the 147 inmates in our sample, nearly a quarter had multiple sclerosis, and the other principal conditions were cerebral palsy, muscular dystrophy or atrophy, paralysis of different kinds, and arthritic diseases. Disability was congenital in about a quarter of the cases, and in a further fifth had occurred before the age of fifteen. Just over half the sample had worked in a full-time paid occupation at some period in their lives; about a fifth had done so for ten years or longer. Nearly three quarters of the sample had not married; and of those who had, 45 per cent of the marriages had ended in divorce or legal separation.

Of the inmates we interviewed, over 80 per cent were unable to walk, even with aids, 39 per cent needed assistance in washing, 49 per cent in going to the lavatory, 52 per cent in feeding, 77 per cent in dressing, and 93 per cent in bathing. Over 40 per cent had speech defects; nearly 20 per cent were incontinent.

The overall ratio of caring staff to inmates was 1:2.4, ranging between 1:1.2 in one of the RHB units to 1:3.9 in the local authority unit. The ratio of trained nursing staff to inmates was about 1:6. Again, the RHB unit had the highest concentration – 1:2.4 – while the others had between six and ten inmates per nurse.

We divide the remainder of this paper into five sections. First, we describe the way in which this project began. We then outline two characteristic approaches to residential care. Neither seems adequately based on reality, and in the third section we relate this to difficulty in coming to terms with the function that society implicitly assigns to institutions of this kind. In the fourth section, we suggest the system characteristics of an institution that are likely to provide the best fit to the needs of inmates, and in the fifth, we briefly discuss the position of leadership.

THE ORIGINS OF THE PROJECT

Our involvement began as long ago as 1962 when we received a copy of an article from the Le Court Cheshire Home. It argued the case for deploying trained social workers to help residents in homes such as this 'to adjust to their disabilities and to each other'. The writer of the article, in a covering letter, advocated the development of the homes into 'therapeutic group communities', referred to the work of Elliott Jaques at Glacier (Jaques, 1951), and suggested that the Tavistock Institute could 'be of immense help' in a process of change. Our response was lukewarm: we were heavily committed elsewhere and also we could not see where the money would come from to finance such a project. We suggested a discussion in London. The reply was, in effect: 'Yes, we should like to come to see you, but we are all in wheelchairs, so it would be quite an undertaking.'

This letter was a shock. We had taken it for granted that we were corresponding with someone involved in the management of the home. We were astonished that instead it was a crippled inmate; and we felt guilty at the unrecognized prejudices that had led us to be astonished.

Although it was difficult at first to see beyond the disfigurement and deformity, we found at Le Court a small group of lively-minded people whom we grew to like and respect. They were less concerned with the capacities they lacked than with the problem of making the fullest use of those they still had. They believed that potentially an institution could provide the severely disabled with a richer life than if they were living in hospitals or even, for many of them, than if they were still at home. Yet they found that institutional life in many ways reinforced their dependence and they had to fight for the right, taken for granted by other adults, to take ordinary, almost trivial decisions, such as when to get up or go to bed. They were disturbed at the prospect of an imminent change of staff: they feared new routines which could disrupt the pattern of everyday life and different values which might more subtly strip them of the hard-won elements of self-determination to which they clung.

Their fears proved well-founded. A new matron was appointed and she, coming from a background of conventional hospital nursing, found the regime of Le Court not merely liberal but anarchic. Backed by some members of staff and of the management committee she re-imposed strict rules on, for example, bed-times and television viewing. Residents protested violently and tried to enlist the support of outsiders. There were counter-threats to remove some of the protesting residents as trouble-makers.

Ultimately, a truce was reached, the matron resigned and a more liberal régime was reintroduced. But it was a precarious truce and there were further periodic eruptions when certain staff members were accused of authoritarian or sadistic behaviour.

Although we had only a tenuous relationship with Le Court at the time of those early troubles, we felt very identified with the residents. They seemed to be in the impossible bind of being physically almost totally dependent on the very staff members who were taking away their freedom. It was difficult to resist being caught up in a crusade on their behalf. Yet we were plainly ambivalent, for it was three and a half years after the initial contact before we made a serious effort to get research funds and more than four years before we started work.

During the early part of the study in particular we felt a deep sympathy and pity for the disabled, seeing them as doubly persecuted by their physical handicaps and by the destructiveness of their institutional environments. But at times we would feel strongly identified with the staff, who could be seen as victims of the insistent, selfish demands of cripples who ill-deserved the money and care so generously lavished upon them. The difficulty we have had in working through our own conflicting feelings is symptomatic of the ambiguous place that the disabled and institutions for them have in our society. At one moment, the cripple is treated as mentally subnormal or refused admission to a restaurant in case his presence should upset the other diners; at another, he is privileged, yet also infantilized, by being given free admission to a place of popular entertainment.

APPROACHES TO RESIDENTIAL CARE

In the institutions we visited and studied in more detail certain patterns repeated themselves so consistently that we were able to identify two quite distinct approaches to residential care. These were related, explicitly or implicitly, to two opposed ideologies, which we call here 'the warehousing ideology' and 'the horticultural ideology'.

We can illustrate the warehousing approach by describing one of the RHB units. It contained several wards, each sleeping five or six patients. Few personal possessions were to be seen in the wards, which were out of bounds by day. Apart from meals in the dining room, inmates spent most of their time either in the occupational therapy room (where many just sat), in the TV room, or in a corridor between them. Another large room was kept locked except for weekly film shows. Conversation and mobility were minimal. Many inmates depended on staff to move them (and it is not easy for a person with a speech defect to communicate with a non-English-speaking orderly), and those who could propel their own wheelchairs could not go into the grounds because a connecting ramp had long since crumbled. Visiting hours were restricted, excursions infrequent, and if an inmate was to be taken out by a friend or relative, special dispensation was needed for return after 6 p.m. One inmate was refused permission to use his record-player (even though he could have played it in the locked room without disturbing anyone) and when he persisted in asking was transferred to a psychiatric hospital. He returned quite changed, and then fitted into the prevailing mode of inmate behaviour, which was either withdrawal and apathy or, at best, overt depression. In the latter category, one ex-dentist with multiple sclerosis was reprimanded by the matron over a short story he wrote for the unit's flimsy monthly newsletter: she said that it introduced a note of depression into 'this happy home'. Staff carefully regulated each inmate's intake of food and drink and normally used suppositories to regulate the day of week and time of excretion. Visiting days, they complained, were often followed by vomiting and diarrhoea. They saw their regime as being in the best interests of their patients. 'We have to do their thinking for them.' And if their patients were considered as creatures with purely physical needs, the treatment was appropriate. It was designed to keep them alive as long as possible.

This indeed is the primary task implicit in the warehousing approach: to prolong physical life. It translates the ethos and methods of the hospital into the setting of the residential institution. The intake into the system is a patient defined in terms of physical malfunctioning. He is processed through the system by being given medical and nursing care. This is facilitated if he accepts his dependent and depersonalized role. Any attempts by the inmate to assert himself, or to display individual needs other than those arising from his specific disability, are constraints on task performance. They are, therefore, to be discouraged. The 'good' inmate is one who accepts the staff's diagnosis of his needs and the treatment that they prescribe and administer.

One of the voluntary homes can be used as an example of the horticultural ideology. Instead of wards, there were bed-sitting rooms which, though usually shared, were full of personal belongings. There were no rules about the use of rooms: an individual seeking privacy to study, for example, might use the small chapel. During the day, most of the inmates would be busy. There was much more conversation and purposeful movement. Though not significantly less disabled than those in the RHB unit, many had electrically-operated wheelchairs, and other gadgets to make them more mobile and independent. Inmates could receive visitors at any time and entertain them to meals; they could also come and go quite freely themselves and arranged their own transport.

Here, in contrast to warehousing, it is the needs for physical care that are the constraints. The intake into the system is conceived as a deprived individual with unsatisfied drives and unfulfilled capacities. The primary task is to develop these capacities. Thus, the conversion process (if we use an input-conversion-output model of an institution) is concerned with providing encouragement for individual development of inmates in the direction of greater independence – in complete contrast to the dependency orientation of warehousing. The role of staff that follows from this is therefore not to treat the disability but to provide opportunities for the development of abilities.

Unfortunately, if we take Le Court as an example, some staff, especially nursing staff, find difficulty in accepting this role. Not only is their status diminished, but they can argue, sometimes justly, that inmates' aspirations for independence may jeopardize their delicate physical condition. When they seek to impose constraints on inmates' activities, however, this is interpreted as a threat to independence. Commonly there is collusion to elect a particularly controlling member of the nursing staff as scapegoat. Sooner or later she is isolated and ejected from the system. We have scraps of evidence to suggest that the underlying fantasy is that with her removal the physical dependency which she represents will also vanish.

THE PROBLEMS OF REALITY

The shortcomings of the warehousing approach are obvious. It is not difficult to infer that in an institution adopting such an approach the social system has a significant function in defending its staff against the anxieties of the task they have to perform (see Menzies, 1960). In the process, some of the needs of the inmates are neglected. The horticultural approach is such a welcome contrast that at first one may fail to notice that it too may have a defensive function and be a means of avoiding reality.

Let us look at some of the realities in terms of the task that the institution is being called upon to carry out. First, of course, those who are admitted are by definition so disabled physically that they cannot look after themselves. The physical disability has psychological – even perhaps psychopathological – accompaniments. We have not time to explore these here, and will merely point out that they will derive from three types of factors interacting with each other: the effect of an impaired body-image; the effect of dependence on others equivalent to the infant's dependence on the mother; and the effect of society's ambivalent attitudes towards disability.

Besides being heavily disabled, those admitted are also rejected. For many it is a personal rejection. For example, admission may have been precipitated by the desertion of a spouse, or by the inability of an ageing mother to provide the necessary care at home. All, however – and this includes those who admitted themselves – are socially rejected. In other words, by crossing the boundary into the institution they have demonstrated that they lack any role that is socially valued in the outside world. They are not breadwinners or housewives; nor do they any longer have even the vicarious social participation of dependence on someone who has such a role. They are defined as social dropouts, parasitical upon the wider society. Once admitted they have a minimal chance of ever leaving

the institution at all, let alone being restored to a valued role outside.
The harsh reality, therefore, is that by the very fact of committing
them to institutions of this type, society is in effect defining them
as socially dead, and (barring serious illness for which nursing
resources are inadequate) they will stay in an institution until they
are physically dead. Yet these are by no means institutions for
terminal care, for, like Charles II, many inmates take 'an
unconscionable time dying'.

Impinging on the institution and its inmates are the ambivalent
social values: on the one hand, that they are cripples – inferior
beings to be despised or infantilized – and, on the other, the more
'correct' liberal view, that they are 'really normal', 'just like us', and
should not be discriminated against.

Given these realities, the need for defences is obvious and the
form they take becomes easier to explain. The warehousing
ideology reflects the attitude that cripples are non-normal
members, or non-members, of society who, out of humanitarian-
ism, are to be kept alive, and perhaps even indulged, so long as they
are kept apart and not seen too often by the rest of us. The
horticultural ideology reflects the more modern liberal outlook, but
what it denies is the reality of differences between the disabled and
the able-bodied. As a defence, its function is to preserve the fantasy
of rehabilitation; and, as in football pools, there are always the
occasional, highly-publicized success stories to give credibility and
hope to the others. Moreover, the norms of achievement that this
ideology promotes, while they keep at bay the apathy and
withdrawal of the warehousing institution, may frustrate satisfaction of the real dependency needs of some inmates, especially
those in the terminal stages of progressive diseases.

If we are correct in our interpretation that, by the very fact of
committing people to institutions of this type, society is defining
them as socially dead, then the essential task to be carried out is to
help inmates to make their transition from social death to physical
death. Denial of the meaning of this boundary between the
institution and the wider society must lead, it would seem, to a
denial either of inmates' remaining capacities or of their incapaci-
tation. The warehousing approach provides only for a regressed

dependency; the horticultural approach idealizes achievement and is impatient of dependent needs.

THE MODEL FOR AN APPROPRIATE ORGANIZATION

There is a fundamental difference between the institutions we are describing and most other enterprises with a human throughput. The modal outputs of a hospital are cured patients (though some die); of a college, graduates (though some fail and drop out on the way) and of an airline, passengers who reach their destination (though a few miscarry). The modal outputs of these institutions, however, are dead inmates; those who leave in other ways are exceptions, and the inexorableness of this boundary at the output end of the system gives rise to many of the problems encountered both in running institutions of this kind and in living in them. In particular it leads to difficulty in agreeing upon their primary task.

Since the primary task of the institution cannot be defined in terms of exporting rehabilitated inmates to the external world, then the quality of living within the institution must be an end in itself. We, therefore, argue that it is the task of the institution, without either destroying the inmate's individuality or denying his dependence, to provide a setting in which he can find his own best way of relating to the world about him and to himself. The institution must at the same time accept the reality that he is likely to remain in it for the duration of his life and accept too his anxieties about deterioration or death.

In this section we outline a model organization appropriate to this task. The conceptual framework used here is derived from Rice (1963) and Miller and Rice (1967).

We postulate that performance of the task requires three systems of activity: these cater respectively for psycho-physical dependence, psycho-physical independence, and support. The system as a whole and the three constituent systems are shown in Figure 3.1. The individual inmate occupies roles in these systems of activities and the arrows indicate that from hour to hour he may be continually moving from a role in one system to a role in another. All his activities as a member of the institution derive from his role in one or other of these systems.

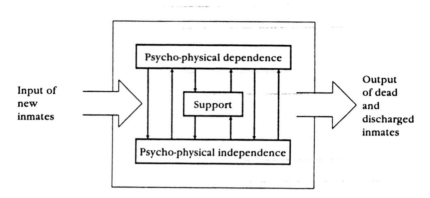

Fig. 3.1 The institution as an open system showing constituent systems of activities

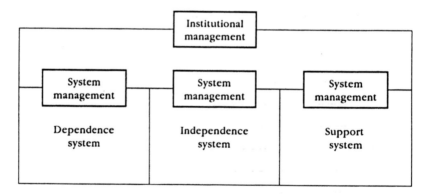

Fig. 3.2 The basic organizational model

Each of the systems has a distinctive task and a distinctive method of task performance. It therefore requires its own management. The task of the institution as a whole is carried out by relating the activities of these systems to each other and to the environment. The basic organizational model is shown in Figure 3.2. Institutional management is depicted as straddling the boundary of the institution and the outside world; the management of each constituent system straddles the boundary between that system and rest of the institution.

The system of psycho-physical dependence is the easiest to think about in conventional terms. It is here that are located the physical resources of caring, catering and cleaning staff, through which the activities of providing physical care are carried out. Inmates in their dependent roles are the throughput of this system. To take a trivial example from one of the many sub-systems of activity, the input may be an inmate needing a bath, the conversion process consists of bathing him or helping him to bath himself, and the output is a clean inmate. Virtually all these sub-systems are directed towards providing the inmates with help in their daily living activities – dressing, bathing, feeding, going to the lavatory, moving from place to place – together with occasional nursing in times of illness.

Difficulty arises, however, if this system is regarded as coterminous with the institution as a whole. If the other systems shown in our model are suppressed, the individual as an independent being has no room for existence and so management of the individual inmates' boundaries – their ego functioning – is also taken over by the institution. The apathy and listlessness endemic in a warehousing institution arise from the fact that once the inmate has been 'processed' through one of the dependence sub-systems – for example, he has been converted from an inmate needing a bath into a inmate who has been bathed – there is no other role in another system into which he can move. He can only wait to become an input of a further dependence sub-system, through which he will be dressed, fed, dosed, given occupational therapy, and put to bed.

In the model we propose, the dependence organization provides for only one set of roles and occupies only a part of the inmate's life-space. Between moving out of one dependence sub-system and into another, he has to be able to leave the dependence system entirely and take up a different role within a different system – one providing for psycho-physical independence. Its primary task must be to provide opportunities for inmates to satisfy their needs as independent individuals.

A simple example would be a workshop run and staffed by inmates. If this workshop were in a separate building, the inmate's change of role, as he moved from the dependence system to the independence system, would be marked by the crossing of a physical boundary. Individuals plainly vary in their independence needs. Therefore, multiple sub-systems of activity are required to provide for psycho-physical independence. Some may be readily identifiable as 'work' – for example, operating a typing–duplicating bureau, or painting and selling pictures. Others – for example, arrangement of outings, or internal delivery of mail and newspapers – may seem trivial if they are not recognized as a means for the individual to experience an independent role.

A system concerned with psycho-physical independence cannot fully perform its task unless it provides some roles from which inmates can influence the running of the institution as a whole and its transactions with its environment – for example, through fund-raising, through participation in a consultative system, or through taking roles in institutional management itself. Although few may be both willing and able to take such roles, it is important that the opportunities should exist and be perceived as existing.

In one sense, it may be misleading to talk of a system with the task of providing for psycho-physical independence, for it is plain that in the sub-systems of activities that arise inmates, like any other members of a work organization, will be expressing and satisfying their dependent as well as their independent needs. Correspondingly, of course, within the caring system, which is concerned with providing for psycho-physical dependence, there will also be activities in which the inmates are expressing their independence. What is important is that the primary tasks of the two systems are fundamentally different and that the institution gives organizational, and also cultural, acknowledgement of the need for both.

The model that we are developing here for a residential institution has something in common with a university. The university offers the undergraduate dependent roles in the teaching and residential systems; and, partly through project work in the teaching system and partly through an array of student-led activities, it also offers him independent roles. The educational process is carried out through the student's movement from role to role in these systems. Universities also recognize, explicitly or implicitly, that they are engaged in a maturational task – they are converting schoolchildren into adults – and that undergraduates may need support in navigating their way through these systems, in dealing with problems of identity, and in planning future careers. Some universities organize a tutorial system around this need; almost all nowadays provide a student counselling service.

A corresponding support system is required for inmates in these institutions. Although the opportunity for movement between dependent and independent roles provides for a richer and more mature mode of living, which is closer to the experience of ordinary adults, it does not eliminate all the pain of being a cripple. Interpersonal support is part of the fabric of healthy institutional life, but specialist resources are also required – for example, psychotherapy and counselling – which for these institutions are almost completely lacking.

We would emphasize that what we are discussing here is support for inmates. Staff too need support and it is a responsibility of institutional leadership to provide it for them. Such support will undoubtedly benefit the inmates. However, to provide support only to staff, without creating a distinctive support system for inmates (preferably linked to external professional bases), implies that their personal difficulties can be dealt with entirely *en passant*, as it were, in the context of providing physical care. The inmate is then barred from the opportunity, which is open to other adults and for which his need is often greater, of taking a client or patient role from which to work at his problems.

INSTITUTIONAL LEADERSHIP

It is the task of overall leadership – whether this role is occupied by an individual or by a group – to relate the constituent systems of activity to each other and the institution as a whole to its external environment. Here we discuss only some of the internal problems of leadership.

The most important task is to maintain the separate integrity of dependence and independence systems and a clear boundary between them, so that the inmate may move from one role to another. However, this is also difficult to achieve. Dependence of the institution on the wider society promotes a dependent culture internally. This can readily preclude anything else and lead to the collusive 'basic assumption dependency' behaviour (see Bion, 1961), in which inmates express only dependent needs, staff exist only to satisfy them, and it is the role of the leader to be an omnipotent source of succour to all. Underlying and reinforcing such behaviour may be a fantasy that the leader is potentially capable of curing the incurable. Such collusion becomes a little easier to resist if leadership of the whole institution and leadership of the part concerned with dependency are recognized as separate roles and assigned to different people. This separation, however, can readily be accompanied by primitive splitting processes, whereby the overall leader is preserved as a benign figure and the badness is projected into the person in charge of the caring activities.

It is also difficult to build up a second system of activities around the positive task of independence. Counter-dependence is more readily mobilized. This is related to another kind of basic assumption behaviour – in Bion's terms, 'basic assumption fight/ flight' – in which the inmates are united in fighting against or fleeing from an external enemy, who is again likely to be the head of the caring system. Counter-dependence is inimical to genuine independence, since it involves inmates in participation at a primitive emotional level and not as mature, reasoning individuals.

No leader can prevent the social structure from being used in this way as a defence mechanism. Inmates and staff will inevitably try to deal with some of their internal conflicts by projecting them into the structure. In this respect, members of residential establishments differ from members of any other organization only in degree: their problems over dependency are more intense. But whereas most people outside belong to multiple social systems between which they can, so to speak, distribute their projections, these inmates and many of the staff have only the one: it is, to use Goffman's terminology (Goffman, 1961), a total institution. It is this which generates such strong collusive pressures to settle for a warehousing model or a horticultural model – structures which meet the defensive needs but inhibit task performance. Therefore, even if the values of the external society were more congruent with the task we have defined, the organization through which it needs to be carried out would still be precarious, since it is a task that calls for the examination of conflict – especially intrapersonal conflict – rather than the avoidance of it. What the leader has to resist is the temptation to take over and erode the ego functioning of others by making their decisions for them and resolving their internal conflicts for them. Indeed, the effective leader serves as a model, both for inmates and for staff, of a person who clings to reality, and who does not need to use the institutional structure as a means of dealing with his own internal conflicts.

Concluding Comments

Our work at Le Court and our experience of some other institutions suggest the model outlined here, though undoubtedly demanding, is not an unattainable ideal. Although we have yet to discover any but the most rudimentary form of support system, a few institutions have found it possible to cater effectively both for psycho-physical dependence and for independence. Observations and comments from the people concerned suggest that these are better places both for inmates to live in and for staff to work in.

While we have been dealing specifically here with institutions for incurables, it seems likely that this way of looking at organization, especially the stress on making clearly separate provision for dependence and independence, may have some relevance to residential institutions of other kinds.

4 GERIATRIC HOSPITALS AS OPEN SYSTEMS

THE PRESENTING PROBLEM

The trigger for this study was an approach to the Ministry of Health by the director of nursing of a teaching hospital group. She was concerned about nursing staff in a geriatric hospital within the group. A year or two previously a committee of inquiry had been set up following complaints about maltreatment of patients. Although the hospital had been found 'not guilty', nurses continued to show signs of severe stress and she had problems in retaining and recruiting staff. Could ways be found, she asked, to alleviate this situation?

The Ministry responded by inviting us to submit a proposal for research into the problems of geriatric nursing. After talking to the director of nursing and to the matron and clinical director of the hospital itself, we prepared an outline proposal which they endorsed and which the Ministry agreed to fund.

THE APPROACH

In our outline, we suggested that the study should not be confined to the nursing staff alone but should be extended to include the whole institution within which the nurses worked, including its

A previously unpublished paper. Other members of the research team were Tim Dartington, Penny Jones and Sheila Scott.

relations with the external community from which patients were drawn. We believed that unless we developed some understanding of the place of the hospital within the wider system of geriatric care in the community as well as the system of care within the hospital itself, we would not be able adequately to diagnose the problem and to devise possible ways of alleviating it. We hoped very much that the study would take the form of an action research project in the course of which we would become involved with experimental changes – for example, in forms of work organization – both in that particular hospital and in geriatric hospitals elsewhere. In that way it would be possible to find practical tests for some of the hypotheses that might emerge. In the event, for reasons which we shall outline later, we were relatively unsuccessful in getting into an action research role.

Essentially, then, we were proposing an analysis of the hospital as an open system. Seen in these terms, an enterprise or institution takes in certain 'raw materials' (in this case patients), engages in some kind of 'conversion process', and exports the products. A further element in the open system model is the notion of exchange. Not only is the institution receiving intakes from the environment and exporting outputs into it, but it must carry out this process in such a way as to satisfy relevant sectors of the environment. In the case of a manufacturing company, its capacity to sell its products and make a profit provides a relatively simple yardstick. In this way it is enabled to generate the resources to acquire further raw materials and supplies and to maintain the system. In the case of service institutions, such as a hospital, the criteria are less direct. Ultimately, however, a hospital must to some extent continue to satisfy certain needs in the environment if it is to continue to attract patients and resources. Also, unlike a manufacturing company, the hospital, along with prisons, public transport undertakings and so on, is a 'people-processing institution'. In these, the human throughputs – the patients, prisoners, passengers, etc. – to some extent place themselves in the hands of the staff of the institution and the 'processing' that occurs is in part the result of interaction between the staff and the throughput. It is a commonplace problem in such institutions that the type of 'batch processing' that effective operation of the institution tends to require interferes with the full expression of the individuality of the people passing through the system. While some of their needs – for treatment, or for transport – will be satisfied, others may well be ignored or frustrated.

In analysing a hospital as an open system, therefore, we have first to ask questions about the characteristics of the intake: where the patients come from, how they are defined, how they get into the system. Second, we have to trace the nature of their experience in going through the system: what sort of processes they are subject to, how long they stay, how much they move between one sub-system and another within the system. Third, we have to examine the processes whereby they leave the system and the destinations to which they go. At the same time we have also to examine the experiences of the staff on their side of the transaction and in particular to consider discrepancies between what staff think should be happening and what is actually happening.

In this particular case, we used four main approaches in the research. First, we undertook a statistical study of a year's admissions, tracing the origins of patients by age, sex, etc., their various routes through the hospital and their length of stay and the outcome of their discharge. Second, we interviewed members of the staff both in groups and as individuals. Third, we carried out interviews with patients' families, GPs, social workers, and others involved in the initial referral of patients and their subsequent discharge. Finally, we followed up in considerable detail twenty consecutive admissions to the hospital. We used these methods both in the first hospital we worked in and in another to which we subsequently moved.

SOME CHARACTERISTICS OF THE FIRST HOSPITAL

This hospital, with just over 200 beds, had in the past catered mainly for long-stay patients. In 1950 some 80 per cent had been bedfast for more than one year. At that time the clinical director had begun to introduce a rehabilitative approach to geriatric hospital care. This orientation could be described as socio-medical. Even if the medical conditions that might initially have prompted admission to the hospital could be successfully dealt with, psychological, social and physical factors in the environment might still inhibit discharge.

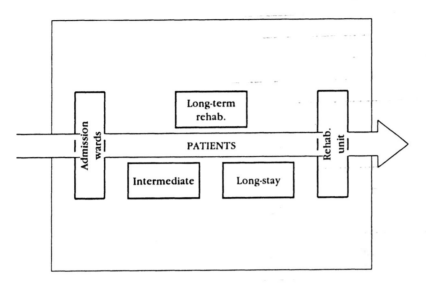

Fig. 4.1 A geriatric hospital as an open system

The rehabilitative approach had to take these into account. The director introduced a system of progressive patient care in which, optimally, the incoming patient moved from a situation of maximum care early in his stay to minimum care towards the time for discharge. These phases of treatment were carried out in different wards with different kinds of resources and different technologies. The accompanying diagram (Figure 4.1) shows the hospital as an open system together with these various sub-systems through which the patients passed.

At the time of our study, the annual number of admissions was around 1000 and, instead of 80 per cent, only half of one per cent of the patients had been bedfast for more than a year. Almost all new patients came in to one of the admission wards, also known as the acute wards, where about a quarter of them would die. (Three-quarters of all the deaths in the hospital occurred in the admission wards.) Most commonly patients who had survived their stay in an admission ward would be transferred to a rehabilitation ward and then discharged. Some would be discharged directly from admission wards. 'Intermediate' and 'long-term rehabilitation' wards were used for patients who no longer needed the relatively intensive care of the admission wards but at the same time were not yet ready for rehabilitation. A few patients for whom the prognosis of discharge seemed poor were transferred into long-stay wards.

About 40 per cent of the admissions were men and 57 per cent of the patients were admitted from home. Slightly over 30 per cent of the admissions ended in death and 13 per cent in transfers to other hospitals. Of all admissions, 55 per cent were for less than four weeks, 3 per cent remained continuously in the hospital for a year or more, and the mean length of stay was between eight and nine weeks.

So much for the general characteristics of the first hospital. Although the figures just given were derived from our statistical study, the outline corresponds closely to the picture we were given during an initial visit while we were still preparing our research proposal.

PRELIMINARY HYPOTHESES

At that time we had also formulated some preliminary hypotheses about the particular problems that a geriatric hospital like this, and therefore the nurses in it, might be expected to experience. In our thinking we were drawing upon previous work by Isabel Menzies in general hospital situations (Menzies, 1960) and by Miller and Gwynne in residential institutions for incurables (Miller and Gwynne, 1972, 1973, see Chapter 3 in this volume). We were also drawing on our work in other institutions with a human throughput, such as airlines (Miller and Rice, 1967, see Chapter 2 in this volume). On this basis we postulated that there would be certain problems arising from the characteristics of geriatric hospitals in general and we foresaw particular types of problem associated with attempting to operate a rehabilitative strategy in such a hospital. We could predict first of all that the geriatric patient would be importing into the hospital hidden 'baggage' not dissimilar in some respects to that of an airline passenger. Dependency in particular was likely to present problems. Some patients would have been clinging to independence in their lives outside and could be expected to be resentful of the illness or the breakdown in external support that had precipitated their admission to hospital. Others would be seeking to be totally looked after. Problems of helplessness and incontinence, combined with the move into an alien setting, would make it even more likely than in an ordinary general hospital that the emotional states of an infantile dependency would be reactivated – 'second childhood'. Closely related to this – again as with the airline passengers – primitive fantasies about separation, especially separation from the mother, would be likely to be evoked at admission. Such anxieties would be reinforced by the real doubts in many instances as to whether the patient could be restored to the home that he or she had come from. Again similar to the case of the passengers' complex fears about flying, geriatric patients would be likely to bring into the situation at both a reality and fantasy level fears about undischargeability, deterioration and death.

In such a situation, we envisaged that staff were likely to be subjected to extreme swings of hopefulness and hopelessness, both leading to some degree of mismatch. On the one hand, they would have invested in them hope that they could produce magical cures and even rejuvenation; and on the other hand, they would be confronted with fears – some justified, some not – that no improvement at all would be possible. We foresaw that confrontation with death would be a particular problem for staff in these hospitals. Menzies had shown how far anxieties about death were an issue for the staff in general hospitals, leading to the mobilization of both personal and social defence mechanisms, and plainly death was much nearer at hand in geriatric situations. The staff would be constantly confronted with mortality, while the successful cures which provide compensating satisfactions in the general hospitals would be much fewer and further between.

We postulated that the policy of progressive patient care leading towards an aim of rehabilitation could pose special problems in the area of dependency. Very many patients would be asking directly and indirectly to be looked after, to be dependent. It could be seen as 'natural' both psychologically and in terms of social values for the nurses to respond to these demands. On the other hand, in a system of progressive patient care the nurse's role would often require her to resist such demands in the interests of encouraging the patient to do things for himself and so advancing his mobilization. The nurse, then, would be subjected to conflict. The organization would need to help her to suppress the 'natural' responses. To the extent that it failed fully to achieve this – and full achievement seemed unlikely – some stress would be inevitable.

Moreover, prevailing social values relating to the care of the elderly are themselves by no means uniform and consistent. As members of the general population the staff of the hospital could be expected to be importing the varying values of the society at large, some of which would be appropriate to the hospital's strategy and others not. One social norm, still widely prevalent in the rural parts of the hospital's catchment area, was that 'families should look after their own'. This could be seen as consistent with the aim of the hospital in trying to mobilize patients and get them back to their families, though equally it could have somewhat punitive overtones for families which perhaps for very good reasons felt themselves lacking the resources to cope with an infirm elderly person. The other set of norms, which supported the families who felt unable to cope, was linked to contemporary attitudes to the welfare state: responsibility for the care of the old and infirm belonged to the 'authorities'. Such norms were more prevalent in the industrialized, urban areas close to the hospital. We could see then that the hospital might well have the problem of trying to discharge patients in the face of family and community demands that it should look after them until they died.

INITIAL FINDINGS

Evidence from our field work largely confirmed these hypotheses and in particular enhanced our understanding of mismatch, both at the interface between the hospital and its community environment and also between patients and staff.

When we came to examine the processes of admission and discharge, it became clear that the hospital was operating under considerable environmental pressure. Some discharges of course were straightforward: patients had been sufficiently mobilized as a result of their stay in hospital; they wanted to leave; and there was a place for them to go to. In other instances, there was much more difficulty. The hospital's definition of 'adequate mobilization' might be quite inconsistent with what the family or the old people's home would regard as adequate – and this was notwithstanding the fact that the hospital, through its medical and social work staff, made substantial efforts to arrange the necessary support services in the community and also offered guarantees of re-admission should the patient fail to readjust to the outside world. Often, then, the social workers and more particularly the doctors were in the position of applying pressure on reluctant families or perhaps striking bargains with the heads of old people's homes: if the home would accept a discharge from the hospital, the hospital would accept an admission from the home. Precious hospital beds were blocked while these negotiations took place.

This had ramifications for the admission process. Analysis of referrals, which were usually through general practitioners (though some patients were transferred from other hospitals, notably the large general hospital in the nearby city), showed that the precipitating factor was very often some breakdown in the system of support in the community. For example, it might be the daughter-in-law who was ill; it was the dependent mother-in-law who had to be admitted to hospital because the daughter-in-law could no longer look after her. There was some tendency for families and GPs to suppress or play down such social factors, apparently on the assumption that the hospital would be more chary about admission if it foresaw substantial problems in subsequent discharge. Thus, although the precipitating factor was, as we came to put it, the loss of 'social space' for the elderly person in the family and the community, and although too the orientation of the hospital was socio-medical rather than merely medical, with an explicit recognition that psychological, social and physical factors in the environment had to be considered as well as the medical state of the patient, GPs nevertheless tended to present their patients predominantly in medical terms. Consultants would be called out to make domiciliary visits and to give second opinions on medical conditions – and it is seldom difficult to diagnose multiple pathologies in an elderly person. Social circumstances would not be fully disclosed. To some extent the patient therefore was being admitted under false pretences and the problems arising when the time came for discharge had not been anticipated by the hospital. In the absence of attempts – by social workers, for example – to hold open the social space in the community, the door was still more firmly closed by the time the patient was, from the hospital's standpoint, fit for discharge. Some GPs avoided the difficulty of direct negotiation with the geriatric hospital by referring their patients as emergency admissions to the general hospital from which they would subsequently be transferred to the geriatric hospital 'for rehabilitation'. Geriatricians would then complain with some justification that the nursing régime in the general hospital was itself not oriented towards rehabilitation, with the result that patients coming from there were more helpless and less competent than if they had been nursed in the geriatric hospital from the outset. As a result, they would require a longer stay in the geriatric hospital.

These transactions at referral and discharge inevitably had their effects within the hospital and thus on the operation of the sub-systems within it. For example, if the rehabilitation unit was to be successful in carrying out its task, which was associated with the provision of minimal nursing care, then it was necessary that patients transferred to that unit were, say, capable of going to the lavatory by themselves and not incontinent. At the same time it is in reality difficult to define such standards rigorously, especially as an inter-ward transfer within the hospital may be experienced by the patient as somewhat disruptive and lead to a temporary set-back – for example, one or two days of incontinence. The appropriate question to ask was: 'Is this patient ready to be moved to the rehabilitation unit?' The pressure on beds in the admission wards was such, however, that the question tacitly being asked was: 'How soon can we vacate this bed for a new patient?' An almost imperceptible decline in the competence of patients entering the rehabilitation ward could lead to a significant increase in 'regressive' transfers into, say, the long-term rehabilitation ward.

The nature of the hospital's relationship with its environment also had other effects on the patient/nurse relationship within the hospital. In particular, the admission of patients 'under false pretences' meant in effect that they were misdescribed both to the nursing staff and to themselves. The image presented by the case-notes often did not correspond to their self-image. There were simple distortions of reality: grandmothers became 'Miss', lifelong spinsters 'Mrs'; but beyond that reasons for admission could be inconsistent with the course of treatment. Patients admitted for manifestly social reasons could feel that the hospital's medical interventions were more related to staff needs than their own.

The difficulty in coming to terms with death was certainly a problem for staff but perhaps not quite in the way in which we had predicted. For example, in the admission wards, where the death-rate was highest, it was a less unspeakable subject than in some of the other wards: death was a much more normal and predictable part of the nurses' working life. Moreover, given such a death-rate, one would reasonably expect the staff to be less concerned about possibly fatal consequences of their own treatment. The issue in these wards was over the prolongation of life. Nurses believed that in some cases death was the obvious, natural and appropriate outcome of admission. They then protested when doctors ordered treatments that were uncomfortable for the patients, distressing for the nurses to administer and only marginally likely to postpone death. Their protests, however, were seldom if ever voiced to the doctors themselves: these were matters to be grumbled about and worried about within the nursing staff.

This underlines one further finding from the research which had not been so evident in our preliminary visits. The multi-dimensional approach to rehabilitation prevailing in this hospital was expressed in multi-disciplinary teams of medical and nursing staff, physiotherapists, occupational therapists and social workers, all, at least in theory, pooling their information about individual patients and jointly developing and monitoring treatment strategies. Nurses' preoccupations (such as the one mentioned above concerning the prolongation of life) were, however, not taken up in the inter-disciplinary case meetings. At least part of the reason lay in the asymmmetry of the division of labour. Some of the disciplinary groups – the doctors in particular – were involved with the patient during the whole of his trajectory through the hospital from pre-admission to discharge. Nursing staff, on the other hand, were

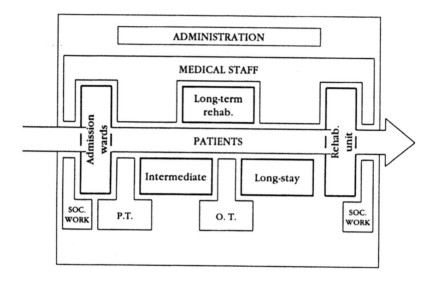

Fig. 4.2 A geriatric hospital: transactions between staff and patients

operating within the various ward sub-systems so that nurses on the admission wards lost sight of transferred patients and often did not know the outcome of discharges; while, correspondingly, nurses in the rehabilitation unit were confronted with families at the time of discharge without being familiar with the processes of admission and early treatment. Despite the theory, one could not conceive that in practice the medical and nursing staff involved with patients on, say, an admission ward constituted a sub-system that was differentiated from another sub-system of medical and nursing staff for the rehabilitation unit. The nursing staff were confined to the boundaries of their sub-systems; the medical staff by contrast were omnipresent. This is illustrated in the re-drawing of Figure 4.1 in Figure 4.2 above.

Each of these wards had a manifest task in terms of providing a distinctive type of treatment for patients. Each also had a latent task in terms of providing and reinforcing defences for the nurses operating in it against the stress of the manifest task. One of the more important defences that we identified was conflict displacement and scapegoating. We mentioned above the dilemma arising over the issue of postponement of death as against easing the process of dying, and we noted that the nurses tended to blame the doctors for persisting in treatment and in refusing to allow patients to die in peace. On the other hand, when we talked to the doctor involved in such a situation he often expressed a view that was in no way discrepant with that of the nursing staff. The nurses, by holding on to their belief that the doctor was ruthless and inhumane, were better able to sustain a belief in their own gentleness and humaneness. This would be one way, then, of coping with the mismatch between the needs and expectations of the patients on the one hand and what the nurses were actually able to do on the other. Similarly, conflict between sub-systems allowed nurses to believe in the validity and goodness of what they were doing within their own sub-system and to project the notions of incompetence and of inability to cope onto others. Thus there was mutual scapegoating between the admissions wards and the rehabilitation unit. Nurses in the latter protested that patients were sent before they were ready for transfer; nurses in the admissions ward, on the other hand, complained that those in the rehabilitation unit only wanted to deal with patients who were already effectively better. Furthermore, medical staff could always plant their blame on the nursing staff.

A particular difficulty within the philosophy and strategy of progressive patient care is acknowledgement that a sizeable proportion of patients will neither die nor recover. They are the failures of the system and to some extent call the efficacy of such a strategy into question. It is therefore an awkward reality to accept and, to avoid accepting it, it may be claimed that the situation need not have arisen if suitable treatment had been given. Blame can then be directed on individuals or groups within the system for alleged inefficiency in carrying out their task. Here again, the nursing sub-systems become natural scapegoats for the medical staff. It may be comforting for a doctor to believe that if only the nursing staff had been more adaptable, better trained, better managed, then this patient need not have deteriorated, or that another one might have been rehabilitated.

What we have tried to do in this section of the paper is to give some examples of the data and analysis that emerged in the course of our initial fieldwork.

FEEDBACK AND RESPONSE

These findings were progressively fed back to the senior medical and nursing staff in the hospital in the form of a series of working notes. The notes were intended as a basis for discussion and hopefully as a basis for moving later into an action research role, whereby possible experimental changes might be designed and carried out. In fact, these discussions were not very successful. We ourselves felt sympathetic towards the staff of the hospital in their efforts to tackle the dilemmas they were in; on the other hand, our working notes were frequently perceived as being critical of what they were doing.

We could put forward some explanations for our difficulty in getting into a collaborative relationship with these staff. One factor was that as a result of certain changes at senior staff level, we had done less than we should have in cultivating regular meetings with them. Another obvious factor was that since the hospital had been the subject of adverse criticism leading to a committee of inquiry, staff might still feel particularly sensitive to any hint of a complaint, even though the hospital had been absolved.

However, these explanations were clearly not good enough, for when we moved to work in a second geriatric hospital setting, we encountered difficulties of very much the same kind. Yet there we had been fairly meticulous in maintaining liaison with the senior staff, particularly the consultant in charge; moreover, in that hospital there had been no previous history of public complaints or committees of inquiry. While in this second hospital we did make somewhat better progress in terms of developing a collaborative relationship with the consultant and with one or two groups of nursing staff, we had a precisely similar experience of our written report being regarded as destructively critical. This could be taken as possible evidence that we had not fully understood all the factors in the situation.

FURTHER ANALYSIS

Although the second hospital was different in a number of superficial respects, our study substantially confirmed all our findings from the first. However, it would appear in retrospect that we had not given sufficient weight in either setting to the significance of the discrepancies between

1   what the hospital was trying to do
2   what the environment wanted it to do
3   what it was actually doing
4   what it 'ought' to do

We have already said something about what these hospitals were trying to do: to carry out a socio-medical strategy for rehabilitation. What the community wanted them to be were custodial institutions which would remove intractable problems from distressed families, overworked GPs and overcrowded old people's homes. The outcome of these pressures was that what they were actually doing was somewhat different from what they were trying to do. For example, one of their functions was to serve as a clearing-house for elderly people who had lost 'social space' in the community. Of the patients who were admitted from home to the first hospital and who survived, some 75 per cent were discharged back to their homes. However, 25 per cent went on to other hospitals or to residential institutions. It was the function of the hospital to negotiate such movements. Moreover, in order to get as many as 75 per cent of survivors returned home, the hospital staff, notably the consultants, were very often forced to act in the role of moral arbiters, reminding reluctant sons and daughters and their spouses of their obligations towards the old. Just as in the admission phase the images of prospective patients were edited by families and GPs in order to conform to what was believed to be a profile acceptable to the hospital, so the hospital itself in discharging them again edited the data, albeit not deliberately, in order to make these ex-patients more acceptable to external institutions. This was undoubtedly difficult to look at.

Essentially then, these hospitals and particularly the consultants in charge of them were faced with powerful and difficult pressures and a constant struggle therefore to maintain a precarious *status quo*. They were dedicated people, indisputably doing their best; but what they were actually doing certainly diverged from their intentions.

If we turn now to what these hospitals 'ought' to be doing, it is clear that our analysis suggested that, in both the community settings in which we worked, the geriatric hospital was one of a set of institutions and services concerned with the care of the elderly which, for all their good intentions, were in effect treating the elderly people as 'problems' to be dumped from one system to another. In this process the identities and needs of individuals got distorted or lost. The implicit 'ought', then, was not something that any geriatric hospital could achieve unilaterally: it needed to become a part of a collaborative set of systems that were concerned with identifying the special needs of elderly individuals and developing conjoint strategies to meet these needs. For this to be achieved, however, it would be necessary for the hospital and for some of the other systems radically to reconsider their aims and functions. A critical question in this field of care was and is, not how to make the best use of the resources that are available but, starting from the other end, how to provide resources to fit the needs of the elderly in the community.

We had noted in both hospitals a very powerful dependency culture centred on the consultants. This dependency had a basis in reality in that it fell particularly on the consultants to maintain the boundaries of the hospital as an institution by regulating admissions and facilitating discharges. We have seen how difficult this task was. Beyond that, however, we had probably underplayed the extent to which this powerful dependency culture needed to be maintained in order to cope with the discrepancies identified above. One could see that it might be difficult for staff working in such a situation to remain sufficiently convinced of the value of what they were doing if they really confronted the full extent of these discrepancies. To hold on to a sense of worthwhileness and value made it the more necessary to elevate the consultant to the role of someone omnipotent and omniscient. It would follow then that if the consultant was used in this way to maintain a belief in the validity of the existing system in the face of powerful and conflicting pressures, it would be difficult for him to entertain any radical re-examination of the way in which the hospital was operating. To contemplate the possibility of radical change would be to undermine that belief. To put it another way, the consultant in both these settings not only occupied a role in leadership of task performance but was the focal point of the defence systems of the hospital. And from our analysis it will be clear that in situations of this kind, where there is such a manifest mismatch between the needs and demands of the throughput, the pressures from the environment, and the capacities of the staff to satisfy both constituencies, powerful institutional defence mechanisms are necessary and inevitable. As Menzies showed, however, such defences, like many drugs, only partly treat the ailment and also produce debilitating side-effects.

UPSHOTS

In conclusion, therefore, this application of an open system framework to the analysis of a geriatric hospital indicates that there are limits to the usefulness of intervention at the level of the hospital itself. Our findings suggested that alternative forms of organization might be available to fulfil a strategy of progressive patient care and that some of these might be relatively less stressful than others for the nursing staff in the system. Such changes might have a marginal effect in reducing the discrepancy between what the hospital was trying to do and what it was actually doing. Moreover, our work with groups of nurses in the second hospital, in which we helped them to understand more clearly the nature of the pressures they were under from the environment, particularly in terms of the expectations from families and others that were being imported as part of the 'baggage' of the individual patients, suggested that some alleviation of stress could also be found in this way. However, any significant reduction in this mismatch would require a much more radical change of the kind we have indicated above and to achieve this the hospital would have to enter into coalitions with other institutions and services which were jointly prepared to get rid of the current knock-for-knock arrangements of the dumping syndrome in geriatric care.

PART THREE:
ANALYSIS AND
DIAGNOSIS

INTRODUCTION

I decided that this volume should include examples of material actually produced for clients as part of the working relationship, and not exclusively the more polished pieces put together later for a wider public. As with some other colleagues, it has long been my practice to produce 'working notes' for clients: these summarize where we have got to so far and offer working hypotheses. They then serve as an agenda for a further round of discussions and possible action.

When I took that decision I had no idea how difficult the choice would be. The privilege of having worked with a very large number of organizations, immensely varied, coupled with a less than adequate system of document retrieval, meant that when I ransacked old files I found some that were barely remembered, including the client of my first solo consultancy after I joined the Tavistock Institute – a company in the business of leasing juke-boxes and pinball machines. Some rejected themselves: the issues were too confidential, or too much contextual explanation would have been needed. Even so, the short-list was long.

Of the four offerings that follow, one – 'A Prison in Northern Ireland' – is actually not so much a working note as a proposal for a project that never happened. The other three relate to interventions in very different kinds of system.

5   A Church of England Diocese

This piece of work was commissioned in 1973 by the Bishop's Council of the Diocese of Chelmsford. The initial approach came from the Vice-Provost (later Provost) of Chelmsford Cathedral, Canon Richard Herrick. From the mid-1960s on, he had been actively involved in the group relations training programme at the Tavistock Institute – he regularly worked on conference staffs – and he had recently established the Chelmsford Cathedral Centre for Research and Training as a vehicle for extending Tavistock-type training and consultancy into the Church. This had followed a brief preliminary study of the Cathedral organization, carried out in 1969 by my colleague, Ken Rice, shortly before he died. In the Church of England the cathedral is formally independent of the bishop of the diocese in which it is located; but Herrick was approaching me in another role he had at that time, Director for Religious Education in Chelmsford Diocese, and as such he was the Bishop's adviser on educational matters.

Essentially the request was to help to rationalize the organization for education and training in the Diocese, which was a tangled web. A current proposal was that a newly appointed Suffragan Bishop should be given oversight of this area. (The

---

The working note reproduced here was co-authored with W. G. Lawrence in 1973; a postscript, written in 1991 by A.W. Carr, has been added.

Diocesan Bishop was at that time assisted by three Suffragans, each with responsibility for a territory – a substantial set of parishes – and also for a function.) I was sceptical about taking on this assignment. As a paper exercise, there was no particular problem in designing a 'rational' structure; but to design a structure that would actually work one needed to understand much more fully what lay behind the manifest irrationalities of the existing structure. Training has to be directed towards a task: what was the task of 'ministry'? The Bishop had recently launched a 'Call to Mission', a kind of publicity drive involving all the clergy and laity: what was the Church 'selling'? With a colleague, Gordon Lawrence, I put forward some of these reservations at a further meeting with Herrick and the Bishop and we eventually negotiated a more open-ended brief.

Our first working note (entitled 'A preliminary study of the Organization for Education and Training in the context of the task of ministry'), was based on interviews with all the key people at diocesan level and (with the help of three associates from the Cathedral Centre) a sample of parish priests and curates. A second note (not reproduced here) put forward some more specific proposals.

A person closely involved in the follow-up was Dr Wesley Carr, then a Canon at Chelmsford Cathedral and Deputy Director of the Cathedral Centre. Now Dean of Bristol, he has kindly volunteered to add a postscript.

THE WORKING NOTE I: FINDINGS

OUR INITIAL EXPERIENCE

It is not unusual for us to experience some confusion when we move into an institutional setting that is new to us. It takes time to grasp essential features of the technology and the language. We also expect to absorb something of the conflicts, dilemmas and uncertainties of the organization without at first being able to clarify the issues involved. In this particular study, the experience of confusion was considerably greater than usual and therefore becomes part of the data that need to be examined.

First, we found it hard to comprehend the proliferation of quasi-independent educational and training activities. We were told that the same group of people met in one guise as the Diocesan Council for Religious Education (DCRE) and in another as the Diocesan Education Committee (DEC). This was widely regarded as an unsatisfactory arrangement, but the people concerned felt powerless to change it. There was a Director for Religious Education accountable to the DCRE; but he evidently had no authority in relation to the Director for Church Schools, who was accountable to the DEC – except that work with teachers on such matters as policy for religious instruction perhaps came within the orbit of the adult education activities of the DCRE. What was the meaning of 'Director' in this context? What made it necessary to maintain these two truncated roles? At the time we began the study, Canon Herrick's resignation from the former role had just become effective. He was already, however, Director of the Chelmsford Cathedral Centre for Research and Training. This Centre was in a position to pursue relatively independent policies in the training of both clergy and laity. For clergy, however, in-service training could also be regarded as an extension of Post-Ordination Training, which now covered the first five years after ordination instead of the first three, and which was the responsibility of the Senior Examining Chaplain. As for laity training, the diocesan Department for Lay Training and Action had become defunct; but the DCRE and the Bishop's Adviser for Social Work were also doing significant work with adults, there was an immense amount of voluntary activity in training, and it was put to us that the parish priest himself was, or needed to be, a local chief training officer. How did all these activities relate to each other? Indeed, should they? Did the conventional definitions of training, as being concerned with enhancing the capacity of the staff of an institution to do their jobs, make sense in a setting where much of the work of the Church was expected to be carried out by the laity?

Second, apart from this manifestly complex, if not chaotic, array of educational and training activities, we found ourselves confused by what people were telling us about their roles. At first we attributed this to our unfamiliarity with the language. The Church has a rich vocabulary, in which, for example, terms such as 'clergyman', 'parson', 'minister', 'priest', 'vicar', 'rector' and 'incumbent' can be used largely interchangeably to refer to the same role. It began to appear, however, that the greater difficulty was that some of our respondents might be using the same terms with somewhat different meanings. Most of those we interviewed were ready and able to talk about their roles in terms of the activities in which they spent their time, but in many cases they were unable to convey – or at least we were unable to grasp – the way in which they conceptualized the roles. In their explanations they used terms, then, such as 'the Church of Christ', 'the Kingdom of God', 'the Holy Spirit' and even 'faith' as if there was a shared understanding of what these terms meant. At times the terms seemed to have a sloganistic ring, and we began to wonder whether the confusion was all in us or whether some of the confusion resided within the institution itself, in that different people were in fact attaching different meanings to the terms. Our hunch that the shared language might be used to disguise such differences was confirmed by our experience of the parish interviews. There, differences of approach and of values became much more manifest.

Our central argument, on which we enlarge below, starts from the observation that in this diocese the task of ministry is being interpreted and carried out in diverse ways and that there is a reluctance to examine these differences. The diversity can be seen as a response to the difficulty that the contemporary Church has in continuing to satisfy dependent needs while remaining relevant to the experience of living in today's changing society. In the absence of any one manifestly right strategy, it may be institutionally useful to generate diversity; but this is stressful for individuals, who have to find their own ways of coping with uncertainty. The diocesan organization generally and the fragmented arrangement of education and training in particular have the function of allowing the individual member of the clergy to feel that his own way of coping is, if not positively endorsed, at least tolerated and certainly not threatened or opposed. In Part II, we begin to consider some of the implications of this analysis.

The Task of the Church I: The Question of Dependency

The demand upon the Church to cater for dependent needs is something that has to be confronted realistically in any consideration of reorganization. Some of those we interviewed had a clear grasp of this issue; others were worried by the demand and uncertain about their own proper behaviour; while yet others seemed unaware that there was anything here to be examined and understood.

Certainly, the culture of dependency within the Church was something that we directly experienced ourselves. Alongside the confusion that we felt during the first part of this study, we also had the paradoxical sense that undue reliance was being placed on us, as 'experts', to produce definitive solutions to the presenting problems. Again, while dependency on us as consultants is not unusual in our work with other institutions, here the degree of deference towards us and of hope invested in the outcome was unusually high. Correspondingly, we felt more than customarily anxious about not doing a good job that would match our clients' expectations.

In this respect, our experience seems similar to that of many clergy. The minister, as he goes about his job as a representative of the Church on the boundary with the rest of society, has a great deal of hope invested in him. He is asked to show dependability and reassurance, while recognizing at times that within the Church and within himself there is much uncertainty and confusion. Obvious though the point may be, it is perhaps worth restating that people turn to their church as representing the possibility of control over events which they themselves cannot control. In particular, it is asked to cope with fear of death. This means that there is inevitably an element of childlike dependency in the relationship to the Church, and thus to its representatives, in that to some extent they are being asked to solve the insoluble, cure the incurable, make reality go away. Indications of this dependency are evident even among non-believers, for whom the Church symbolizes the hope of security and continuity; and so they use it for their *rites de passage* and protest when an undistinguished church building is threatened with demolition. Ministers of the Church, then, have to receive this dependency. Sometimes they get stuck in a paternalistic posture; sometimes they are able to help their parishioners both to recognize the dependency and to discover their own resources and capabilities. But for the Church, the dependent posture is itself a reality that cannot be made to go away – without it the Church as an institution could scarcely exist – and so it is something to be constantly worked with.

We are labouring this point because of the implications of the dependency culture for diocesan organization. The kinds of expectations that the wider society, albeit implicitly, reposes in the Church are reflected, within the structure, in the expectations that laity repose in clergy and that clergy repose in those above them in the hierarchy. Thus the parochial minister is likely to be seeking within the hierarchy two kinds of support that are potentially contradictory. On the one hand, he seeks confirmation that he is in fact as dependable as his parishioners would wish him to be. On the other hand, he is asking for a figure on whom he can rely to deal with his own feelings of inadequacy and dependency. It would seem to us – and we shall come back to this point – that some of the current proposals for diocesan reorganization are responses to the culture of dependency rather than to an analysis of task requirements.

The Task of the Church II: Ministry

As we have already hinted, we conceive 'ministry' as a boundary function: the minister operates as representative of the Church on its boundary with the rest of the world. Our working definition of the task of ministry would run something like this: 'To illuminate the interrelatedness of the teachings of the Church with the contemporary experience of members of society'. (Such a definition would apply equally to parochial and to specialized ministries.) Thus we see it as essentially a teaching, and more specifically an interpretive, role. To be effective, it must at once be looking back into the teachings of Christ and of the Bible, and into the traditions of the Church, and outwards into the problems and preoccupations of contemporary society. Unless it can continue to demonstrate relevance the Church as an institution is doomed. Moreover, the minister, in his own behaviour, is required to set a personal example of this relevance.

Yet, as we have also suggested, at a latent level the Church has to cater for dependency needs, both individual and communal. It is required to maintain a belief in institutional, social and natural order, in dependability and in continuity, in the face of the actual social realities of discontinuity, rapid change and disorder, involving individual experience of isolation, alienation and fragmentation. This belief too the minister is asked to exemplify.

DIVERSITY IN THE CONCEPT AND PRACTICE OF MINISTRY

Seeing the problems of the task in this light, we should perhaps not have been so struck as we were by the very different ways in which, explicitly or implicitly, the task of ministry was conceived and carried out among the incumbents and curates interviewed in our sample. It was a small sample and was in any case selected for diversity as to the variety of parishes encompassed by the diocese (for example, urban/rural) and different types of churchmanship (high/evangelical). However, the diversity we identified as most significant was along quite a different dimension, directly related to the task of ministry as we have provisionally defined it. This had to do with the difficulty of maintaining the boundary position.

So far as the individual parish priest is concerned, we would look upon the problem in this way: To maintain the boundary position, from which 'to illuminate the interrelatedness', he needs to be in touch with *un*certainty, within the Church and within himself. The dependency culture denigrates uncertainty; and within the Church it is liable to be labelled 'a crisis of faith'. In that sense there are social and institutional pressures against sticking to the role that the task requires of him. These pressures encourage him to operate from a position either further inside the Church and relatively encapsulated from society on the one hand, or further into society and correspondingly less in touch with the Church on the other. Those towards the former end of the spectrum may be called fundamentalists, to the extent that for them the maintenance of the traditions of the Church or the exposition of biblical texts become ends in themselves, with little concern for their perceived relevance. From this standpoint, the Bible needs no re-interpretation. Towards the other end of the spectrum are those who are so immersed in real social problems that, while they have not gone so far as taking on full-time jobs in secular institutions, they may nevertheless fail to sustain the task of relating contemporary experience to the teachings and traditions of the Church. This is not to discredit, of course, their achievements in, say, the social work or educational fields: we are merely concerned here to question their relevance to the task of ministry. From the standpoint of our definition they, like the fundamentalists, can be regarded as having moved away from the uncertainty of the boundary role into a position in which they can feel more secure.

Many of those we interviewed could be located along this dimension on one side of the boundary or the other; but this classification does not, of course, exhaust the variety of individual interpretations of the task. For example, there are those who find some security in a perpetual round of parish visiting or in participation in numerous committees.

Our evidence that the taking up of roles somewhat removed from the boundary is related to the need for security is rather indirect. For example, a number of clergy seemed to become quite uncomfortable when we tried to explore how they saw the link between their activities and their concept of their role. Those whom we identified as operating on the boundary, by contrast, were in no way personally threatened by such an exploration and indeed welcomed it as an opportunity to discuss their dilemmas and difficulties.

INSTITUTIONAL ENCOURAGEMENT OF DIVERSITY

When one adds to the diversity we found in interpretation of the role of ministry the various other differences, in churchmanship and even in personal style, it is plain that the variety is immense. Notwithstanding the fact that the 'freehold' of the parish priest has always given scope for individualist approaches, we would suspect that the variation is greater than in the past. It is also likely to be more publicly apparent. People move house more frequently; widespread car ownership has expanded the choice of where to worship. The fact that parish boundaries are diminishingly related to the sources of congregations is well recognized; and of course it makes the job of parochial ministry all the more difficult when one's own parishioners feel an allegiance to another priest. Some of the parish clergy we met seemed to be relating more to congregations than to parishes, and one said explicitly that he did not recognize that belonging to the Established Church differentiated his role from that of ministers of other denominations.

It may be entirely appropriate for this diversity to be encouraged within the diocese. If the parish has ceased to mark a relevant community boundary, then one could argue the case for the Church deliberately 'marketing' an array of 'products' (styles of worship; approaches to ministry) to match the variety of 'consumer' needs. It is not within our brief to consider the pros and cons of such policies. What our observations do suggest, however, is that various factors in the diocese at present encourage diversity not as a matter of policy but almost by default. The implicit policy is one of laissez-faire and of avoiding examination of the differences.

Thus the freehold, which is designed to protect the parish priest from arbitrary intervention, appears to be used as a way of avoiding questioning what he is doing. The nature of the hierarchy is such that each parish priest, if he needs counselling and support, has access to a variety of superiors: a Rural Dean, an Archdeacon, a Suffragan Bishop, the Diocesan Bishop. Given such a choice, he is likely to go to the one who will not basically question his approach to his role. By and large, however, he does not go to the Diocesan Bishop, who in a sense is asked to endorse and legitimate everything done in the parishes without examining anything. The notion of 'the Holy Spirit at work' has a positive connotation in respecting individualism; but it can also be used – albeit unintentionally – as a catch-phrase to avoid the confrontation of differences that may be institutionally important. By the same token, the Bishop's Call to Mission, which was plainly designed to mobilize the clergy and laity of the diocese in a united purpose, may also unwittingly foster diversity, in that it is essentially a call to do more effectively the things being done already, leaving any questioning of the appropriateness of these activities to the groups and individuals involved.

Our hypothesis is that the organizational dispersion of educational and training activities is itself consistent with the implicit policy of *laissez-faire*. It leaves the options open. In particular the parish priest is largely free to decide whether the programmes offered are relevant to himself and his laity. In the case of church schools, it would seem that the separation of the DCRE and the DEC enables the diocese to discharge its statutory and financial responsibilities, while avoiding potential controversy over the locus of responsibility for setting educational policy: the relationship of the parish priest to the local church school remains unexamined.

THE WORKING NOTE II: IMPLICATIONS

EDUCATION AND TRAINING

At the time we started work, it was the intention of the Bishop of Chelmsford to give a newly appointed Suffragan Bishop a general oversight in the area of education and training, and it was hoped that we might help in the definition of his brief. At first sight, the Bishop's Council might justly accuse us of posing more questions than we have answered. In light of what has emerged so far, however, it seems to us that priority needs to be given to the formulation of a policy for education and training; any organizational rearrangements must flow from that.

In the first instance, the analysis we offer in Part I, although it gained some acceptance from the Bishop and the other three members of the Council when we outlined it to them, needs to be checked, refined and confirmed against available knowledge and experience. If our hypothesis is correct, then it is important to recognize that the existing organization is related to an implicit policy of *laissez-faire*. This encourages, by not questioning them, diverse interpretations of the task of ministry. And to question them, we have suggested, may also be to question the very personal accommodations – even defence mechanisms – that individuals have adopted to cope with the uncertainty and insecurity of their roles.

This is to be construed as an argument not for inaction but for caution, in the sense of predicting and being prepared for the consequences of possible actions.

One possibility is to maintain the *status quo* by making the policy of encouraging diversity more explicit and then mobilizing diocesan services to help make each of the various approaches to the task of ministry more effective. A difficulty about this is that, as with the Call to Mission strategy, it would imply that the Bishop and his advisers endorsed each of the approaches as equally valid; and we doubt whether this is or should be the case. In particular, if we are correct in believing that many parish priests have not so much chosen to operate their roles in specific ways but have fallen into them, as it were, as a means of dealing with anxiety, then such a policy would in all probability be reinforcing inappropriate choices.

This does, however, open up a perhaps more positive and creative policy. How can clergy (and also laity) be helped to make better decisions about their approach to ministry? And, in line with our definition of the task of ministry, how can they be supported in remaining in the boundary position in the face of the uncertainties? Our study offers some clues to possible answers. First, an aspect of post-ordination training found useful by many curates is the opportunity to meet in groups, whether at their annual residential training week or locally with a tutor, in order (to quote one) 'to thrash things out . . . and really to work out what ministry means for oneself'. Generally, it would seem, the curates do not have the feeling of a view of ministry being imposed on them: they have a sense of choice. A second clue also comes from the experience of curates: this is the value they attach to the mutual support and counselling element of the residential week. Many feel that they are in difficult or isolated positions in their parishes and welcome the opportunity to compare notes with others. Many parish priests would themselves also welcome support, but, as we noted earlier, find it difficult to acknowledge their need in the face of the pressure from their parishioners to be superhumanly dependable. As a way of getting round this, one vicar proposed workshops of a kind that were formerly convened to tackle a 'respectable' shared problem – such as confirmation training for the eleven to fifteen age-group – but would also indirectly furnish support for incumbents in tackling their own separate problems. The third clue from our study is that one or two of the incumbents quite evidently gained some benefit through talking to us, in a way they had not talked previously, about the nature of the task of ministry in relation to the characteristics of their own particular parishes. This led us to feel that there was a lack of what might be called a 'sociological' conceptualization of the systems in which people were intervening in their roles as ministers. (This also made us wonder, in passing, how fully the Bishop and his advisers, when they are making appointments, take into account the characteristics of the specific parish, the nature of the outgoing incumbent's ministry and the orientations of potential candidates.)

If we put these points together and consider them in relation to parish priests in the first instance, then we are led to the proposition that what is required is more in the nature of a diocesan consultancy service than training in a conventional sense. Its focus would be on helping incumbents to identify the opportunities and alternatives open to them and to make and implement more informed decisions. A useful preparation would be to conduct research in order to clarify the various models of ministry actually being operated and also to begin to build what we have termed 'sociological' models of parishes – that is, models that identify parameters of the community that are relevant to the task of ministry. The Cathedral Centre might be encouraged to press forward with research of this kind. Indeed it might also be able to muster a small initial consultancy cadre which could be gradually enlarged. While it would be essential for such a cadre to develop the capacity to work with local clergy and laity in tackling the problems of a particular parish, intensive consultancy is obviously expensive and it would be necessary to adopt other techniques, such as conferences and workshops, designed for incumbents only, for mixed parish groups, for specialists and so on. The orientation, however, would remain consultative. In the educational area, work with teachers and schools might be approached in a similar manner.

The orientation we are outlining here does not eliminate the need for conventional training of a more specific kind. We recognize, too, that some of these activities are already going on – for example, in the Cathedral Centre and in elements of post-ordination training. What is perhaps new is the concept of a unifying policy which positively encourages the examination of divergent approaches and helps to sustain people in their boundary roles by acknowledging that their uncertainty is something to be legitimately explored and worked with.

THE ORGANIZATION OF THE DIOCESE

While a Suffragan Bishop might be charged with redeveloping training and education along the lines we have indicated, it is clear that in talking about a policy in this field we are ultimately discussing the way in which the Diocesan Bishop himself chooses to exercise his leadership. Ministry is itself an educational activity and the Bishop is the chief teacher of the diocese. But beyond that, it is not enough that a policy for education and training is consistent with the Diocesan's philosophy: it is an instrument through which he discharges his episcopal role and not merely supports but exercises surveillance over parochial and specialist ministry in the diocese. Thus, although it was not in our own brief to study diocesan organization as such, we must inevitably comment on our observations in this area.

The image of the Diocesan Bishop that emerged from the parish interviews was of a shadowy figure, whose function was to authenticate what was happening in the parochial ministry and to be available as a kind of long-stop in times of crisis, or possibly a scapegoat in case of failure. There was little sense that parish priests were acting on the authority of the Bishop, as agents of the diocese. He was rather a figure to be kept off-stage, except when required for ceremonial occasions, and the possibility of his wanting to analyse and question the exercise of ministry in his diocese was kept at arm's length. If differences or conflicts occurred, his job was not to examine them but to smooth them away.

In other quarters too there seem to be strong pressures to keep the Diocesan in a largely administrative-cum-ceremonial role – perhaps a managing director who has delegated authority to suffragan bishops to do all 'real' work as divisional managers, with the possible sop of a small mini-diocese to manage himself to satisfy his needs to be an executive and to take a pastoral role . . .

We are deliberately caricaturing the picture as a way of asking what these processes mean. We see them as part of the general phenomenon of seeking a *modus operandi* and a form of organization which will defend its members against the anxiety of change rather than helping them to face it. The anxiety must be taken into account, but the task of the Church is to face change, and it is for this task that forms of organization need to be built. The picture we have at present is of the simultaneous pursuit of two different organizational approaches which cancel one another out. The one form postulates that the essential task is being carried out by substantially autonomous parish priests: it then becomes the task at diocesan level to mobilize the supports and services that they can draw upon to help them be more effective in the parishes. This form, which one might term the 'independence model', might be appropriate if the communities served were substantially self-contained; but the reality is of course that they are overlapping and interconnected, and moreover that the Church in the diocese needs to relate to many institutions that transcend parochial boundaries. The other form, which we may call the 'delegation model', presents a hierarchy in which authority is delegated from the Diocesan through Suffragans and Rural Deans to incumbents in the parishes, each of whom is then executing, in his own territory, the sub-tasks assigned from the top. This model is not consistent with the autonomy that the parish priest actually has; nor does it fit the pattern of synodical government.

If neither model is tenable by itself and if, as it would seem, they cannot be validly combined, is there a viable alternative? We believe that potentially there is; but to work towards it, it is necessary to consider more thoroughly the influence of the dependency culture. There seems to be an assumption that potency is a commodity in limited supply. If the parish priest is to be potent, then the bishops have to be shadowy; if the Diocesan exercises leadership and direction, he is removing potency from the Suffragans and the rest; and so on. It is inevitable in this culture that the 'leader' at any level will feel pressed to be more omnipotent and omniscient than he can in reality be; and that he will seek from those above him the confirmation that he is as potent as his followers would have him be. If he is helped to examine and understand this phenomenon, then he becomes correspondingly more capable of helping his followers move from less mature to more mature modes of dependency. We would postulate that one factor in the demand that Suffragans become more autonomous in their own mini-dioceses is pressure from their constituents to meet their dependency needs; and that if the Diocesan and the three Suffragans allow themselves to be fragmented in such a way the potency of their episcopacy will in fact be diminished. Certainly we would recommend that they should meet regularly as a College of Bishops to examine their separate and joint experience of what is happening to their episcopacy. If they can work at the way in which the dependency culture is affecting them, they will be both setting an example to others and also enhancing their capacity to work with others on these issues.

It becomes possible then to consider an alternative model for diocesan organization in which ministry is exercised conjointly at different levels. At the parochial level, the incumbent is both discharging his own ministry and providing the consultancy and support that will enable his junior clergy and laity to discharge theirs in a mature way; at diocesan level, the bishops will both minister to the diocese at large – especially *vis-à-vis* the supra-paro-chial institutions – and provide corresponding consultancy and support for the parochial ministry. Besides being an exemplar, the Diocesan would exercise an integrative leadership in the conjoint examination of the experience of ministry at the various levels so as to enrich them all.

We must end with a caveat. The scope of our study has been limited; we were not specifically considering overall diocesan organization; and so the tentative ideas we have sketched out in the last section obviously need much fuller and more informed consideration. On the other hand, we remain convinced that organization for education and training requires a policy, and that the policy flows directly from the way in which the Bishop elects to carry out his episcopacy.

POSTSCRIPT: AFTER THE MILLER/ LAWRENCE WORKING NOTE (1991)

BY DR WESLEY CARR, DEAN OF BRISTOL

The above Working Note, together with its follow-up, proved classics of their type. They are short and because of that some people dismissed them. Yet they presented an interpretation of aspects of the life of the Church in the Diocese of Chelmsford that were of greater significance for the client than the specific questions of education and training. For some years afterwards these papers were a point of reference, although often disputed and sometimes ignored. They were written when a number of concerns which were coming together in Chelmsford were also of growing importance in the Church at large.

In Chelmsford A.K. Rice had produced a First Note on the working of the Cathedral. It was not very full and his death precluded the further study that it implied. There was, therefore, some suspicion about the Tavistock Institute and the quality of its work. This was matched in the Church at large, where, after the excitements of the 1960s, bishops and other leaders were looking for a more stable way ahead. They were wary of innovation. These anxieties, as is often the case, were focused in questions to do with the education and training of lay people and clergy. Group work was still being offered in the Church, some sponsored by the Board of Education at Westminster, some derived from T-group and similar approaches. Bruce Reed, then of Christian Teamwork and later of the Grubb Institute, was also in the field. At Chelmsford the various strands – consultation, the Cathedral, education and group studies – were held together by Canon Richard Herrick. He was a Canon of the Cathedral, Diocesan Director of Education, as well as being associated with the Tavistock Institute and with Bruce Reed. It was against this background that the Notes originated.

Several people in the Church were exploring how to create a model of in-service training (later called 'Continuing Ministerial Education' – CME) for the clergy. Old patterns were based upon leisurely study and self-discipline. But these had largely decayed.

New forms of pre-ordination training were being offered in the colleges. So the clergy coming to the parishes had different, but nevertheless unclear, expectations of their further training. Simultaneously, lay people were being assigned new roles and prominence. They were demanding more competent clergy. But post-ordination training for the clergy was still confined to the first few years of ministry and even then in a haphazard fashion. The Miller/Lawrence Notes were thus opportune not just for a diocese which was wondering what to do, but also more widely for the Church.

Their immediate impact, however, was as intended on the Diocese of Chelmsford. The client, the Bishop, was sceptical about some of the material to do with the authority of bishops and the organization of the diocese. But the suggestions about education and training were accepted. The staff of Chelmsford Cathedral Centre for Research and Training was invited to develop these ideas into a structure and to create a programme. Richard Herrick and Wesley Carr produced a series of detailed proposals which were endorsed. People outside Chelmsford heard about these and they were widely circulated in other dioceses. Because of this theoretical work and the practical working at CME that resulted (Carr was appointed Director of Training) the Diocese of Chelmsford at that time offered the Church at large a distinctive and challenging model for creating a system for CME. It was frequently disputed, but it was not ignored.

Miller/Lawrence's description of the task of the Church and the role of the clergy has proved especially perceptive. It was developed by Carr (1985a) and is still discussed in CME circles, seminars and lectures. It has recently been quoted again in a book in which the Miller/Lawrence ideas about the church remain prominent (Carr, 1992). One national document on CME proved seminal for the Church of England and was widely studied by other churches. This was *The Continuing Education of the Church's Ministry* (Advisory Council, 1980). The Working Party which produced it was chaired by a Chelmsford person (John Taylor, then Archdeacon of West Ham and later Bishop of St Albans) and Carr contributed. The group used the Note. The Report is still in print and is used as a guide in setting up CME programmes. Its organizational setting was also interesting. The Working Party recommended, and it was agreed, that work on CME should be subject to a five-yearly review and report direct to the House of Bishops. This remains the only area of the Church's work which has had such direct contact. Others work through committees. The argument was based upon discussion in the Note of the working relationship between the Bishop and his clergy. In addition to this Report, a number of Diocesan Officers for CME have been advised in their thinking by those who worked at Chelmsford during the 1970s and 1980s. These ideas also influenced the study of Herrick and others on the organization of the Diocese of Southwell (Herrick and Carr, 1975). Echoes can still be heard in similar reports such as, for instance, a recent study of the Diocese of Bradford by the Archdeacon of Craven.

In 1978 a book from another source (Reed, 1978) contributed to the study of the Church and its ministry in dependency. These ideas have been used by, among others, the Archbishop of York (Habgood, 1983). A subsequent collection of essays by a range of authors (Ecclestone, 1988) illustrates the effect of the confluence of ideas derived from this Note and that of Reed. In a number of published writings, as well as several unpublished essays, Carr has brought the two strands together and developed their application to the Church's ministry (Carr, 1985b, 1989) and to thinking about the church and society (Carr 1987; Shapiro and Carr, 1991). In addition group relations work and coherent CME programmes have continued.

It is difficult in a necessarily dependent institution (as Miller/Lawrence showed) not to be perceived as being dependent and as overestimating the influence of these Notes. It would, however, be equally wrong to underestimate their direct impact around the time of their publication and even more their subsequent indirect repercussions. After a period of uncertainty about the handling of dependence there are signs that the Church of England may be recovering a sense of this task. If so, the clarity of perception and range of comment in this Note is likely once again to prove valuable.

6 A PRISON IN NORTHERN IRELAND

Towards the end of 1974, a letter arrived from the Northern
Ireland Office, which was in some desperation about the
notorious Maze prison. This housed an explosive mixture of
political detainees and of prisoners granted certain privileges on
the grounds that their offences were politically motivated. The
problems of management and control, already acute, were
further exacerbated in October 1974, when inmates succeeded in
setting fire to it and destroying most of the buildings.

The letter was seeking 'professional help in the resolution of
these very intractable problems'. Would I pay a visit and talk to
relevant people in order to put forward a proposal? My colleagues
in the Tavistock Institute were deeply divided over the ethics of
accepting such an invitation and one or two were worried that
it might make our building the target for a bomb. For my part, I
was by no means free of anxiety, but felt that if there was even
the slightest chance of contributing to dialogue in Northern
Ireland, then it should be taken. Also at that time I was trying to
set up a conflict research programme.

It was an intensive visit. Apart from discussions at the Northern
Ireland Office and an illuminating tour of the Dantesque prison
itself, where I talked mainly to the governor and the chief welfare

---

The previously unpublished proposal reproduced here was written in
1975.

officer, there were other significant people I had to try to meet. Luckily, my networks were able to procure introductions to a few priests, lawyers and community workers. These in turn established my professional credibility with key gatekeepers on both sides of the political divide. My recollection is of being escorted after dark by devious routes for meetings with anonymous individuals. I explored with both parties the ideas that I was beginning to formulate and, somewhat to my surprise, both saw them as a positive way forward. I was therefore fairly confident that they, and through them the leaders of factions within the Maze itself, would accept and work with the scheme that I put to the Northern Ireland Office.

The scheme also attracted a lot of interest and support in the Office itself. In the end, however, the Minister decided not to go ahead. Shortly after my submission came the announcement (which I had been expecting) of a temporary ceasefire; the Government for its part was quietly preparing to phase out detention; and it was also planning to build a new Maze. As so often in Northern Ireland, there was a temporary optimism; the sense of urgency subsided – and a significant opportunity was lost. There was at that time a widespread feeling – evident in the discussions I had on both sides – that political processes should move away from terrorism and violence. The Maze, as I saw it, was a potential forum in which the alternative of political discussion and negotiation could begin to be rehearsed. If my projected experiment did not work, little would be lost; on the other hand some degree of success would have wide ramifications outside the prison.

What follows, therefore, is a proposal in January 1975 for an initiative that was never taken.

INTRODUCTION

In a discussion at the Northern Ireland Office on January 10th I outlined a possible developmental strategy for the Maze. In preparing the present document, I try to make those initial ideas more precise. The first section of the document briefly sets out the nature of the problem as I understand it. A second section identifies some factors that need to be taken into account in designing possible changes. Particular emphasis is given to the relatedness of the Maze to the wider society of Northern Ireland and to its characteristics as a 'political prison'. It is suggested that these factors, which from one perspective pose major difficulties for the prison population, might provide the basis for a positive developmental strategy. This would be designed to give inmates an opportunity to use their time in prison in ways that would be directly relevant to the current realities of Northern Ireland and to the roles they may take when they are released. The next section sketches a scenario of the process by which the strategy might be implemented. Specifically, it suggests that inmates might take on a major role, alongside staff, in managing their own education. The final section discusses a possible consultancy relationship between a Tavistock Institute team and the prison. It proposes that the Northern Ireland Office should consider sanctioning an initial phase of work in which the team would try to collaborate with the total prison population – staff and inmates – to explore the feasibility of such a developmental strategy.

This strategy is in my judgement worth testing regardless of shifts in the currently fluid political situation. I see it as independent, for example, of political decisions to end or continue detention.

THE PRESENTING PROBLEM

The problem as seen by the Northern Ireland Office is that the Maze accommodates some 500 detainees, held under the Northern Ireland (Emergency Provisions) Act of 1973, and over 500 'special category' prisoners, who 'cannot be made to carry out useful work and live in large groups in compound conditions with very little supervision. The opportunities for positive rehabilitation are extremely limited and in addition there are very serious problems of management and control.' These latter problems were epitomized in October 1974, when the inmates burned down most of the prison, including medical, educational and other facilities. Detainees and convicted prisoners are segregated in different areas and, within each area, by faction. Each compound has its own authority structure and representative system and operates with a good deal of independence in relation to the prison authorities, while retaining close affiliation to the external body from which its members are drawn. There are fifty or so in the separate category of young prisoners and many of these too identify with the political factions. The Prison Service does not have the training and experience to operate a 'political prison'; it has had to recruit many new staff, some from outside Ireland; the nature of the site – a dispersed encampment on a disused airfield – is totally ill-suited to the development of relationships between prison officers and individual inmates; and the consequence is that the prison staff are in practice little more than gaolers. Moreover, even for this function they need the back-up of the Army, which tightly controls the outer perimeter of the prison and which is brought in to reinforce the prison staff when, for example, searches are carried out.

Correspondingly, the inmates, though in some respects more autonomous than ordinary prisoners, are also deprived of some other potentially beneficial experiences of prison life. For example, they are exempt from work; counselling opportunities are limited, partly by shortage of resources and partly also by the control that compounds exercise over their individual inmates' contact with staff and visitors; and in other respects as well rehabilitative provisions are very restricted. More importantly, it is recognized that this is not a setting in which conventional definitions of rehabilitation apply; yet there is no obvious alternative. Certainly, few of the inmates are or regard themselves as 'ordinary prisoners'. The experience of the detainees is of having been interned without trial, while the sentenced prisoners have acquired 'special category' status through arguing successfully that the crimes for which they were convicted were politically motivated. In many respects, therefore, the prison authorities are regarded as representatives of 'the enemy'. The fact that this is a shared view, across the boundaries of factions, may have positive connotations, but it certainly limits the capacity of prison staff to act as resources to inmates. This is not a situation in which an individual inmate can readily ask for and receive help from staff; and correspondingly staff are seldom able to identify individual needs and offer acceptable help.

Morale is particularly low among detainees – evidenced, for

instance, by low standards of personal and environmental hygiene in their compounds. This can be substantially attributed to the processes by which they are brought into detention and to the indeterminacy of their length of stay. There appears to be a pervasive feeling among both staff and inmates that the problems of the Maze are intractable and that any significant changes within the prison must await political stabilization outside. At that time, it is felt, the detainees will be released and the Maze can either be closed or begin to operate as an ordinary prison again.

My brief, therefore, has been to advise on whether in fact this problem should be regarded as intractable, or whether there is a possibility of effective professional intervention in the internal situation without waiting for external changes to solve the problem.

SOME CONSIDERATIONS IN DESIGNING A STRATEGY FOR DEVELOPMENT

Among the factors that need to be taken into account in designing an effective strategy for change and development are the following:

1 Any attempt to introduce such a strategy would depend on mobilizing a sufficient degree of sanction both from prison staff and from all the main groups of inmates.
2 This would imply establishing a professional relationship in which the consultants would refrain – and, more difficult, be seen as refraining – from working in the interests of any one prison group at the expense of another. In other words, the prison population as a whole would need to be regarded as the 'client' of a professional intervention.
3 The starting-point has to be the situation as it exists in the prison itself: the strategy must not be dependent on prior external changes.
4 At the same time, the Maze is anything but a closed system. Members of the various groups of inmates for the most part see themselves as, and are regarded as, members and representatives of active political factions outside. Their perceptions of prison and army authorities at the Maze are likely to be heavily influenced by the views that their

respective factions take of the Government and Army in Northern Ireland as a whole. In a sense, therefore, the Maze is a microcosm of the political structure of Northern Ireland.

5   A political prison is by its nature informally an institution of political education. Typically, inmates are engaged in ideological indoctrination and perhaps also practical instruction in tactics of violence and revolution. Moreover, it can be assumed that a significant proportion of detainees and prisoners, when they are discharged, will be politically significant and active figures, at least in their own local communities and perhaps in the wider system.

The fourth and fifth factors in particular are obviously experienced by staff as central to the difficulty of operating the prison and as preventing them from moving beyond the basic prison task of confinement.

The challenge therefore is to explore how far it would be possible to modify the institution in such a way that it could provide for the inmates, individually and in association, opportunities for development relevant to their future roles in the social, economic and political systems of Northern Ireland – while at the same time (given that the total population of the prison is to be regarded as the client) providing more positive roles for staff. To put the point slightly differently (and more ambitiously): given that the Maze is a kind of microcosm of the problems and conflicts of the external society, can the prison become a place in which these issues are worked on rather than regarded as disturbances which ought somehow to be kept at bay?

If this objective were adopted, then some of the factors now regarded as problems and constraints would be redefined as resources and opportunities. For example, one of the detrimental features of what sociologists call 'total institutions' (and prisons are a prime example) is that the individual is deprived of opportunities for choice and decision-making. I have argued in another context (Miller and Gwynne, 1972) that this problem can to some extent be mitigated by creating systems of activity within which inmates can exercise some authority in managing aspects of institutional life, including, if possible, management of some transactions across the boundary of the institution with the external environment. Thus, inside the Maze, a degree of inmate self-determination within the compounds, which can be seen only as a constraint while the task of the prison is defined solely in terms of confinement and control, can be regarded as an asset to be used and built on if the prison also takes on the task of providing inmates with developmental experiences relevant to their future roles outside. Those involved may find it very hard to acknowledge, but the fact is that, within a rehabilitative framework that emphasizes the importance of opportunities for self-management, the compound system makes the Maze potentially more advanced than most other prisons.

An Approach to Change

I want to emphasize that this section should not be regarded as a specific blueprint for action. Professional experience of working with institutions is that changes are unlikely to take hold unless the members have a chance to 'work through' the consultant's initial propositions, with him and with each other, and reach their own conclusion. Often they identify constraints and also opportunities that the consultant has not taken into account. Consequently, what I am offering here is not a firm recommendation but a possible scenario, which could provide a basis for discussion with the people concerned.

I have suggested that it is highly likely that a political prison will also have an implicit function as an educational institution for its inmates. Alongside this, the Maze operates an 'official' educational function, using its own small education staff, together with paid and voluntary part-time teachers from outside. If, as I have proposed, the prison were to take on as a major task the provision of opportunities for inmates' development, these two functions would in some way need to be brought together within a single more comprehensive framework, in order to tap the motivation attached to the implicit function. There is much evidence – Paolo Freire's work on adult education in Brazil being one example – that capacity to learn is strongly dependent on the individual's internal experience of a degree of freedom and choice. The problem then is how to attain, in a setting of physical imprisonment, a sense among the inmates, collectively and individually, that they are managing their own learning – the more especially in what is seen as a political prison, where educational initiatives by prison authorities are subject to suspicion as attempts at indoctrination.

One possible starting-point is through establishment of a Prison Education Committee. This would be composed of representatives of all compounds together with the Education Officer. (The Governor might either attend himself or treat the Education Officer as his representative on the committee.) The aim would be for this committee to take over management of the educational system and in doing so to try to mobilize the resources in the total prison population that could be applied to the educational task. For this the committee would have to make a census not only of educational needs of inmates but also available skills among inmates and staff that might fit those needs. The notion that inmates might take teaching roles under the auspices of the committee, and not simply student roles, is a departure from conventional thinking and may be experienced as threatening by some staff; but it is an innovation with potentially very positive consequences. The personal benefit for inmate-teachers is that it would use aspects of their skills and experience that might otherwise be neglected or suppressed in prison – and for some detainees this might be especially construc- tive. Inmate-students, for their part, would have a potentially larger reservoir of resources to draw upon; and some might find it less inhibiting to reveal educational deficiencies to fellow inmates than to staff.

Initially, there may be diffidence about forming classes with members from different factions. To put it another way, establish- ment of such classes would be significant evidence that the work of the committee was gaining acceptance and sanction from the total prison community.

Let me anticipate one possible objection, and in doing so illustrate how the committee might function: What if the inmates demand courses on, say, guerrilla warfare? One option would be for the Governor or his representative on the committee to veto the proposal on the grounds that the Northern Ireland Office could not afford to be seen as officially endorsing such activities. A more constructive alternative would be for these grounds to be put before the committee and discussed there as an example of the various conflicting pressures on different sections of the prison population, staff and inmates. To do its work, the committee has to find a way of examining and reconciling differences.

It will be evident that I conceive of the committee as serving an educational function at two levels. At the obvious level, it is providing further education and vocational training for inmates. Less directly, in its own operation, it is providing its members and the constituencies they represent with the experience of working across factional boundaries for a specific task. (Some constituents may also be experiencing this in 'mixed' classes.) In this way, inmates would have an opportunity to rehearse, as it were, in the microcosm of the prison, their participation in the necessary political processes of the larger community.

From this latter standpoint, the education committee would not be the only collaborative forum. Indeed, if it remained so, it would too readily become a vehicle for other matters that inmates wanted to air with the Governor and his staff, thus reducing its effectiveness in its direct educational task. Correspondingly, the raising of such matters might indicate that it was timely to set up other specialist committees: to take an obvious example, complaints about food might be the basis for a Food and Hygiene Committee. Each committee, of course, would provide additional inmates with opportunities for representational experience; but it would be counterproductive to use this as a reason for forming committees for tasks not widely regarded as important.

A further development might be the formation of a Prison Council which, among other things, might oversee the activities of the various committees. However, that is unlikely to happen until one or two more specialized committees have shown themselves to be effective.

So far this scenario has concentrated on potential benefits for inmates. What of the 'more positive roles for staff' referred to earlier? Initially, staff would find their job more difficult. While it is clear that the emergency imposed on the Prison Service a job for which it was not equipped and that rapid expansion to do the job has been a set-back for the professionalization of the service, and while too some prison staff complain at this loss of a professional role, it also has to be recognized that the limited gaoler role is in key respects simpler. This is not to underrate the burdensome problems of security and control that face prison staff. But at least there has been no doubt that security and control are the primary task. Staff are therefore not having to wrestle with the role dilemmas of an ordinary prison, where they are called upon by society to perform perhaps three tasks - punishment, confinement and rehabilitation - which are often in conflict with one another. What I am proposing reintroduces that kind of complexity. I should therefore be surprised if this did not generate anxiety: staff are likely to feel initially that the new approach threatens security and control. Such fears will be partly grounded on reality. Some inmates may see the changes as evidence of staff weakness and will test how they might be exploited. Beyond that, to the extent that the approach leads to the beginnings of cautious collaboration across factional boundaries, and inmates become to some degree united by their common identity, staff will feel more outnumbered and thus weaker.

It is predictable, therefore, that the first stages of change would be difficult and demanding for prison staff. They would need to be assured of full backing from the Northern Ireland Office; and they would probably be helped by professional support. For example, they would need opportunities to talk about their anxieties and to tease out how far these were based on reality and how far on the uncertainties of the changes themselves.

However, the experiences would not be all negative; and certainly, once the preliminary hurdles are crossed, there is the potential satisfaction of being engaged in a highly innovative process. The innovation would, of course, be relevant far beyond the Maze and beyond Northern Ireland. It could well provide a basis for the re-professionalization of the Prison Service. I would therefore expect many of the staff who are dissatisfied with being only gaolers to welcome the development of their role and to find the experience rewarding.

To sum up: I have proposed that an effort should be made to make the Maze into an institution that provides the inmates with opportunities for development going beyond (though not pre-cluding) the vocational training and counselling of ordinary rehabilitation and that attempts to give them experiences relevant to the whole range of problems they will face in taking up roles again outside the prison as citizens in the political realities of Northern Ireland. I have suggested that a key means of achieving this would be the participation by inmates themselves in the management of their own education. I have also shown how this might come about and put forward the proposition that the process would give staff a more demanding job to do, but a job that is more professional and potentially more satisfying.

However, I repeat that what this section has offered is a scenario and not a specific set of recommendations for action.

THE CONSULTANCY ROLE

My proposal at this stage is that the Northern Ireland Office should commission a professional team from the Tavistock Institute with the limited objective of exploring, with the various groupings of staff and inmates within the Maze, whether the kind of development strategy I have outlined could be viable. This would be a process, referred to above, of 'working through' these propositions and so giving the people concerned (including the Northern Ireland Office) an opportunity to examine issues that would be raised by the strategy. This phase of work, then, would end with a decision on whether to proceed further or not.

It is, of course, impossible to forecast precisely how long this would take. At present, I am thinking in terms of about three months.

As I also indicated above, we would foresee many difficulties in establishing a professional role in relation to the total prison population. An undertaking by the team that it would not align itself with any grouping would not ensure that the team would be perceived as non-aligned. Arrangements of an ostensibly trivial nature – for example, where the team was based and where it ate – would have to be carefully examined and worked out. The other side of this coin is that the struggle to establish a consultancy role would in itself yield valuable data about the problems of implementing the development strategy.

It is an aim of the Tavistock Institute to combine research with professional practice. While the needs of the client system – the total prison population – would unquestionably have priority, the team would not be professionally effective if its members were not also learning from the experience and examining its possible wider implications. This, then, is another aspect of the consultancy relationship that would have to be worked out with the client system.

As I have implied, I would propose to deploy a small team of professional staff on a part-time basis rather than confine the work to, say, two people. This is partly for a practical reason: staff cannot be released from other commitments. However, there are two technical grounds for preferring the team: first, the variety of perspectives tends to be productive in itself; and second, our experience of operating in other institutions where stress is relatively high – for example, various types of hospitals and residential establishments – is that our staff become vulnerable to institutional pressures and therefore require periodic relief. I would take responsibility for the work myself on behalf of the Tavistock Institute.

If the project were to develop into a second phase of implementation, I should want to plan for the inclusion of Irish members in the professional team and the progressive phasing out of non-Irish staff.

7   SOME REFLECTIONS ON THE ROLE OF THE DIPLOMATIC WIFE

INTRODUCTION

In January 1976, I was approached by the Diplomatic Service Wives' Association (DSWA). Its Committee had for some time been concerned about the emotional strains on wives abroad. The incidence of more obvious symptoms of stress – broken marriages, alcoholism, psychological disturbance – was not documented but was almost certainly increasing. Underlying these symptoms, the Committee was aware of more widespread unhappiness, anxiety, loneliness, despair and bitterness, which were mostly contained and occasionally bubbled up to the surface. It could be and was argued, with some justification, that very many women found the life satisfying and rewarding, that the frequency of divorce or of individual breakdown was probably no greater than in the population at large and that Service wives, because of their backgrounds and of processes of self-selection, had a greater than average capacity to cope with stress. On the other hand, it was also true that only in a very small minority of posts did families have access to the kinds of support services that would be available to them if they lived in Britain – marriage guidance, psychiatry or even

The introductory and concluding sections in the original working note are here condensed and slight editorial changes have been made in the main sections. The note was reprinted in full in the *DSWA Newsletter* (Miller, 1978). It is followed here by a summary of outcomes.

the sympathetic GP – and they were usually also cut off from the informal support of parents, sisters and intimate friends.

One specific suggestion was that the Tavistock Institute might be able to help through some form of training which would develop the counselling skills of wives of Heads of Chancery. I was told that as a counterpart to the 'personnel function' of the Head of Chancery (the 'number two' in an embassy), his wife is conventionally regarded as having a special responsibility for the welfare of mission wives. However, it seemed to me that special training for women in this particular category might be reinforcing distinctions of rank that were becoming obsolete. Should they have this welfare role at all? Even though they might be well trained, would they be trusted? And in any case, I wondered whether the sources of stress were sufficiently understood. Perhaps we needed to know more about the dilemmas that wives faced.

The next step was a meeting with the Committee of the DSWA in December 1976. There was a frank exchange of experience and certain issues began to be articulated more precisely. I had the impression that some of the problems and feelings that came to the surface in that discussion are usually bottled up, perhaps being treated as the private problems of individuals rather than as reflecting the nature of the Service as it is today. If that were so, I could see that one positive function that the DSWA might have would be to make the open examination of these issues more legitimate.

As part of the process of widening the debate, the outgoing Chairman reported on these discussions to the Annual General Meeting and also arranged a one-day seminar, to explore the issues further. There were about fifteen invited participants, widely ranging in age, length of time associated with the Service and husbands' rank, and including two 'single girls' (see below, p. 139).

By then, eighteen months had elapsed since the initial approach. I believe the time-scale indicates the uncertainty of the Committee about how to proceed – and, even, whether to proceed – in what is felt to be a delicate and controversial area, and doubt also about seeking professional advice from outside the Service. This hesitancy may reflect a paradoxical aspect of the culture of Service wives: on the one hand, it is recognized that the life can be stressful and that support should be provided; but, on the other hand, the individual feels that she is expected to be able to cope, and hence to seek help is a sign of personal weakness and failure.

For my part, I take it as a compliment that the DSWA believes that I may be of some help as an outside consultant; but I have also felt at times that unrealistic hope is being invested in me - as if I were going to be able, after these few discussions, to produce solutions to problems that have received a lot of intelligent consideration within the Association itself. Possibly my main contribution, as I hinted above, is to help legitimate the more open discussion of this whole problem area. Beyond that I may be able to draw attention to some underlying factors that it is more difficult to identify, or at least to talk about, from the inside. But the Association has to find its own solution.

Accordingly, this document is very much a working note, intended to contribute to the ongoing debate. In the section that follows, I try to summarize the main areas of concern. I then go on to put forward some more tentative observations and hypotheses, which are intended to contribute towards a somewhat fuller and deeper understanding. I hope that readers will use the evidence of their own experience to test, develop and modify these hypotheses (and possibly reject them). The final section, which is also tentative, suggests possible next steps for the Committee to consider.

WIVES' PERCEPTIONS OF THE PROBLEMS

The role of the diplomatic wife is commonly seen as combining two main strands. First, there are the problems - and satisfactions - of living abroad for extended periods in several countries. These she shares with many other women whose husbands are employed in, for example, international companies. Second, there is the issue of being married into an institution in which, as in the Church, the wife has traditionally been expected to take on responsibilities that are an extension of the husband's role. The nature of these responsibilities within the hierarchical structure of a British mission abroad is a source of uncertainty and sometimes resentment.

Living abroad implies separation - from family of origin, from close friends, and above all from children. This is a sacrifice the wife makes for the sake of her husband's career. Unhappiness and guilt about leaving children in boarding school are repeated themes. Letters from the child or the matron may contain disturbing news; but the mother is impotent to do anything and is expected to keep up her regular activities and put a good face on things. (Fathers, it is implied, suffer less.) A time of particular concern is when the child is leaving school: that is when there is a special need for parental support, or at least availability; but that is also when the thrice-yearly holiday visits are no longer subsidized. So there are repeated separations to face. As one person put it, the experience is of a series of small-scale bereavements, each requiring some degree of mourning and readjustment. This is related also to the movement from post to post (or, as it is sometimes felt, from pillar to post), which means that the Service wife is constantly making and breaking relationships.

'Abroad' comes in many different guises. The main contrast that seems to be drawn is between the small Third World country, with a difficult climate and few amenities, and the large posts in the older Commonwealth, the United States and Western Europe. The former have some compensations in the exotic surroundings and often in the cohesiveness of a small western community. The latter offer the advantages of a more familiar culture – it is easier to make friends in the host country and perhaps to get a job – but, because the missions are larger and the cities more dispersed, one risks feeling more isolated. Some posts fall into neither category and may combine the disadvantages of both. I have the impression, for example, that one requires an unusual combination of resources and interests to enjoy a posting to Moscow. Difficulties are also caused by the occasional unexpected transfer, at short notice, to a totally different environment – for example, a sudden posting from Belgium to Bangladesh.

For newcomers, whatever the location, the reaction to the structure and culture of the Service, and of the specific mission, is often puzzlement, if not resentment. In the words of one woman: 'I was astonished that anybody could tell me what to do.' The hierarchy, with its elements of paternalism and even authoritarianism, is out of tune with the values of many younger women, who regard distinctions of rank, class and sex as outmoded. One of the first things they encounter is the ritual of 'courtesy letters', which they read about in Sir Stanley Tomlinson's *Handbook on Diplomatic Life Abroad*: it may be acceptable for the husband, as a careerist, to send a courtesy letter to his new boss; but why, his wife asks, should she be expected to write in similar terms to the boss's wife?

The new wife, then, moves into a society in which her status is determined by her husband's rank: the hierarchy of the husbands is visited upon the wives. If her husband's job is in security or communications, she discovers that, regardless of her age and previous experience, she will be permanently labelled a 'junior wife'. (She will also find that her husband's allowances are lower and may therefore protest that cost of living depends on the place, not the grade; but it is the status differential that rankles more.) If she has married into the right grade, no matter how young, she will be a 'senior wife'; but she too will be reminded in subtle and not so subtle ways that she has a location within a hierarchy. On the one side, if she consorts with a security officer's wife, she may be told directly, as one woman was, that she is entertaining below her grade. On the other hand, she owes some kind of deference and obligation to the wife of the head of mission and perhaps, in a large mission, to the wives of one or two other senior officers. The nature of the obligations is sometimes specific – to help with the preparations for an ambassadorial party – but this is becoming less common, and it more often takes the form of a veiled moral pressure. Indeed, some women said they would prefer a 'list of instructions', so that they knew where they stood. However, the notion of the mission as a family, with the ambassador and his wife (sometimes, incorrectly, called 'ambassadress') as the parental figures, still seems quite persistent.

There is also uncertainty about representational responsibilities. Contrary, perhaps, to her expectations, the new diplomatic wife will not – unless she has married very well indeed – be plunged into a round of glittering embassy parties and responsible for entertaining important guests. Official entertainment becomes obligatory (or virtually so) only at the top of what are called the 'representational grades'. But this is another classification that arouses irritation, because even the woman whose husband is 'non-representational'

finds that in some ways she is taken as being representative, both
by the local population and indeed by the mission itself. If a wife is
fortunate enough to find a job she may not accept it without
permission from the head of mission, and she is caught up in
security constraints which would in most countries, for example,
prohibit her from consulting a psychiatrist. If she prefers to educate
her children locally, only one particular school may be 'approved'.

'Loneliness' and 'emptiness' were words frequently used in the
discussions to describe wives' experience. If the climate is hot and
the bedroom is the only air-conditioned part of the house, that is
where many daytime hours are spent in isolation. 'Who cares?
Nobody cares.' A number of women are evidently faced with
identity problems. In Britain they had jobs and counted as persons
in their own right. Now they derive their status wholly from their
husbands: as individuals they don't exist. Men have the 'scaffolding'
of their jobs to sustain them; wives are left to their own devices.
Lonely and depressed though they may be, several factors make
wives wary about confiding in others. Leading a transitional life,
they learn not to make close friendships, since this leads to painful
separations. Relationships, then, become superficial; and because
of this defence some women become not unwilling but unable to
engage in fuller and closer friendships. The hierarchy, in any case,
restricts the range from which friends can be safely selected. And
given the unacceptability of revealing mental stress it is safer not to
confide in anyone within the mission. There is a pervasive belief
that any such signs of weakness affect one's husband's standing and
career. In this situation, as one woman put it: 'Your husband is your
only best friend.' But even that is a friendship that some women are
reluctant to lean on too much: he too has his problems in the office;
and the prevailing ethos is that it is for the wife to support the
husband, not vice versa. Some marriages break down, it is said,
because the husband is asked for more support than he is
emotionally equipped to give. Moreover, fellow wives are not
always responsive to the needs of a woman in trouble. If her
loneliness is noticed, she may get invitations. But if she is observed
to be drinking too much or to be in manifest difficulties in her
marriage, it is not considered proper for others to intervene.

As I said earlier, the incidence of individual and marital

breakdown is not known; but it is evident that most wives adapt to Service life, some very successfully. The conventional adaptation is through close identification with the husband's job and career. These wives effectively join the Service. The husband's career is 'our career'; they accept the pecking order of seniority among the wives; they take their representational responsibilities seriously. Apparently successful adaptations may nevertheless come under pressure again later on, at the time of menopause, the late adolescence of the children, or the husband's promotion to head of mission – all three perhaps coming together. It seems that the wife of the head of a mission in one of the more important countries has a particularly demanding role. It is often described as living in a fishbowl. It is almost mandatory in this role that relationships are held at a superficial level: entertainment is obligatory; the residence may become a hotel for a succession of eminent visitors; the wife feels she is always on parade. At the same time it is a seductive experience. One moves in the most distinguished company and receives almost royal treatment at times; and there is a risk of coming to believe that the honours accorded to the *role* of ambassador and extended by courtesy to his wife are instead a response to her *personal* attributes. This then produces the imperious relationship towards other mission wives that is so much resented. At the other extreme, there is the wife of head of mission who finds the burdens onerous, but does not feel that she has any right to seek help, and labours on under increasing strain. Other wives for their part collude in maintaining a distance from the wife of the head of mission – they tend to treat her as someone special and separate – and across this gap it seems exceptionally difficult to sustain any interpersonal relationship that is uninfected by the status difference of the husbands.

I have spoken of commitment to 'our career' as the conventional adaptation. In other words, the conventional processes of socialization in the Service have tended to produce this kind of wife. And many have found it satisfying. Younger women are more sceptical. They do not feel that they will be satisfied in old age to look back on a life in which they have simply been the wives of their husbands. They recognize that by having 'married into the Service' they have diminished their options: as it says in the

Handbook, 'a professionally qualified woman who is determined to exercise her profession full time should clearly think twice before she marries a Diplomatic Service Officer'. At the same time, it should be possible to be married to a member of the Service without taking on a major role as a diplomatic wife. They point out that, since some wifeless men are apparently successful in the role of head of mission, then surely it is not necessary for any wife to become deeply involved either in representational entertaining or in the ancillary activities, such as charitable work, which are still expected of wives in some missions. Even if they are lucky enough to get jobs outside the mission, they are often made to feel that they are not pulling their weight. They are pushing, therefore, for a more flexible culture in which neither the employed wife nor the full-time diplomatic wife is denigrated.

Another frequent protest, partly related to this, is against the arbitrariness of postings. Special skills and interests of the husband, family commitments and problems, and even medical factors, are not adequately considered by the Foreign Office: I was told of one wife in great distress because her husband's health had broken down in one tropical post and now he was being sent to another. It seems to be an unquestioned belief that any promotion offered must be accepted, regardless of circumstances: to say 'no', or even to express a preference for an alternative, might incur a black mark on one's record. But don't husbands consult wives before accepting? Yes, they do; but the wife normally goes along with what he thinks is best, just as he goes along with what (as he sees it) the Office thinks is best for him. It is the wife who carries most of the resultant anxiety.

'Single girls' is the term used for women employed abroad as secretaries and personal assistants. The diminutive term 'girls' is consistent with the family model of the mission, and it seems quite common for them to become, as it were, the 'adopted' daughters or younger sisters of married couples. This device may be seen as coping with two aspects of concern about them. One or two wives have said to me privately – this is not easily acknowledged in public – that they are worried about possible affairs between husbands and 'girls' working alongside them in the office, and there are reports of such affairs leading to broken marriages. At the same time the senior staff of the mission feel some responsibility, on security and personal grounds, for discouraging associations between British female employees and local men. 'Adoption' is a method of containing these two problems.

FURTHER REFLECTIONS

Much of what I have said in the previous section is an account of the overt concerns that have been voiced in discussions. Some of the points could be amplified, and there are probably others I have missed. Since the discussions I have read a recent article by an American Foreign Service wife, Margaret W. Sullivan (1977). There is a striking similarity in the problems and preoccupations of wives in the two services, and she analyses them well.

In this section, I want to offer tentative hypotheses about some underlying factors, which get alluded to only occasionally or obliquely but which nevertheless need to be elucidated if the role of the diplomatic wife and the difficulties of it are to be properly understood.

One hypothesis is that the difficulties and uncertainties of the wife's role are an expression of uncertainties about the diplomatic role itself. Another way of putting this is to say that unresolved difficulties within the Service get projected into the wives. Some of my evidence for this comes from things that were *not* said. In the July discussion, for example, the review currently being undertaken by the Central Policy Review Staff (CPRS) was hardly alluded to, and yet I know that there are widespread anxieties in the Service about the recommendations that may emerge. Wives of some heads of mission were criticized for the way in which they patronized the mission wives; but there was no criticism of the behaviour of heads of mission towards their staff. In other words, it is not the hierarchy among husbands itself that gets questioned, but only the effects of it on wives. Indeed, wives seem to put a protective screen around their husbands. When in the course of discussion I raised the possibility that at least some of the problems that wives experienced might be exported into them from their husbands, the conversation moved rapidly away to other topics. Occasionally it is acknowledged that there might be problems in the office, or that husbands might do a little more to help; but by and large the wives regard their problems of adjustment as their own and therefore to be sorted out individually or at best among themselves.

To a considerable extent, this is reflected in the aims and activities of the DSWA. In addition to linking wives together and giving practical assistance, it is one of the stated aims of the Association 'to provide a corporate means of approaching authority to bring about practical, desirable reforms in the conditions of service'; and it has done a lot to ensure that problems of wives are communicated to the Office and that posting practices and regulations generally become less arbitrary and more benign. But the Association does not see it as part of its function to comment on more basic aspects of the task and structure of the Service.

The fact is, of course, that the role of the Diplomatic Service has altered radically over the last thirty years. Seen from the outside, there are three obvious trends. First, Britain has suffered a decline in economic and political power, in relation to the rest of the world. Second, the ambassador has a diminishing role in major international negotiations, which are much more often conducted at Foreign Office and minister level and through conference diplomacy. Third – related to this – there is a much increased emphasis on commercial and consular activities. (The second and third factors apply to all the older Foreign Services; the first is specific to Britain.) The CPRS are not the first to question whether the Service has adequately reconceptualized its task, its structure and its culture in response to these changes. Accusations of elitism and traditionalism are familiar enough. In the past, these could more easily be written off as expressions of envy: members of the Service could pride themselves on carrying out an important job for their country with dignity and professionalism in conditions that were sometimes difficult and even dangerous. Nowadays, the importance is not quite so obvious, and more doubts are being felt within the Service itself. I have been told of growing cynicism: it makes less sense than before to dance attendance on the ambassador and to make sure never to walk on his right, but if that is the way to get promotion, then one goes along with it.

My proposition is that, with these changes, the established coping mechanisms of the wives are threatened. Traditionally, the sacrifices they had to make – long periods of exile and separation – were compensated by both the important responsibilities and the high standing of British missions abroad; and the hierarchical mission structure provided a means through which wives could contribute – each according to her level – to the representational task. As I indicated in the previous section the idea, or ideal, of sacrifice, for the Service and for one's husband's career, is still prevalent. However, the sacrifice today is either less or different. Certainly many wives are anxious and guilty about separation from children; but they see them every holiday, and one or two wives acknowledged privately – to say it in public would be out of tune with prevailing values – that they probably have a better relationship with their children as a result: holidays mean treats, and they are not with the children for long enough at a time to become nagging mothers. Sacrifice of the wife's career is increasingly mentioned and again some women feel this deeply, but it is also asked (usually by those who have stuck to the wife-and-mother role) whether all those who complain would really be pursuing careers if they had stayed in Britain. So the idea of sacrifice remains important as a way of coping; but, on the one hand, the sacrifices, though talked about, are less now than they used to be; and, on the other hand, the husband's career and the Service justify sacrifices less than in the past. I am not suggesting that the husband's career has lost its force to motivate wives. The ambition of eventually occupying the Residence in Paris or Brussels can make it all seem worthwhile. But if your husband has a not very responsible job in a hierarchical system to which he is not wholly committed, then your basis of coping is jeopardized. I suspect that this is hard to face; and hence there is some denial – the protective screen that I mentioned. It is difficult to acknowledge, even to oneself, that one's husband's job and the role of the mission are anything but important and positive. Negative feelings are more safely deposited in the Office, which is branded as insensitive to human needs.

Let me try to put this in a slightly different way. Loyalty of wife to husband and the expectation that she will do what is necessary to service him in return for dependence on him as a breadwinner have been taken-for-granted behaviour in our culture. Questioning of it is very recent and the wife who departs from the traditional norm – allowing him to cut his own sandwich for lunch or to wash his own shirt – is in most British sub-cultures still frowned upon as deviant. The Diplomatic Service has used this loyalty and dependence and incorporated it into the organization of the missions; and in return it has given the wife certain rewards and privileges, including diplomatic immunity, and has conferred an identity on her through the hierarchical system. Many wives are now, I postulate, becoming caught in a bind – one might call it the 'loyalty trap'. The husband is communicating to the wife, openly or perhaps implicitly, depression, anger or cynicism about the state of the Service and about his position in it. She absorbs this and her own commitment to the Service is diminished. Personal loyalty, however, and support for the husband's career, imply that she continues to endorse the hierarchy, since that still represents his ladder of promotion and the justification of her sacrifice. Loyalty to the husband therefore has the effect of distancing her from other wives, and maintaining status distinctions among them, even though many may feel a similar predicament. There may be a connection here with the strong need to go on believing, despite reassurances to the contrary, that the husband's standing and career will be prejudiced by signs of 'weakness' in his wife. One can see that it must be necessary to believe this in order to continue to believe in the converse – namely, that the wife's strength and support will have positive consequences.

Perhaps this is also linked with the apparent convention that one does not intervene if a fellow wife shows signs of becoming, for example, an alcoholic. This seems to contradict the notion of a mutually supportive 'family', especially in a small mission. One possible explanation is that if the husbands, and therefore derivatively the wives, are competing with each other in their careers, then the 'failed' wife implies that one potential rival has been removed. Human groups are often cruel, despite the good intentions of their individual members, and it has frequently been observed that the identification of a casualty within a group gives the other members a feeling that they are more robust and better adjusted than they actually are: their weaknesses are projected into the casualty.

The family model of the mission, with the ambassador and his wife at the head, authoritarian but benevolent, has a Victorian ring, yet it seems curiously persistent. Presumably it is still linked to some ideal of loyal wife and dutiful daughter-in-law. Since 'family' is a 'good' word in our culture, it may seem almost blasphemous to question it – as if this would evoke only the opposites of disloyalty and anarchy – and there is evidence that this picture of the mission is still found supportive by some women. On the other hand, it is a model that seems to have diminishing relevance and perhaps it actually obstructs more objective examination of the current realities of the mission as a social system.

Possible Next Steps

What I have postulated in the previous section is that some of the stress on Service wives comes from discrepancies between past and present, myth and reality. In particular, problems of the changing Service and husband's questioning of it are carried by the wives and derivatively by the Association. This is a working hypothesis, for which I have offered some evidence. Since my observations are not based on an intensive study, I would suggest that as a first step the Committee should examine my propositions, as dispassionately as it can, in the light of members' own experience. If the propositions withstand this initial test, then ways might be found of getting them examined more closely and more widely. One medium is the Newsletter. Another is a direct request to a sample of liaison officers to solicit views from the members of their 'branches' and to report back to the Committee. It seems to me that the DSWA is already fulfilling an important function of identifying and representing common interests among wives – wives in general, and wives at different ages, different phases of family development and different stages in their husbands' careers. It has begun also to have a function of legitimating open discussion of the experience of Service wives, including ambiguities about the role and problems of adjustment to it. I believe a further extension of this function to be highly desirable. I see it as a process of demystification of Service life – pinning down the myths and fantasies inherited from the past and asserting the realities. However, the wives and the Association cannot go very much further on their own. If problems of the

Service are being carried by the wives then it seems inescapable that the DSWA actively involves the Service in the debate and in the process of diagnosis . . .

That working note went on to list various other points for practical action. Among those implemented was the creation of posts of family welfare officer and staff and family counsellor. In the posts, the local chairperson of the Association has taken over the welfare role from the wife of Head of Chancery. But the note achieved its greatest effect simply by being published in the DSWA Newsletter. *This sparked off a great deal of debate and correspondence. The predominant reaction was one of relief that there was now sanction to speak openly about feelings and issues that had previously been unspeakable.*

My own follow-up was a set of long interviews with five wives at the apex of the hierarchy. The resultant paper, 'The role of the wife of Head of Mission', was also published in the Newsletter (Miller, 1981). It seemed to me that these women were confronted, in quite an extreme way, with two dilemmas. First:

> *'How do I maintain my identity as an individual while at the same time responding to the demands of a role that require me to be someone quite different?'*

The second dilemma was shared by husband and wife:

> *'The closed hierarchical community generates a dependent, familial culture. There is pressure on those at the top to meet the dependency needs by taking on parental roles. If they resist this pressure, they will be charged with being non-caring; if they succumb to it, they will be accused of treating people as children instead of as mature adults.'*

The debate (in what is now the British Diplomatic Spouses' Association) has continued. In October 1992 its magazine included three articles by wives reviewing the original working notes. They endorse the analysis and point to the positive steps the Association has taken since. One had chaired the DSWA committee at the time of the initial study and now, fifteen years later, was wife of the ambassador in Rome, then about to retire. The problems inherent in the role, she says, 'haven't gone away, but perhaps because of Dr Miller we are better able to confront them'.

8 GOVERNMENT AND WATER

INTRODUCTION

Organization is a means of carrying out a task. In order to design and implement an effective form of organization, we have to understand clearly the nature of the task and the conditions under which it is to be performed. This note is written primarily for my own benefit, to clarify my thoughts about the task of water management and to begin to develop a conceptual framework within which it can be examined.

First, I put forward a general proposition about the task and role of government. I then explore what light this proposition may throw on the specific case of hydrological systems. In a third section, I consider the meanings attached to water, since these too will have to be taken into account in organizational design.

This is, then, a preliminary exercise in model-building. Much of what I say will be obvious; some of my assumptions may be wrong. It is certainly not going to offer recommended organizational solutions. If it leads to a clearer conceptualization of the task and to preliminary propositions about organizational requirements, it will have fulfilled its purpose.

Reproduced here is an unedited working note prepared in 1975 for the Mexican National Water Planning Commission. It is followed by a summary of later developments.

The Task of Government

I start with the premiss that the primary task of government is ultimately to ensure the long-term survival of the country. More specifically, the government of a developing country such as Mexico has the task of providing the conditions within which a balanced process of development will be carried out to advance the well-being of the people.

Its task, then, is essentially one of regulation. By 'regulation' I do not mean only the making and enforcing of rules, though that is part of it. Regulation involves acting in such a way as to promote and encourage certain kinds of outcome and to discourage or prevent others, in relation to national objectives.

What government exists to regulate is the multiplicity of systems in which people conduct their lives and which in various ways serve their needs. There are systems of interconnected transactions for the production and distribution of goods; communication systems; educational systems; kinship systems; and many others. Boundaries of these systems often do not coincide with the administrative boundaries of state and local government. Some are relatively isolated, with limited spread; others extend even beyond national boundaries. Nor does the range of activities of a given system necessarily correspond to the functional boundaries of governmental administration. For example, the operation of a given agricultural system may be of concern to a number of different government departments.

To a large extent, these systems are self-regulating: that is to say, they themselves manage their boundaries with other systems in their environment from which they receive intakes and to which they transfer outputs. They have a degree of resilience, in terms of being able to adjust to environmental changes or even to induce such changes for the sake of their own survival. Adjustments, therefore, are constantly occurring within and between systems, without requiring governmental intervention.

Broadly speaking, there are two kinds of situation which require regulatory action by government. First, a system may lose its capacity for self-regulation (for example, the collapse of the

Mexican sugar industry a few years ago) or in some other way transmit disturbances to other systems, thus having a negative effect on the well-being of the people. Here governmental intervention is reactive. Second, to pursue national developmental objectives a government may need to intervene proactively through modifying or abolishing existing systems and promoting the formation of new ones.

I would suggest that the task of government in all such cases is to promote the boundary conditions within which new or modified systems can again become viably self-regulating. Another way of putting this is to say that in so far as system boundaries are drawn in such a way as to provide restricted capacity for self-regulation and to require continuing external regulation, then system effectiveness will be lower, regulatory costs will be higher, or both.

REGULATION OF HYDROLOGICAL SYSTEMS

In considering the government's task in relation to water, we have to start from the physical characteristics of the hydrological system. Mexico, as a hydrological open system, can be seen as 'importing' water as precipitation from the atmosphere, receiving the water into its soil, vegetation, lakes, rivers and aquifers, and 'exporting' it again as vapour into the atmosphere and as effluent into the ocean. This is shown in simplified form in Figure 8.1.

It is evident that the import–export boundaries of the hydrological system are only marginally susceptible to regulation. Virtually nothing can be done to affect the quantity and timing of precipitation. Desalinated water from the ocean is too expensive to provide more than a minute supplement to precipitation. Limited action is possible to retain water in the system by reducing evaporation and discharge. As Figure 8.1 hints, government regulation may be needed with neighbouring countries to prevent the mining of aquifers or contamination of Mexican waters at the frontiers; and the government may need to engage in international negotiation to prevent atmospheric contamination (for example, through radioactivity).

Government's concern, however, is not with regulation of the hydrological system for its own sake. The relevant point is that this

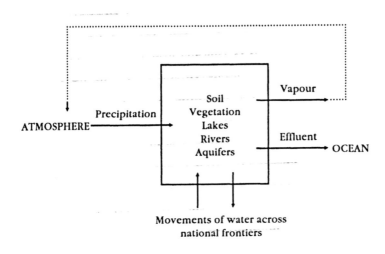

Fig 8.1 Mexico as an open hydrological system

natural system constitutes a significant environment and resource for numerous internal systems. These can be thought of as 'socio-hydrological systems' or perhaps 'socio-technico-hydrological systems', to help us keep in mind that the movement of water in and out of these systems occurs within the context of complex sets of social and technological interactions. For convenience, I shall call them 'user systems'. For most user systems, water is not the primary throughput: it is a supply ancillary to the primary process. The two principal exceptions are systems of hydro-electric generation, which use water to produce energy, and distribution systems, which 'retail' water.

Therefore, following from the premises in the preceding section, we have to define the primary task of government in relation to water in some such terms as these:

To regulate the external boundaries of the hydrological system and the internal boundaries between the hydrological system and user systems in such a way as to ensure the long-term survival of the country, and more specifically so as to provide the conditions within which a

User systems

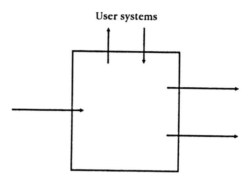

Fig 8.2 The boundary between the hydrological system and user systems

balanced process of development will be carried out to advance the well-being of the people.

Perhaps a less cumbersome definition could be found; but the important concept here is that of boundary regulation. The primary focus of regulation is on the quantity and quality of what users take out of the hydrological system and of what they put into it. This is illustrated in Figure 8.2.

Thus the kinds of regulatory activity required on the boundary of the hydrological and user systems will include: regulation of ground-water use to avoid mining of non-renewable resources; improvement of soil management policies to avoid erosion and silting; control of contamination; construction of dams to regulate availability of water over time and for flood control, etc.

A further area of regulation is between users. When water is in abundant supply, this is mainly confined to ensuring that one user's discharge does not contaminate another's intake. Differential pricing of water for different uses, for example, is in these conditions not a relevant mechanism for governmental regulation of development. This and similar mechanisms become relevant only when scarcity of water leads to competition between users for the same or different uses. Water policies may then be adopted to

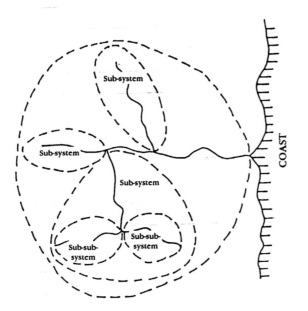

Fig 8.3 Sketch of hydrological system, showing sub-systems and
sub-sub-systems

favour some uses and to discourage others. Measures may also be
taken, of course, to reduce competition by making more economic
use of the available water through industrial zoning and other
water-saving schemes.

So far I have been implying that Mexico can be considered as a
single hydrological system. In fact, it contains a number of such
systems, each of which is hydrologically independent or nearly so.
Thirteen systems have been identified and, through incorporation
in them of small isolated systems, these cover the whole country.
With the major exception of the water supply for Mexico City, these
regions are also mainly self-contained in terms of water consumption. As Figure 8.3 shows, a regional system can be considered as
including a number of sub-systems and sub-sub-systems. Potentially,
these constitute units within which regulation of the boundaries

between the hydrological sub-system and local user systems can be carried out within whatever wider system constraints may be established on quantity of extraction and quantity and quality of discharge. Such units are themselves analogous to user systems in relation to the wider hydrological system. Thus, what I defined as the primary task of government in relation to water is applicable to the boundary of each local hydrological (sub-)system and local user systems. Considerable delegation of the task of regulation therefore seems both possible and indeed advisable.

Strategies for regulation, including the possibility of designing substantially autonomous local systems of regulation, have to take into account the special meanings that are attached to water. These are briefly discussed in the next section.

MEANINGS ATTACHED TO WATER

Water is legally defined in Mexico as a national property, to be managed by the government on behalf of the people of the country.

Water has no intrinsic value: its value derives from its relation to human intentions. In the right place, the right quantity, the right quality, it is a vital resource for survival and development and it may be a scarce resource. In these conditions it is valued at least psychologically and socially; and it may also have an actual monetary value, based on the cost of bringing it to the point of use and, beyond that, if there is scarcity, based on the economic value to consumers competing for similar or different water uses. On the other hand, in the wrong place, the wrong quantity, the wrong quality, it is a nuisance or worse: floods destroy lives and property; droughts bring starvation; contaminated water infects, poisons and kills plants, animals and people.

Water therefore evokes strong feelings, which are often deeply ambivalent: it is both good and bad, a life-giving substance and a threat to life; it is both blessed and feared. It is charged with deep meaning in the ritual and belief of Christianity and of probably all other religions.

The strength of the feelings and the powerful ambivalence in rural societies may be underestimated by city dwellers, most of whose experience is of water that has already been, so to speak, tamed and domesticated by intermediaries before it reaches them: not knowing it in its wild and unpredictable state they can take it for granted as a commodity. It follows that when a peasant and a government official talk about water they will be attaching very different meanings to it. We expect, of course, that the peasant will tend to think of local water as local, not national, property; but beyond that, we have to recognize that water is likely to be more prominent in his life-space, that it has strong personal significance, and that this significance is not only economic, but symbolic and emotional. Unless these meanings are taken into account, negotiations and decisions about water may lead to unanticipated consequences. They may explain, for example, the disproportionate violence of some irrigation disputes. They may also partly explain the common failure to maintain channels and drainage ditches: the idea that water can be tamed, and made to do what one wants it to do, is not deeply rooted – on the contrary. The other side of the coin, of course, is that, with rapidly expanding demand, the city dweller also has to learn that water is not abundantly available.

SOME IMPLICATIONS FOR ORGANIZATION

One proposition, then, is that the psychological meanings of water will have relevance for the organization of water management, at least in the context of rural development. The process of development requires the peasant to regard water as an economic resource whose quantity and quality he can to some extent control. Education and indoctrination will not shift the more deep-seated and primitive feelings and attitudes. Nor will these be shifted by the demonstration that water engineers have the capability of exercising a degree of control. Indeed, what we know of psychological processes suggests that the water engineer's capability may serve only to reinforce the backward peasant's view of himself as being incapable. On this basis, therefore, only the experience of participation in successful water management is likely to convince him that he can have an alternative, more rational relationship to water. To be successful, he requires help; so there is still a need for the water engineer, but in the role of consultant, instead of a remote figure doing the job himself. The peasant as participant can hardly avoid beginning to incorporate something of the water engineer's way of looking at the world, including, for example, the long-term effects of over-extraction, the function of soil conservation, the evaluation of competing uses, the relation between contamination and health.

In other words, the peasant ceases to become the passive recipient of benefits or the object of control (with the attendant problem of superficial compliance or refusal to comply); he himself becomes part of the regulatory process, being self-managing rather than managed by others.

Obviously, these last points have much wider relevance to processes of development and do not relate specifically to water. Rural development almost invariably requires the peasant to give up one set of beliefs, attitudes and relationships and to substitute another set; and this is most likely to occur if (with help) he manages the transition himself rather than having it imposed on him. But the uniquely deepseated feelings about water mean that if a community can learn to bring about a significant change in its relationship to water, this will be a crucial experience in leading it to manage other kinds of development.

These arguments point towards a policy of local management of user systems, such as irrigation areas and potable water systems. And indeed, if we accept the overall primary task as to regulate boundaries *between* hydrological and user systems, it would seem appropriate to encourage the building of resilient local user systems, capable of internal regulation, with consultant help when required, rather than to take over the management of them. If local management of user systems is accepted, it may be useful to re-examine the process whereby federal money is used to install new local facilities of this kind. A community which organizes itself to negotiate for a new irrigation scheme or other facility, the more especially if it is also prepared to contribute cash or labour towards its construction, is much more likely to have the organizational capacity to operate it. Time spent in helping the community to assess opportunities open to it and to decide what it wants to do is likely to pay off in terms of the resilience of the user system when it is built.

The argument against local management of these user systems is that it is less efficient. In a transitional stage from dependence to independence it almost certainly will be. If it continues to be inefficient despite technical aid, questions have to asked about the suitability of the design of the installation for the task in hand. It may be that the design is so sophisticated that only the experts can manage it. Certainly the technology of rural engineering – that is, the design of systems that campesinos can be readily trained to operate – is itself underdeveloped.

To sum up so far: for the federal government to involve itself in the operation of user systems, whether for irrigation or water distribution, is anti-developmental and also a distraction from its primary task of regulating the boundary between hydrological and user systems. The more appropriate policy would be to provide consultancy to help user systems of all kinds to manage their use of water more effectively in conformity with water policies.

To be effective, regulation of the boundary between hydrological and user systems needs to occur as close as possible to that boundary. It follows therefore that the government's task of regulating national water resources will be most appropriately carried out through regional water authorities, corresponding to hydrological systems, and operating with substantial autonomy in regulating these systems.

It also seems worth considering that these authorities should be self-financing, through charges to user systems, whether these are cities, irrigation districts, industrial enterprises, or government-owned bodies such as the Federal Electricity Commission. Charges would take into account such factors as: capital costs that may be incurred in bringing water to a user system; exploitation charges for extraction of ground water; levies on contaminated discharges; etc. Differential pricing for different classes of user would reflect the government's development policies. Thus water might be made available more cheaply to small municipalities. Major user systems, on the other hand, would need to be charged full economic costs, including opportunity costs. Therefore, the relationship between the regional water authority and user systems would be one of negotiation. If the cost to a user system proved to be higher than it could bear, then it should be the user system itself, not the authority, which should be seeking federal aid.

Strong regional participation in the regional authority's planning and policy making would seem advisable. This would fit with the widespread subjective feeling, not restricted to campesinos, that water is local, not national, property; and at the same time it would reinforce the idea that responsibility for development ultimately belongs to the inhabitants of the region, not to the federal government. Thus one would envisage that state governors would sit on the board of the authority. On the other hand, it would not be appropriate for the federal government to abdicate its ultimate responsibility for water regulation. A possible solution would be for a federal minister to serve as chairman of the board and for the full-time chief executive to be a Presidential appointment. However, it is not my purpose in this note to offer a specification, only to indicate that an organizational solution along these lines would seem to fit the nature of the task to be performed.

Involvement of state governors on the board would only go part of the way toward securing regional participation. At least two additional strategies (not mutually exclusive) are possible. One is involvement of the public in consultative bodies. The second is the possibility of the authority redelegating some of its powers. This is most practicable in those hydrological sub-systems that are relatively independent, serving their local populations. As I suggested earlier, a local unit for regulation of a sub-system of this kind is analogous to a user system. It would be feasible then for the regional authority to say in effect to the local population: 'You take collective responsibility, through your representatives, for regulating this hydrological sub-system on our behalf. It is up to you to ensure that negotiations with local user systems lead to an equitable and economic allocation. To help you in this, we can make expert advisers available to you if you wish. The only conditions we impose are that your extraction should not exceed X, your consumption should not exceed Y, and your discharge into the larger hydrological system should conform to the following specification . . .' The promotion of local organizations along these lines, besides providing for popular participation, would have the additional advantage of relieving the regional authority from some of the detail and freeing it to concentrate on the more complex and controversial parts of the system.

Does the creation of regional water authorities across the country mean that no function in water regulation remains at the centre? Certainly, water regulation offers an opportunity for actually putting into effect, in an impressive way, the policy of regionalization of government that is often preached but seldom practised; but I would envisage that a small central bureau would still be required with specific functions. For example, an element of planning must remain at national level. (The concept of developing new agriculture in the well-watered Gulf Coast, as an alternative to extending costly irrigation in arid zones, could only occur through study of water resources from a national perspective.) Other examples would be sectorial manpower planning and the conduct of certain types of specialized research, exploration, etc. for which regions lacked the necessary skills.

Let me conclude by repeating that in this note I have had the limited objective of trying to conceptualize the task of government in relation to water and to make preliminary propositions about organizational requirements. If my general thesis is accepted, then more detailed analyses can follow.

The concept proposed in the working note was fully accepted by the Commission and I worked with them on a more detailed plan for establishing regional water authorities. This in turn was endorsed by the Secretary of State for Water Resources, who was about to present it to the Cabinet when he was offered the governorship of a state. His successor was less keen on devolution and the plan lapsed.

I nevertheless continued intermittent consultancy assignments in the water sector. One major role was in creating a new organization for water supply in Mexico City. That assignment included two unusual elements. One was in designing and helping to run an international conference on the organization of large urban water supply systems, which brought together top executives from about forty major cities. We had to create a setting in which people of very different ideologies could talk freely. I vividly recall my trepidation in chairing a round table that included Leningrad, Los Angeles and Peking. But it worked. The other was the use of a jointly authored book to consolidate the reorganization. The book was designed in a conference of about forty persons with key roles in the organization: engineers, planners, economists, managers, and so on. Authors were assigned to chapters; their drafts were circulated and then reviewed in a second conference; and the outcomes were a worthwhile volume (Aguilar Amilpa et al., 1982) and a significant improvement in working relationships.

Other water-related assignments in the 1980s included an evaluation of a rural development programme in the tropical states of Mexico, linked to a major drainage scheme that made large areas available for new cash crops, and secondly an institution-building role in establishment of a new Mexican Institute for Water Technology. But regional water management remained on the back burner.

This changed abruptly in July 1988. Mexico had elected a new President, who would be taking office in December. He wanted a national water policy and I joined a small team (of people I had worked with in 1975) to provide it. The model we proposed, which not surprisingly included regional water authorities and independent self-financing user systems, was endorsed by the President as soon as he took office and I then consulted to a new National Water Commission set up to implement it. A follow-up in 1991 revealed encouraging progress.

PART FOUR:
PROCESSES OF DEVELOPMENT AND CHANGE

Introduction

The papers in Part III were products of the consultant and they were written for specific client systems in response to specific problems. The working note on diplomatic wives did, it is true, go into print, but only in a publication of and for the wives themselves and few other people will have read it, except perhaps some husbands. Those in Part IV, on the other hand, though arising from research and consultancy in particular settings, were written with the aim of disseminating emerging ideas, frameworks, hypotheses and so on to wider audiences.

The earliest – Chapter 9 – which dates from 1962, draws on a study of setting up a new steelworks on a green-field site and was seen as a contribution towards organizational theory. The other three were all written in 1976–77. Though addressing issues in manifestly different fields – rural development in the Third World, cultural change in a manufacturing company and innovation in a psychiatric hospital – those very differences accounted for this spell of productivity. Throughout my years at the Tavistock Institute I have always been engaged in more than one project at a time. Economically this has been a necessity; intellectually it has been enormously rewarding: I have constantly found my experience in one setting illuminating another. The year 1976 had seen the publication (in Spanish) of a book about the first phase of my consultancy to the Mexican government on integrated rural development (Miller, 1976d). Since writing it, however, I had taken the work further in Mexico and also in Panama. The paper reproduced in Chapter 10 crystallized the progress of my thinking at that stage. It has never been published before, though I drew on it for several articles (for example, Miller, 1979b), and I was able to apply the ideas fruitfully in further consultancy on rural development programmes in the Philippines in the early 1980s. Meanwhile, however, these ideas were sharpening my conception of organizational development in a project in industry. Chapter 11, which includes a case-study, is part of a longer paper I wrote at that time for a readership in the organizational development field (Miller, 1977). (Earlier sections of that paper are used in Chapter 1 of this volume.) At that time too I was involved in an experimental project promoting a 'bottom-up' culture of innovation in a psychiatric hospital. That was the ostensible subject of Chapter 12, but when I came to write it I found myself putting together experience both from rural development and from other settings in order to say something more general under the title of 'Autonomy, dependency and organizational change' (Miller, 1979a).

9 INSTITUTION-BUILDING: A NEW STEELWORKS

The research from which this paper emerged was sponsored by Richard Thomas & Baldwins (RTB). Between 1960 and 1962 the Company courageously allowed a colleague (David Armstrong) and myself to watch the processes through which a large integrated steelworks was built, manned and brought into production. This was the Spencer Works, near Newport in Monmouthshire. Sadly, publication of my book about it was later censored, as being too sensitive; but some papers emerged: e.g., Miller and Armstrong, 1966; Miller and Rice, 1967, Chapters 11, 12, 19, 20.

Practically everyone associated with the building of this works must have learned something useful from the experience. I am concerned here only with lessons *I* have learned, as someone interested in the social processes of building new institutions. And the main lesson for me has been the scale and complexity of the problems involved in an undertaking of this kind. Here I shall be content if I succeed in clarifying the nature of some of these problems.

In brief, my argument is that what is being built in cases such as

From a paper entitled 'Designing and building a new organization: some lessons of a green-field situation', read at the Manchester meeting of the British Association for the Advancement of Science, 3 September 1962.

this has the characteristics of a system, which has to satisfy a variety of differing needs – technological, economic, social and psychological. If in building the system, attention is paid to the technological and economic needs, regardless of the others, then a subsequent process of internal readjustment will take place, whereby the social and psychological factors will reassert themselves, possibly at the expense of the functioning of the system as a whole. There are, therefore, advantages in bringing forward at least part of this process of adjustment into the phase of designing and building the system. The building of the Spencer Works may be regarded as an experiment in doing this. It also throws light on the interrelations of the designing and building processes; some of the experience in this case can be satisfactorily explained only by regarding the designing and building of the works as themselves part of an overall system in which the system being built has a complex role.

My theoretical starting-point is open system theory, and in particular the theory of socio-technical systems which has emerged at the Tavistock Institute during the last few years.

One way of looking at a steelworks (or any industrial enterprise) – a static way – is as a collection of physical resources (i.e. machinery, equipment, transport, etc.) and a collection of human resources (operatives, engineers, managers, etc.). More dynamically one can regard it as a system of activities, human and non-human, through which raw materials are imported, processed and exported as finished products. Such a system brings to life the physical and human resources in a purposeful way – that is, it has certain explicit tasks or objectives. There are also implicit tasks to be performed: for example, the satisfaction of social and psychological needs that individuals carry with them into the organization. The explicit and implicit tasks are not always consistent with each other. Consequently, the form that any particular system takes might be regarded as the outcome of a process of reconciliation or mutual accommodation between a number of competing tasks.

Two such processes concern us here. First, there is the accommodation between the demands of the formal organization and the needs of the people who occupy roles within it, the outcome of which is the social system of the enterprise. Second, there is the accommodation between the social and technological dimensions: a social organization that is viable in one technological setting may be quite inappropriate to another. Clearly these two processes of accommodation – within the social dimension and between the social and the technological – affect each other. And since the enterprise is an open system – that is, there is a two-way traffic between the system and its environment – the processes are never completed, for changes in the external environment are likely to affect the internal relationships between different parts of the system.

If one accepts this orientation it follows that the task of building a new works on a green-field site is essentially the task of creating a new socio-technical system. It is, I think, worth labouring this point, because although this might be regarded as a statement of the obvious, many industrial enterprises, when they extend an existing works or put down a new one, seem to operate on different assumptions. They adopt the static rather than the dynamic model. Indeed, they behave as if their primary task is to design and build a plant – a set of physical resources.

There are fairly straightforward reasons for this. First, initial consideration of a new works is almost inevitably in terms of types and quantities of outputs and this leads directly to technological decisions about the economic manufacture of those outputs. In the case of RTB, for example, it was precisely these dimensions of the ultimate production system that had to be cleared with the Government before the building of the Spencer Works was sanctioned. Second, it is the installation of the physical plant that swallows up most of the expenditure on a new works, and it is this that appears on the company's balance sheet. Thus, externally at least, the works is defined primarily in terms of its physical characteristics. Nor should we underestimate the immense engineering and logistic problems of designing, specifying, ordering, assembling and constructing the plant. In the case of the Spencer Works, this has cost some £120 million [1962 prices] and over 10,000 people were at work on the site during the peak periods of construction.

Insofar as plant is liable to be the main preoccupation, people tend to be regarded as human resources, ancillary to plant. The emphasis is often on numbers, and on the distribution of manual and technical skills required. This attitude, too, is encouraged by the sheer size of the administrative task of recruiting, selecting, training and perhaps housing large numbers of new employees.

Now the consequences of approaching the task of building a new works in this way are, I think, fairly predictable. Where priority has been given to the design of plant, while the organization – that is, the relationships between man and machine and between man and man – is either assumed to be predetermined by the nature and constraints of the technology or else inherited more or less intact from a pre-existing works, then any 'goodness of fit' between the organization and the technology will be largely a matter of chance. Once the physical and human resources are activated and a socio-technical system comes into being, a process of accommodation will inevitably begin. Because by this time it may be too late, or too expensive, to modify the plant in order to improve the 'socio-technical fit', the outcome will almost certainly be a less than optimal performance of the system as a whole.

Now what does the 'socio-technical system' orientation tell us about the task of building a new works? First, it implies that it is not merely the plant – the technical system – that has to be designed, but also the organization – the social system – and that these two designs should be correlated with each other. Ideally, in fact, the system should be designed as an integrated whole. The second implication is that a socio-technical system, unlike a machine, cannot be constructed piece by piece and activated only when it is complete: a system grows organically. As soon as two or three people are recruited, however tightly or loosely their roles and relationships may have been defined in advance, the interplay of their personalities and of the experiences they have brought with them begins to introduce unpredicted and largely unpredictable elements into the situation.

Later I shall come back to the dilemma that this creates. For the moment, however, I want to consider what happened in the building of the Spencer Works, because it represents an unusual departure from the more normal, 'static' approach; and at the same time it illustrates some of the problems posed by the more dynamic 'socio-technical' approach.

The distinctive feature in the case of the Spencer Works lay in a hypothesis put forward by one or two managers in the Company, based on what they had seen happening in new works elsewhere. This was that many of the teething troubles encountered in commissioning and running in, although they may appear as failures in the design and building of plant, may be attributed to inadequate advance work on the design and building of an operating organization. On this basis it was decided that the senior group of managers who were to operate the new works would be recruited one-and-a-half to two years ahead and would actively participate in designing and building their organization. A detailed scheme of conferences and training exercises was worked out in conjunction with a phased programme of recruitment of more junior managers, supervisors and operatives. I have no time here to describe the scheme: it must suffice to say that so far as I know, it was unique in its scope and sophistication. Among other things, serious attention was paid to developing a cultural milieu – 'a philosophy of management' – which took into account some of the assumed needs of members of the future organization.

Let me now briefly outline the course of events. In the 1950s there was a long period of public controversy over where and when a fourth strip mill should be built in Britain. This culminated in an announcement by the Prime Minister, in November 1958, that not one but two new strip mills would be constructed, one by RTB at Newport and one by Colvilles in Scotland. For three years a group of engineers in RTB had been drafting and re-drafting designs for the new plant. By the spring of 1959, the main features of the design and lay-out appeared to have been settled, detailed specifications were being drawn up, and this same team of engineers had been given responsibility for supervising the construction of the plant. Clearance of the site began in the autumn of 1959. Towards the end of the year, the Iron and Steel Board asked the Company to expand the scheme by about one-third. This demanded substantial alterations in some of the plant specifications, and by the time the first work began on the foundations in February–March 1960, firm orders had yet to be placed for some of the major items of equipment.

The first operating managers were brought in during the latter part of 1959 and early 1960, that is, during the period of the last-minute extension of the proposed plant and the earliest work on actual construction. Before this, over a period of six to eight months, some preliminary work had been done on organization design, but this was mainly confined to specifying the top management structure in outline, as a basis for filling the senior posts. Within this limitation, the managers concerned were to participate in writing their own job specifications and in designing, manning and activating their departmental organizations.

Until the early part of 1960 the process of plant design and building and the process of organization design and building had been almost completely isolated from each other. The future operating managers had only a very general picture of the technical system on which the engineers were working; while I think it is fair to say that the engineers, who were wholly preoccupied with the vast problems of construction, could not have cared less what the operating managers were doing. These two processes were brought together in April 1960, when the General Manager for operations was put in charge of the construction organization as well. During the next two months, the operating managers closely scrutinized the engineering designs and recommended many changes. Some of these were adopted; others were turned down on the grounds that they were unnecessary or that they would be too costly in money or time. The principal modifications had been made by June 1960.

The operating managers then turned to the task of designing and building the organization. The first of the conferences mentioned above was held in September 1960. But as they built up their departments, managers kept a watchful eye on construction, and there have been periods of more intensive interaction with the engineers again as various units of plant have been commissioned and run in during 1962.

So much for a brief narrative of events.

RTB's plans for building the new works had two distinctive elements. First, they provided for the systematic design and building of an organization, parallel to the design and building of a plant. Second, the plans were consistent with the organic nature of the process of system building. Since the senior managers were recruited at a stage when organizational design was still fluid, they had an opportunity to design a system that was adaptable to their needs: the formal and informal organizations could be developed together. The progressively lower levels of management, as they were recruited, could also participate in more detailed design – though obviously the lower the level, the less the latitude available. Thus at least some of the processes of accommodation within the social organization, that would otherwise have taken place only after the works began to operate, could be got out of the way in advance.

However, RTB's plans did not provide for accommodation between the technical and social dimensions. The activities of plant design and organization design were separate, and it seemed to be widely assumed that the engineers' designs for the plant were fairly firm constraints on the design of the organization. Some were, of course: for example, the overall layout of the works – three-and-a-half miles long – and the scale of items of plant within it. But when, in April 1960, plant design and building on the one hand and organization design and building on the other were brought together under the General Manager for operations, many people were surprised at the flood of suggestions for changes in plant design.

One way of interpreting what happened at this juncture is to say that, even though it had not been planned, an accommodation between technical design and social design nevertheless took place. Thus some of the incompatibilities between the technical and social that might otherwise have reduced the efficiency of the ultimate operating systems, were reconciled before the technical system had fully 'jelled'. The problems of social and technical adjustment are painful – the early summer of 1960 was an uncomfortable period for everyone concerned – and I have little doubt that by taking some of the difficulty of adjustment in advance, the Spencer Works will have correspondingly reduced dislocation during the operating phase.

This interpretation is valid so far as it goes, but it does not do full justice to the complexities of the real-life situation. For example, many of the technological changes that the managers proposed seemed to indicate that they were judging the engineering designs not against any draft organizational design for the Spencer Works – this had scarcely moved forward at this stage – but rather against their past experience as operating managers, projected in their future operational responsibility at the new works. It was as if the operating system was already activated and asserting itself over the system of plant design. This in turn accelerated the process of organization-building, for the future operating managers were drawn more closely together as allies in opposition to the engineers. But this conflict was also detrimental to organization-building, because some of the senior engineers in plant design and plant building were themselves to occupy roles as maintenance engineers in the future operating system – roles in which they would have to work closely with these same managers.

One could continue in this vein. I hope I have said enough, however, to suggest that the process of building the Spencer Works cannot be fully understood merely in terms of the relations between a system of plant design and plant-building on the one side and a system of organization design and organisation-building on the other. These have to be seen as parts of a larger overall system, *of which the socio-technical system being created was also a part*. This existed not merely as a vision or objective, but as a progressively more concrete reality.

Many individuals occupied roles in two of these constituent systems; some in all three. I plan to deal more fully elsewhere with this pattern of multiple role-holding, which I have called 'counterpart roles'. These were not always explicit; and individuals seemed sometimes to move unconsciously from one to another, but they were nevertheless an essential feature of the process through which conflicts between the systems were both expressed and resolved.

How far might a different approach have eliminated some of the difficulties encountered in building the Spencer Works and led to a more effective result? The senior group of managers who were expected to develop the organization were not only brought in much later than the engineers, but they were recruited into *specific* operational jobs. This effectively inhibited them from making organizational innovations that might threaten the existence of these jobs or their relative status and power. As progressively more people were recruited, so the inhibiting forces were strengthened. In any case these managers were first and foremost system operators rather than designers.

This brings us back to the suggestion I made earlier. Might it not be possible to exploit the opportunities of the fresh start on a green-field site more fully if the socio-technical system were designed as an integrated whole? If, in fact, design were carried out within a separate, self-contained system, in which all the technical and human requirements of the ultimate system could be reconciled before any specific appointments were made at all?

Certain practical difficulties would arise. First, because of the rapid changes in technology and in markets which confront most industrial firms, it is seldom practicable to execute a comprehensive design before building starts. The Spencer Works, in which alterations were made both in the overall capacity and in the type of equipment to be installed, at a time when work had already begun on the site, is probably not unusual in this respect. Second, to design even a comprehensive technical system on paper can be formidably difficult, and errors often remain unnoticed until production begins – or fails to begin. And there is a good deal less reliable knowledge of the social dimension than there is of the technical. However, these difficulties might be overcome: one might be able to design the perfect socio-technical system.

Here one is brought back to the dilemma I hinted at previously. This perfect system would still have to be built, and because the building of a socio-technical system is an organic process, this would inevitably modify the design. Consequently it is fruitless, at least in our present state of knowledge, to try to build such a system to a precise blueprint. System-building has more in common with horticulture than with engineering; though even the gardener has at his disposal more reliable seed and a richer array of fertilizers and pesticides than are available to the industrial enterprise.

In conclusion, let me briefly summarize what we have learnt about institution-building. The first point is that the task of creating a new works is an exercise in creating a socio-technical system. If one approaches this task with any other assumption – for example, that it is primarily a question of designing and building a plant and assembling people to operate it – the 'systemic' nature of the works will reassert itself in unanticipated and probably undesired ways when it is in operation. The operating system both affects and is affected by the processes of designing and building – first as a vision and then as a progressively emerging reality. Regardless of the actual content of designs for the operating system, the way in which design and building are carried out will affect both the form and effectiveness of the completed system. Hence we are faced with a problem of system design and system-building of a higher order: it is a problem of designing and building an overall system within which the design and building of the operating system can most effectively be carried out. I feel that we are just beginning to understand some of the forces that are at work in such a process.

10 TOWARDS A MODEL FOR INTEGRATED RURAL DEVELOPMENT

I was part-time consultant to Secretaría de la Presidencia in Mexico, 1971–76, and from 1973 onwards was especially concerned with a large national programme of investment in rural development (PIDER) being undertaken by the Dirección de Inversiones Públicas. The earlier phases of this programme are discussed in my book (Miller, 1976d). At the time this paper was written in 1977, I had also been advising the Government of Panama on establishing a similar programme.

THE SCOPE OF THIS PAPER

Disappointing results from earlier development efforts in Latin America and other parts of the Third World have highlighted the need for more comprehensive approaches to the problem. There has been a move away from isolated crop improvement projects or health projects towards programmes of integrated agricultural development and, in a few countries, integrated rural development. Such programmes involve a wide range of interventions and investments, in farming technology, rural industry, credit, commercialization, road-building, transport and other areas, designed to bring about economic advancement, and, alongside these, projects concerned with nutrition, health, housing, education and so forth, intended to improve the quality of rural life. Massive effort and

Published here for the first time.

PROCESSES OF DEVELOPMENT AND CHANGE

expenditure are required; but these in themselves do not guarantee effectiveness. Objectives are often confused; methods are inadequately worked out; ministries and other governmental agencies flounder in unaccustomed patterns of delegation and coordination in the field; and results tend to fall far short of intentions. Even where initial results seem satisfactory, the longer-term outcomes are often discouraging: for example, large numbers of rural drinking-water supplies, which are proudly inaugurated as a major contribution to villagers' health and welfare, are out of use within a couple of years because the local communities seem to lack the skill or will to operate and maintain them.

This is the general problem-area that I address in this paper. I shall not, however, be concerning myself with technical issues that are the province of such specialists as agronomists, irrigation engineers, or nutritionists. What I am concerned with is the nature of their relationships – with each other and more especially with the target population. Obviously the technical content of the relationship is significant: if the agronomist recommends a crop for which the soil is unsuitable or for which there is no market, the outcome is unlikely to be successful. But even where the soil is right and the market is available, there are many instances of failure. My general proposition is that the nature of the relationship is a critical factor in the process of development.

I shall begin by offering a definition of the outcome to be achieved through a development programme. This, then, determines the task of the 'development agency' – that is, the agency or group of agencies responsible for implementation. I shall then examine the role of the development agency in carrying out that task in relation to the 'client system' – that is, a given group intended to benefit from the programme. Third, I shall discuss in more detail the identification of different types of client systems. Finally, I shall consider some implications for inter-agency relationships and organization.

OBJECTIVES, TASK AND AN OUTLINE OF THE PROCESS

To begin with, it has to be noted that a government-sponsored rural development programme is usually the product of a diverse set of motives and objectives, ranging from the moral to the pragmatic. It is seen as contrary to social justice that large sectors of the population should be living at subsistence or infra-subsistence levels; continued existence of such underprivileged groups, as they become aware of their relative deprivation, may threaten political stability; migration from the countryside to the cities and the growth of a marginalized urban population pose major social, economic and political problems; greater agricultural and agro-industrial production is needed, both for urban consumption and for export; urban industrial expansion depends on a growing internal, and therefore rural, market for consumer goods; and so on. Obviously, any single act of development may have multiple functions. A new road, for example, permits services to be taken into a remote community and produce to be brought out to the market; thus it may contribute to greater prosperity. Also, however, as many Latin American breweries have discovered, it permits truck-loads of beer to be delivered to the community in exchange for the additional cash now available; and it may facilitate government counter-insurgency measures against guerrillas. I do not intend to discuss the rights and wrongs of these various motives and functions, but merely to note at this stage that contradictions among them are factors that may influence programme design and implementation.

Despite these contradictions, in fact, usually the shared and stated objective is that the target population should become fully connected to the wider social, economic and political system of the country. Development, therefore, can be thought of as a set of technical, structural and cultural transformations through which that outcome is attained. Correspondingly – and this is often explicit – investment in such a programme needs to produce, directly or indirectly, a multiplier effect so that development can become a self-sustaining process. Related to this, it is also often emphasized that the rural community should participate actively in the design and execution of the programme.

Underlying such a statement of objectives, of course, is an implied conception of 'underdevelopment'. This is a word to be used with caution, since it defines the condition of the target community not in terms of the values of the people themselves but in terms of the values of the developers, who regard themselves as 'developed' – whatever that may mean. 'Underdevelopment', therefore, suggests a distinction between, on the one hand, the benefactors, the superiors, those who do not need to change, and, on the other, the beneficiaries, the inferiors, those who need to be changed. The objective is to make 'them' more like 'us'. I shall come back to the implications of this position.

It is nevertheless possible to offer a less value-laden and more operational meaning for 'underdevelopment'. We can arrive at this by considering some typical characteristics of the intended beneficiaries of a rural development programme. They usually comprise a group or community that is relatively lacking in control over its natural environment: it is the victim of its environment rather than its master. Second, the underdeveloped community tends to be a rather tightly integrated system, within which relations to the land are closely tied to social relations and values. This means that any change in one aspect of the system – for example, a new agricultural technology – will produce changes in other aspects – for example, in established patterns of mutual aid among kin and neighbours. These ramifications, which may not be grasped by the well-intentioned agricultural extensionist, often account for apparently 'irrational' resistance to technical innovations: resistance protects valued social institutions that the innovation would threaten.* Third, the underdeveloped community is a relatively closed system. That is to say, it engages in only a limited set of transactions with other systems in its socio-economic environment. Products, for example, may be sold to a single middleman, who thus controls prices and credit and may also control the store in which villagers spend the money they get. In such a situation, the control that the community exercises over its external environment is zero. The forces maintaining the *status quo*

---

* Extensionists may also ignore the pragmatic wisdom of peasant communities that has enabled them to survive. They are not interested in crops that will produce a maximum yield in good years; the varieties they have learned to plant are those that will minimize the chances of a total crop failure in the bad years (see Jennings, 1976).

are therefore very powerful. Over and above this, if there has been a cumulative experience of generations of exploitation and oppression by wealthy landlords and merchants, then the community is highly likely to display apathy and feelings of worthlessness and impotence.

Hence I propose the following operational definition of 'underdevelopment': *relative lack of control over relations with one's environment, where that includes both the local physical environment and the external environment that comprises the wider socio-economico-political system.* Specific aspects of these relations – economic and other – can be identified, analysed and sometimes measured. Development, then, implies a change in such relationships in the direction of influencing and controlling the environment, instead of being controlled by it – a change from impotence towards potency. Following from this, my proposition is that: *the primary task of a development programme is to help the client system to increase its control of its environment.* It is for this task that the development agency needs to organize itself. Four aspects of this task may be identified. Two of these are familiar enough; but I suggest that the significance of the third and, in particular, the fourth is insufficiently recognized. (In this discussion, for the sake of simplicity, I shall assume that the client system is a rural community; later I shall consider more complex alternatives.)

The first aspect is the development of the human resources of the community. Thus it is obvious that education can inculcate new techniques and skills; literacy provides access to alternative values and goals. Similarly, improved nutrition and health potentially release greater energy for existing and new activities.

The second aspect is improvement of the physical resources of the community. This is the goal of many development agencies, which often measure their performance by the number of wells dug, hectares irrigated, classrooms constructed, households provided with electricity, etc.

However, as I illustrated with the example of drinking-water systems, installation is not synonymous with utilization. These projects, therefore, are to be regarded only as means, not as ends in themselves. The criterion of effectiveness lies in my third aspect:

have they helped the community to extend its own control over its physical environment. Sometimes an extensionist works hard and successfully to arouse enthusiasm for a new agricultural technique, which really seems to be moving the boundary between the farmers and their physical environment. It operates successfully for a couple of seasons, and then the farmers regress to previous methods. Assuming that the innovation really fits the needs of the community and that the extensionist has ensured that continuing supplies of seeds, fertilizers, etc. are available, then the explanation has to be sought elsewhere. Often the most plausible explanation in such cases is that the farmers have not learned to manage the new process themselves: they have been dependent on the extensionist, so that only his continuing presence has permitted the innovation to be sustained.

So I come to my fourth aspect, and with it a hypothesis: that the community will not achieve greater control in relation to its local physical environment, or the achievement will not be sustained, unless the change is also accompanied and reinforced by corresponding and more permanent changes in relations with the external environment: the community needs to become more autonomous and influential in managing these relationships also. Many of these changed relationships will be economic: for example, the community sells produce instead of manual labour; it sells its produce in a more profitable processed form instead of selling it unprocessed (for example, cheese instead of milk); it diversifies its products; it extends its control over distribution and so commands higher prices; and so on. Although these points may seem obvious, it is surprising how often they are missed even in so-called integrated development programmes. Extensionists promote higher yields without considering the process of commercialization: they fail to recognize that farmers will have little incentive to increase output if all the extra profits go into the pocket of the traditional middleman. In such cases the farmers may need to be helped to establish their own co-operative marketing arrangements, bypassing the middleman, if they are to obtain a proper return. Along with the economic gains, a less obvious, more subtle and at the same time more significant change seems to occur – a change in the community's identity and self-image. As a result of, for example, bypassing the middleman and managing distribution themselves, the people acquire a different – more potent – image in the external environment, and this in turn reinforces an emerging image of themselves as more potent, both collectively and individually.* In this way, technical and structural changes become confirmed by a cultural transformation. The outcome, then, is a system that has discovered the possibilities of exercising autonomy and choice and has become capable of managing itself in a self-sustaining process of development. That is to say, it can manage its transactions with markets, credit institutions, sources of supply, agricultural extension agencies, etc. on the same basis as the 'developed' sector and hence no longer needs the support of a special development programme.

THE ROLE OF THE DEVELOPMENT AGENCY: PARTICIPATION AND NEGOTIATION

It is towards this outcome in its 'client system' that the activities of an integrated rural development rural programme, such as PIDER in Mexico, have to be directed.

There seems to be widespread agreement that participation of the client population is an important element in the approach of the development agency. Closer inspection, however, shows that the apparent agreement often conceals two very different views of the nature of participation. These differences show up in the following statements:

---

* I witnessed a simple but good example of this in Oaxaca, Mexico. Several families in one village had been helped to take up poultry-raising. Among themselves they organized their production cycles so as to maintain a steady overall output and they manned a stall in the market of a nearby town, where the dressed chickens were sold. The stall bore the name of the village, and it quickly acquired a reputation for quality and reliability. This in turn helped to sustain the collaborative arrangements among the families concerned and was quite evidently a source of pride and added self-confidence in the village as a whole.

A. 'The community should participate actively in the selection, formulation and execution of development projects.'
B. 'It is necessary to secure the close identification of beneficiaries with the goals of the proposed projects.'

Statement A expresses the 'bottom-up' view of development planning, which focuses on helping the client group to formulate its own objectives and strategies for attaining them. Statement B, on the other hand, characterizes the 'top-down' perspective: goals have already been determined; 'participation' is the device through which the client group is to be persuaded to accept and adopt those goals.

In light of my definition of the development task and my outline of the processes through which it may be realized, the bottom-up approach has manifest advantages. Essentially, the client system has to be helped to design and manage the implementation of its own development programme. A top-down approach, with its assumption that the technocrat knows what is best for the client, is in practice unlikely to produce what is best, since either the innovation will not be accepted at all or, if it is adopted, it will be maintained only at the cost of continuing dependency on the development agency; and, as I have indicated, such dependency may prevent mobilization of self-management.

One difficulty, of course, is that at the beginning the client community does not know what choices are open to it – nor even imagine that it is capable of any action. Hence it cannot think meaningfully about a development programme. A possible strategy, therefore – and perhaps the ideal one – is to start with a prolonged phase of education and consultancy. As Freire (1973) points out, where a peasant community starts from a posture of apathy, self-depreciation and ignorance, an initial, possibly essential, task is to help the people to realize that their plight is a consequence not of inherent inferiority but of generations of neglect or of oppression and exploitation. They need to acquire the self-confidence through which to fight back against their oppressive environment. Once the community has been helped to consider its actual and potential resources and the uses to which they might be put, and has conducted, in effect, its own 'cost-benefit analysis', in social as well as in economic terms, it is ready to select from the alternatives open to it and to negotiate with the relevant agency for specific resources required to carry through the chosen strategy. Thus, an advantage of separating the role of educator/consultant from the agencies that actually make investments, construct works, provide credit, etc. is that the autonomy of the client system is cultivated from the outset. By the time it approaches the agency to seek a specific contribution from it, the client system is less likely to be caught in the dependency relationships between beneficiary and benefactor. (If it has some continuing dependence vested in the consultant, this may help it in taking on a more independent and assertive stance towards the agency.) A further advantage is that the work with the consultant gives the community ample time to prepare for the inevitable changes in its internal social system; whereas the top-down approach is more likely to be experienced as a threat to the *status quo* and thus to provoke resistance to innovation.

Government sponsorship of a rural development programme, it can be argued, is ultimately incompatible with pursuit of a bottom-up approach, which leads in essence to overthrow of the established system – to revolution. While this argument must carry considerable weight, there is another perspective that often gets forgotten: by instituting the programme the national government is to some extent committing itself to an alliance with backward peasantry against local exploiters – such as the middlemen referred to above. It is by its willingness or otherwise in practice to implement such alliances, of course, that a post-revolutionary government displays whether it is in fact continuing to pursue stated revolutionary aims or merely engaging in rhetoric. Theoretically at least it is not impossible for a government to support the quasi-revolutionary role of the educator/consultant. In one or two areas of Mexico, for example, this is happening; but it is the exception. One – probably genuine – constraint is a shortage of people competent to take the role. Moreover, once governments embark on a rural development programme they tend to be impatient for action and results – even though the conditions that they now want to rectify so urgently have persisted for many years, or even for many generations.

Whatever the reasons, the development agency finds itself

pressed to take action without sparing time for a prolonged preparatory phase. And it is faced with the dilemma – which requires much more explicit recognition and understanding than it receives – that it occupies two different and potentially contradictory roles in relation to its client systems. On the one hand, the agency itself has to take on the educator/consultant role, which, in a more perfect world, might already have been undertaken in advance by a different party. This role embodies the bottom-up task of helping the client group to design and implement its own development programme. In its second role the agency is charged with pursuing specific national, regional or sectorial objectives and so it is in the top-down position of promoting policies that it wants to see incorporated in the programme. For example, I have seen an agricultural plan prepared by a government for one region, in which it is proposed to make a major transition to rice-growing in a society dedicated to cattle-raising. The same plan, partly to create land-holdings of a more viable size and perhaps for ideological reasons as well, also proposes to introduce collectivized forms of agriculture in a society which has quite strong individualistic values. Given that, in relation to the client system, the development agency has the power to give or withhold financial and other assistance, the pressure on it to adopt an authoritarian, top-down stance is obviously powerful.

The emerging model indicates, in fact, that it will be counter-productive for the agency to exercise the power available in its second role and so to neglect the first. Unless the client system itself takes a thought-out decision to adopt such an innovation as rice-growing or collectivized farming, the programme will fail in two ways: the innovation will either prove abortive or be sustained only through continuing external direction; and second, the client system will not have learned to manage its own development. I contend, therefore, that the development agency must not allow its first role, as educator/consultant, to be swamped by the second. In the following paragraphs I shall explore the appropriate role of the development agency and some of the difficulties it can expect to encounter in managing its relationship with the client system.

Figure 10.1 illustrates the hypothesis that it is a necessary condition for effective development that the client system as it is at

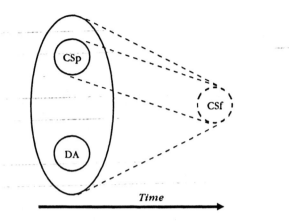

Fig 10.1 Creating a future

present (CSp) should acquire and identify itself with a vision or image of some desirable future state (CSf) which it is capable of attaining. CSf has greater control over its physical and external environment than CSp; it is managing its own continuing development. In relation to this process, the role of the development agency (DA) can be seen as including three elements or phases:

1 the *generation*, jointly with CSp, of an image of CSf which the people are motivated to achieve and also have a reasonable hope of achieving;

2 *negotiation* of the respective contributions of the CS and the DA for the attainment of the CSf; and

3 continuing *maintenance and development* of the image of CSf.

From the standpoint of the client system, one can see this as a process of moving from dependence, through interdependence, towards independence.

The more underdeveloped the client system is at the beginning of this process – that is, the more it is dependent, oppressed and impotent in its relationships with its environment – the stronger the leadership that will have to be exercised by the development agency in the early stages in order to convince the client system that it is capable of achieving potency in relation to its external environment and to show the means by which this may be achieved. Thus the expert from the agency will be in the top-down position of offering an image of a CSf, proposing a development programme and mobilizing support for an initial project. He will be wise to conceive the programme as a draft – a working hypothesis – rather than a blueprint, and to select the first project carefully. It should offer something that the community perceives as valuable; the community should be contributing to it in labour and/or other resources; and it should extend the community's own control over an aspect of its environment – probably the local physical environment. For example, in some communities in Mexico it has been demonstrated that, by adopting an innovative method of drip-irrigation, which uses minute quantities of water and fertilizer, it is possible to grow fruit trees on land that had been regarded as barren. But it is important in such cases that members of the client system themselves should have the experience of contributing to the change – in the case of the fruit trees, for instance, by themselves preparing the ground, constructing the canals and storage tanks (with technical assistance and materials being supplied by the agency), and keeping the irrigation scheme in operation. To do this work for them is anti-developmental. Hence my emphasis on negotiation between the DA and the CS about the contribution that each will make to the process.

The third phase, 'maintenance and development', is required not only to sustain the motivation of the client system – thus regular visits from representatives of the DA demonstrate concern for and belief in CSf – but also to make the image of CSf fuller and more specific. Thus the image initially generated may be of a CSf engaged in cultivation and commercialization of fruit trees. In the continuing visits other projects get added – for example, poultry-raising – and negotiation occurs around these. Then a stage may be reached in which the CS is formulating its own potential projects and negotiating with the DA for help in implementing them.

Progressively, therefore, leadership in the development process needs to move from the development agency to the client system, which becomes increasingly capable of formulating its own development plan and of implementing it with diminishing assistance from the agency.

The difficulty of achieving this transition should not be underestimated. The cost of omitting or abbreviating the preliminary educational phase and moving rapidly towards change is that stronger and more charismatic leadership is used to persuade the client that productive change is possible. The dependency relationship so created then becomes more entrenched and the 'developer' finds it harder, especially in more backward communities, to extricate himself from it and to move towards the situation in which the client system is interdependent with him and finally independent of him. Part of the difficulty will come from within himself, because leadership of a dependent group, who are perhaps excited by the project and grateful to their benefactor, can be a seductive experience. It is tempting to continue in the paternalistic role. Moreover, the developer is reluctant to relinquish control. Here his role-conflict may become quite acute. He may realize that, if development as I have defined it is to occur, then leadership must pass from him to the client system. He therefore has to look out for signs of initiative and leadership within the community and to respond to them. Yet at the same time he may be dissatisfied with the directions that the client system wants to pursue and able to think of alternatives that fit more closely with his own and his agency's policies. He is likely to feel that his own performance is being evaluated by the 'success' of the client system in implementing those policies, and to fear that if he reduces his intervention the client system will make mistakes. Heckadon, a sociologist, gives an excellent example in his study of poultry projects in the District of Sona in the Republic of Panama. Local men were not highly committed to poultry-keeping, which was perceived as a female activity, so the scheme was less productive than it should have been. Gradually the group of young government experts took over more and more of the decision-making until they were effectively running the whole project themselves, 'which in no way contributed to providing the conditions for encouraging the maturation of these groups' (Heckadon, 1973, p. 67). Rationally, we can see that, in relation to the task of development, the opportunity to make mistakes is necessary to the learning and maturation of the client system: in fact, in learning to manage itself and its relations with its environment, the client may gain more from the experience of a failure than from a success. Yet very often the proposal for a tiny rural project is subjected to more stringent evaluation and control than a major governmental investment.

What happens, therefore, at the boundary between the development agency and the client system is a form of negotiation between top-down and bottom-up development planning. The representative of the agency is in an ambivalent position. Bottom-up planning is necessary for the task and he may well be urged to operate within an ideology of genuine participation; yet at the same time he is charged with implementing governmental objectives, including overt or implicit desires to control the course and outcomes of rural development. I shall have more to say about this dilemma. Here I simply want to emphasize the problem that the power of the two parties to the negotiation is unequal. It is too easy for the agency to impose its policies on the client system. Equally, we know that if the agency uses its power to impose policies in this way, the client's acceptance of them is likely to be only superficial. It will remain dependent on the agency and not advance towards self-management; and the projects will probably not achieve the results that the agency has hoped for. The more underdeveloped the community, the greater this problem. Before proposing a project that will predictably make a big change in the social system – for example, the change from cattle to rice – it is prudent to wait until the power of the two parties has become more equal. Only if the client system feels strong enough to say 'no' to an agency proposal can one be sure that its 'yes' really means 'yes'. This presents a problem for management of rural development programmes at all levels. If the agent in the field is quick in obtaining a client's agreement to a project, then the natural tendency is to congratulate him. But how genuine is the 'yes'? Another agent may seem unduly slow; but time spent in this initial phase may well lead to much more enduring results. To return to an earlier example: it is very easy to persuade a village that it wants a drinking-water supply; but does one judge the performance of the agency by the number it installs or by the number still operating after, say, three years? Time may also have been spent usefully even if it produces the answer 'no': this is better than wasting money and effort on a false 'yes'. While I am not suggesting that all quick acceptances will be false, in general I would expect projects requiring active participation of the client population in implementation to mature only slowly.

IDENTIFICATION OF THE CLIENT SYSTEMS

To simplify presentation of arguments, I have been equating client systems with rural communities. This now needs some qualification.

Under certain conditions, the small local community – the village – may be regarded as the basic unit of development and thus as the appropriate client system for an integrated development programme. These conditions include: the existence of a form of community government; communal ownership of land (even though some or all of the land may be parcelled out and cultivated by individual families); and relative homogeneity in wealth (or poverty) and power. Such conditions are to be found in Mexico in many indigenous communities and *ejidos* – rural collectives set up on expropriated land after the revolution. In these circumstances the community is a ready-made client system, with which it is possible to work on a wide range of projects, including both 'productive' projects (for instance, in agriculture) and 'social' investments, such as a school building or a health centre. Usually, the degree of internal organization will enable the community to contribute labour and materials in constructing, for example, a local road or irrigation canals. In this way, the client system genuinely participates in its own development. It may be that, in the longer term, the new linkages formed with the wider socio-economic system will produce disequilibria within the community – for example, through the unequal accumulation of wealth by individuals – but in the short-to-medium term the traditional organization can provide some stability during the process of modernization. The task of the development agency is therefore relatively straightforward and uncontentious, in that it probably needs to work only at two levels: the community and whatever larger unit (micro-region, district, etc.) has been selected as the development 'block', within which investments in infra-structure – for example, roads, a secondary school or a market – support development of the communities concerned.

A pre-existing organization makes the task of the developer so much easier that he tends to fall into certain traps. He may assume that the organization is more robust and active than it is: for example, the realities of *ejido* government may be very different from the written constitution. He may fail to notice internal factionalism, or the domination of one group by another in an ostensibly egalitarian community. And he may be tempted to promote a collectivist ideology in settlements of small farmers whose culture is highly individualistic.

A pre-existing organization makes his task easier not only because the client system is ready-made but also because it saves him from having to make awkward and contentious political choices. It is satisfying to champion the cause of a backward homogeneous community and to help it acquire independence of anonymous external exploiters. When the exploiter lives within the community, the situation feels different. The fact is, of course, that development programmes are designed to rectify accumulated inequalities; hence the clients of development are the neglected districts in a state, the neglected villages in a district and, at the micro-level, the neglected sub-groups in a village. With these clients the development agency has to form coalitions, through which they become capable of acting back upon their environments and so rectifying the inequalities.

Ultimately, then, we return to the dilemma mentioned earlier: the representative of a governmental development agency is faced with making a coalition with one group of citizens against another. Co-optation is one strategy to avoid confrontation: that is to say, the development agent allies himself with the 'exploiter' and attempts to persuade him to make room for development of the 'exploited'. He is likely to do this under two related conditions: first, he perceives the political power of the government as dependent more on the support of the 'exploiter' than of the 'exploited'; and second, he identifies the 'exploiter' as belonging to a social class from which governmental officials and experts, including the agent himself, tend to be drawn. This kind of alliance sometimes works, in that it may mitigate inequalities, but it will not produce more profound politico-economic transformations. Other strategies may also be used, which come closer to, but nevertheless avoid, direct confrontation. Important here is the encouragement of co-operative interest-groups, which transcend village boundaries, for purchase of supplies, credit, marketing, etc. Such groupings then become significant client systems, which reduce the power of 'exploiters'. Quite a crucial point is that the traditional power of landlords, merchants and so on has relied on the absence of organization among the scattered 'exploited' groups in different villages. Any change achieved through a coalition between the development agency and an exploited sub-group within a village is most unlikely to be sustained in the long term unless that sub-group has formed an effective alliance with similarly deprived sub-groups in other villages. Hence, to perform its task, the development agency needs to promote such an alliance as its client system. Ultimately, therefore, development involves reallocation of power; and, while direct confrontation between the development agency and local 'exploiters' may prove unnecessary in bringing about change, my hypothesis would be that no significant change will in fact occur unless the development agency itself feels powerful enough at least to risk such a confrontation.

When moving into a new development region there are nevertheless fairly obvious advantages for the development agency in beginning with the 'easier' client systems, which already have some internal organization and show good potential for change, and in postponing confrontations. In this way, results are likely to be achieved more quickly and cheaply; the agency learns from its experience before moving into more complex systems; and the idea of development and change is disseminated and may lead to demands for help from other potential client systems. (The importance of this last point, of course, is that the community or group that offers itself for development is more likely to make effective use of investments and technical advice.) Politically, too, such an approach is less likely to provoke organized resistance from existing vested interests; and moreover, as rural populations discover that they can have an independent political voice – for example, that they do not necessarily have to follow the voting instructions of the traditional *caciques* – the power base of the government begins to shift and the development agency can afford to be less cautious about antagonizing the older rural establishment.

THE ORGANIZATION OF DEVELOPMENT AGENCIES

It follows from the preceding section that the development agency needs to be able to engage with an interlocking and overlapping set of client systems. Some correspond to boundaries of *ejidos* or communities; others lie inside these boundaries or cut across them. Some already exist; others have to be brought into existence and become viable groupings through the help of the development agency itself.

Although I have been using the global term 'development agency', the reality in most integrated programmes of rural development is that multiple agencies are involved. For example, in any one of the micro-regions of the Mexican PIDER programme, the participating bodies are likely to include: the Ministries of Agriculture, Agrarian Reform, Public Works, Water Resources, Health, and Education, together with such other public agencies as the Federal Electricity Commission, the National Corporation for Staple Commodities, the National Fund for Promotion of Village Enterprises, the National Institute for Rural Community Development and Popular Housing, and others besides. PIDER coordination is vested in yet another body, the Ministry of the Presidency. Each participating agency has its own experts and has certain sectorial objectives and policies to pursue. On the other hand, I have defined the primary task of the development agencies in terms of helping each client system to extend its control over its environment and thus to become capable of managing its own development. If that definition is accepted, then it follows that the specialized projects are only means to that end. Members of this micro-regional team, therefore, in their transactions with client systems, have to reconcile the top-down and bottom-up approaches. The requisite organization is one that will allow and encourage this to happen.

What this appears to demand is a form of 'project organization' (see Miller and Rice, 1967). The basic unit of organization is the team – usually multi-disciplinary – that is responsible for managing the relationship with one client system. The composition of the team will vary, both over time and between one system and another, according to the nature of the projects being undertaken. One member – usually the member in closest and most regular contact with the client – needs to be nominated as team leader. Thus if the agencies involved in a PIDER micro-region are working with fifty client systems, the basic operating units will be fifty multi-disciplinary teams. The individual, of course, is only a part-time member of any one team. Sometimes one team will handle a number of clients; or the same individual may work in several differently composed teams with different client systems.

This implies that management of the programme at, say, micro-regional level, should be primarily concerned with monitoring the progress not of the sectorial projects but of client systems. The crucial criterion of effectiveness is not, for example, the construction of the irrigation scheme as such but whether the group of farmers using it are moving towards autonomy. It is, of course, part of the managerial task to make sure that the necessary resources are available for completion of the physical works; but even more important is to give the team in the field the requisite support – including 'political' support – in building and managing an appropriate relationship with the client system.

A hospital analogy may illuminate this way of thinking about organization. In, say, an orthopaedic hospital, several different disciplines are involved in care and treatment of patients: for example, medicine, nursing and physiotherapy. If each discipline pursues its own independent strategy, the effects on the patients are unlikely to be beneficial and may even be fatal. In a well-organized orthopaedic hospital, by contrast, the doctor, nurse and physiotherapist agree together on a treatment strategy for each patient and perform their specialized functions as members of an inter-disciplinary team in the light of that strategy – which, of course, they review regularly. As the patient moves towards discharge, a social worker may be drawn into the team. Each of these specialists has a distinct clientele. The nurse may be looking after twenty in-patients on one ward; the doctor and physiotherapist may have responsibility for a larger number of both in-patients and out-patients; the social worker's clients will be a set of families in the community. But the primary unit of treatment is each individual patient, and it is those professionals involved with him who need to organize themselves around the task of getting him better. I must add, however, that this analogy is defective and even misleading in one important respect: unlike the client systems discussed here, the patient himself does not usually play an active part with the team in designing the treatment strategy.

The distinctive professional skills of each team member therefore have to be used in the service of a development strategy that the team as a whole has devised with the client system. This strategy is the unifying factor, the basis for co-operation. The same applies to the overall team at the level of the micro-region: the contribution of every specialist within it has to fit the wider development strategy for that region, which is the overall client system. If the individual pursues the goals of his own specialism without regard for the shared strategy, it is probable that his activities will be wasted, or even damaging to the development process.

The approach that I have been describing requires the team to negotiate with the client system. It has to hear, interpret and respond to the needs of the client. If it is to be able to do this, then its own voice needs to be heard by programme management. Government agencies normally operate in a hierarchical, top-down manner: people at the top decide; people at the bottom execute. Such a culture is not appropriate to the task of rural development. On the contrary, programme management needs to encourage active participation of all field staff in designing the development strategy and in monitoring the progress of the programme. In this way, the field staff themselves are more likely to make room for genuine participation of the clients. If, on the other hand, programme management is authoritarian in relation to field staff, they in turn can be expected to be similarly authoritarian towards their clients.

In a large programme such as PIDER in Mexico, which has one hundred micro-regional development programmes, the open kind of negotiating relationship between the team and micro-regional programme management also needs to be replicated between the micro-regional group and central management at national level. It is the task of the centre to provide encouragement and support, rather than specific direction.

The form of organization described here is sometimes called a matrix organization. Each person within it has, in effect, two bosses. In one direction he is accountable to an inter-disciplinary project team, working with a client system; in another direction he is part of a specialized functional group within a government agency. My proposition is that, if the organization is to operate effectively in its task, the inter-disciplinary ties have to be stronger than the functional ties. However, I am also aware that this is a sophisticated form of organization in which the loosening of functional ties and the requisite delegation and decentralization represent a sharp departure from the traditions of governmental bureaucracies. Consequently, explicit and continuing attention needs to be given to the problem of building and sustaining an organization that is appropriate to the task.

CONCLUSION

In this paper I have proposed a definition of the primary task of a development programme – 'to help the client system to increase its control of its environment' – and I have described a model of the transactions between a development agency and a client system through which such a process of development will be achieved. I have also outlined the organizational conditions necessary to enable the representatives of the agency or agencies working with the client to take up the roles that the task requires.

My approach has been for the most part normative – 'if you want to achieve this, then you ought to do that' – because I judge that to be the most useful way of communicating to practitioners in rural development. Scientifically speaking, what I have offered is nevertheless the beginnings of a model, in that it includes a series of propositions about the effects, within and between different systems, of various kinds of action and interaction. Consequently, it can be tested, modified and refined through more intensive scientific research. While this may be useful, however, it may be much more productive if practitioners actually working in ongoing programmes can themselves become involved in the process of model-building. They can do this by testing my propositions against their own experience or by using my model as a basis for experimental changes in their own practices. So much is still unknown that it is imperative to build into every rural development programme, and indeed into every practitioner, mechanisms for monitoring and analysing successes and failures and for learning from experience.

11 AN INTERVENTION IN A MANUFACTURING COMPANY

My work on rural development in Mexico in the 1970s, discussed in the previous chapter, was interleaved with other projects. One of these was with a British manufacturing company, starting at the beginning of 1975 and continuing over several years. The main architect of this innovative intervention was an internal consultant, Andrew Szmidla (AS), who, with a colleague, Olya Khaleelee (OK), had already achieved a good deal, both conceptually and practically, before I came on the scene as an external consultant. In our work together, I am sure I learned at least as much, if not more, from them and from the client system as they from me.

'Industrial democracy' and 'organizational development' were fashionable in the mid-1970s, and because we were doing something novel in this field I made a presentation of work in progress to the August 1976 meeting of the US Academy of Management and then made it part of a longer paper (Miller, 1977). The later phases of this intervention are described in Khaleelee and Miller (1985), Chapter 13 below.

The company, which I shall call 'Omicron', manufactures equipment widely used in the engineering and construction industries. Its main factory is about twenty miles from Central London and it

---

This chapter has been extracted from Miller, 1977.

employs 800 people. Historically, by all accounts, it had been a successful company. It had an international reputation for the quality of its products, many of which were tailor-made for specialist applications; and it was profitable. In the middle 1960s it was taken over by a large British-based group ('Omega'), which itself owned a company ('Kappa') manufacturing similar equipment. Omicron's name was retained (presumably because of its higher reputation); Kappa was merged into it; sales were incorporated into a large Omega sales department which covered other types of production; and Omega put its own men into senior managerial positions. Other changes followed. Manufacturing processes in the two companies were rationalized. A two-shift system was introduced. This led to the loss of a large part of Omicron's female labour force and to their replacement by inexperienced male labour. Profits turned into increasing losses; redundancies became necessary; and a series of general managers appointed by Omega attempted to introduce their own solutions without success. Omicron was seen in Omega as a major problem.

Towards the end of 1973, the most recently appointed general manager sought advice from AS, a psychologist. As an internal consultant employed by Omega, AS's services were available to companies within the group. As a starting-point, AS designed a diagnostic questionnaire which was distributed to all employees of Omicron during February 1974. It was based on Levinson's approach to organizational diagnosis (Levinson, 1972). Many questions were open-ended and some were projective – for example:

> 'Tell me about Omicron. What do you think is its greatest strength and greatest weakness?'
> 'What kind of people would be likely to apply for a job here?'
> 'If you were to make changes that would make the company a better place for you to work, what would you change?'
> 'Make believe Omicron is a person. Think about that person for a minute. Describe the person to me so that I can get a good idea of the picture you have in mind.'

The response rate was high – 70 per cent – though, of course, not all the respondents tackled every question. The results were analysed over the next four months and presented for discussion in a series of six open meetings. These were attended by about a hundred of the employees.

The ways in which members of the organization saw Omicron were in many respects a direct consequence of the history I have outlined. Omicron was perceived as having four potential strengths: its membership of the large Omega group; the technical excellence and reputation of the product; its social amenities (its active social club being an important focus not only for the main factory site but for the local community outside); and the workers. But these potentialities were not being used. Externally, there was a lack of co-operation and communication between Omicron and Omega. The core employees of Omicron saw Omega as having grossly violated the boundary of their organization by, on the one hand, foisting Kappa on them and, on the other, by depriving it of an essential element – its sales force. Related to this were several internal splits. There was rivalry and antipathy between the old Omicron and Kappa factions. Omicron staff saw the old company's distinctive competence for specialist applications being whittled away by emphasis on Kappa's standard 'bread-and-butter' lines: in recollection, differences between the two companies were much greater than they had been in reality. To some extent this split fed into interdepartmental relations, which were characterized by isolationism and back-biting. There was also a worker–management split, 'experienced by the individual worker as an isolation and detachment from the management of the site and symbolized by the roadway running between the factory and the offices, so that although management actually worked on both sides, they were perceived as only working on one side.'* Management was seen as top-heavy; there were too many management changes, which deprived the organization of stability and continuity; and there was a feeling that Omicron was being exploited by serving as a stepping-stone for Omega managers on their way to senior positions

---

* This and subsequent quotations, along with the survey findings summarized here, are taken from working papers prepared by AS and OK.

in the group. Additionally, management's preoccupation with union relationships – which were said to be good – left staff employees feeling neglected and unappreciated.

Overall, there was a sense of inefficient use of resources, both material and human: the scrap rate was excessive; people felt themselves treated as numbers; and departure of experienced people was seen as having created a dearth of expertise.

> Both individuals and departments within the organization were extremely confused as to what their objectives were and how they related to the organization's objectives . . .
>
> Omicron thus presented itself to us as an organization split up into departments, each trying to exist as a separate entity, each having little awareness of corporate objectives, each apparently expending energy in competition with other departments within the organization rather than in competition as in integrated entity with the outside world. This internal competitiveness seemed to take up so much time that Omicron often appeared to be out of touch with aspects of its environment such as its competitors or knowledge of market share. Overall, either very little mention was made of outside factors, or else a grossly distorted view of certain parts of the environment, such as Head Office, was presented to us.
>
> Thus the fragmentation of the site seemed to operate at all levels: at the level of the individual relating to other individuals; at the group level, where departments needed to relate to other departments; and at the level of totality – that is, the relationship of the organization to its environment.

I have quoted at some length from the conclusions that AS and OK drew from their survey, because these led directly to the strategy of intervention that was adopted. They conceived Omicron as a system. Inefficient and precarious though it was, it was nevertheless surviving. Its behaviour as an organization had to be seen as the result of a collective belief – by no means explicit – on the part of the people in it that it was necessary to behave in this way in order to achieve organizational and personal survival. And I think it is worth reiterating here a point that sometimes gets forgotten: that an enterprise has no independent existence as an entity; it is a product of the actions and interactions, beliefs and assumptions, of people located inside it and outside. Before any change was possible, therefore, it was necessary to discover the implicit 'rules' which were guiding people's behaviour. 'Because the rules were in the minds of the people who worked at Omicron, it was only with their help that they could be discovered and only with their co-operation that they could ever be altered.' A further related conclusion was that the work to be done at Omicron would eventually have to involve the whole organization. The question was: how?

Out of this emerged the idea of what came to be called the 'People Programme' in Omicron. As one element in this, the General Manager formed an Employee Consultative Group (ECG), consisting of elected and appointed representatives from the principal levels and areas of the organization. He envisaged this, or a successor body, as potentially taking on more than a consultative role and assuming at least some of the responsibility conventionally regarded as the prerogative of 'management'. That was an open question. But it is worth noting that the General Manager conceived it at the time not as a carefully controlled device for providing token worker participation, but as an open-ended experiment which might have unknown and quite radical outcomes.

The other main element of the People Programme was designed to give as many employees as possible an educational experience akin to that of the Tavistock group relations training conferences (see Chapter 1, pp. 20ff).

Our thinking at this stage was that in any system which has more than a small number of people, there are three quite distinct boundaries at which interaction takes place and work gets done: between individuals; between groups; and between systems (i.e., across the external boundary and with the outside world). The People Programme was designed to provide members with an opportunity to examine these boundaries, in order to learn about themselves in relation to other people, in order to learn about the underlying dynamics of groups, and finally in order to look at the way the organization as a whole related to the outside world; and overall, to be able to distinguish form from content so that employees of the company would be able to stand back from their situation and look at *processes* which were operating as distinct from merely acting out the work role. In this way we hoped that a self-consciousness or self-awareness would develop, initially on the individual level and later on a departmental and organizational level, so that the process of fragmentation could be replaced by more meaningful interconnections between the different parts, and this in turn would lead to improved effectiveness of the system as a whole.

But there was a problem of numbers. I recall that my first meeting with AS was at a Tavistock Conference in September 1974 (he and OK had also attended a conference in the previous year), and the question he put to me there was essentially this: 'How does one consult to a Large Group of up to 1000 people?' OK had left the project in May 1974 and, although she was to rejoin later in the year, for the time being AS was single-handed. If one accepted the logic that one had to start by giving people an opportunity to study the first of the three boundaries identified – that between individuals – then the appropriate medium was the Small Group (of about twelve members); but to provide small group experience for 800 people would occupy more time, consultancy resources or both than seemed reasonable. A further constraint was the size of the Large Group which was the selected medium for working at the third (inter-systemic) boundary: practically and technically the upper limit of membership was around one hundred. Hence a critical decision was made in the autumn of 1974 to limit participation in the initial stages to a group broadly defined as 'management' at the main site – a group of about 120 people from general manager to supervisors and including some specialists in non-managerial roles. Participation would be voluntary. Given that this was the largest number which could be encompassed at that stage, an alternative strategy would have been to make the programme accessible to a cross-section of the total organization. That might have helped in working at the split between management and workers. However, the selected strategy had two strong arguments in its favour: the 'management' group constituted a meaningful sub-set of the total system and it was potentially the most influential sub-set in terms of the possibilities of change.

For the Small Group exercise they were formed into nine groups, each meeting for one and a half hours weekly over twelve weeks.

I myself became involved in the design and operation of two residential weekends, held at Omega's management college, for the study of inter-group relations. Other outside consultants were also introduced for these events. I have discussed elsewhere (Chapter 1, p. 23) the way in which this type of exercise can illuminate the culture of an institution: here one pervasive characteristic of Omicron managers – one of the tacit 'rules' of the organization – seemed to be a sense of their own powerlessness in influencing their individual and collective futures. The 'real' management was somewhere else; because it was ignorant of local factors its decisions would probably be bad; but there was nothing that Omicron managers could do about it except to acquiesce and obey. The notion that they themselves by default were bestowing power on this 'senior management', through failing to exercise their own authority, was discomfiting.

Following the inter-group weekends, participants returned to their small groups for four more weekly sessions, in which they reviewed and consolidated the learning that had taken place and began to apply it to their understanding of Omicron and their own roles within it.

The Programme then moved into its third phase at the end of March 1975 for the study of inter-system relationships. For this, six weekly meetings were arranged, open to the whole of the management in a 'Large Group' configuration, with AS and myself in the role of consultants. Whereas in the small group and inter-group exercises the task was defined as the study of the actual processes occurring in the 'here and now', the Large Group was asked to examine the relationship between Omicron and its environment. A seventh working session was added with the explicit task of discussing a review document prepared by OK.

At the time, the Large Group was not a wholly satisfactory experience and we wondered whether we had the design right. We felt some uncertainty about the consultant role. The task required us to act as consultants to the Omicron management group as they engaged in their task of examining their boundary with the environment, and we were able to make some comments about their perceptions of each other and of external systems; but we found it hard to discover and to use as a data what they were projecting into us, who could be perceived as representatives of the environment actually present in the room. For participants, too, the experience seemed disappointing. At the first session attendance was substantial and there was an air of high expectancy; subsequently absences increased. We were therefore somewhat surprised by the outcome of the final session. The ending of the Large Group marked the end of the formal educational phase of the People Programme that AS had initiated in the previous October. The stance we had taken was that if there was to be any continuation or extension of the Programme, its leadership could come only from the client group. They had been given their opportunity to learn and reflect: what they now did as a result was up to them. No doubt the discomfort of both members and consultants in the Large Group was partly attributable to anxiety about this impending transition. Throughout the final session the mood suggested that the Programme was going to end 'not with a bang but a whimper'. Only in the concluding minutes did a few participants recognize that our statement that it was the last session was not binding on them – that they could exercise their own authority to continue. They rapidly appointed a convenor and agreed to meet the following week. And in fact the group has continued in existence up to the time of writing [1976].

OK, who had a role in monitoring the Programme, was at this time interviewing a sample of one-third of the group who had been, as it were, on the books of the Programme since the previous October, including the small minority of persistent non-attenders. OK's interviews and report (which was distributed to all participants in the People Programme) were not, however, focused only on the Programme, but included the state of the organization as seen through their eyes. Thus it was a partial follow-up of the survey a year previously.

One impression that emerged was that many of the dissatisfactions that the survey had exposed were still very much alive: the Omicron/Kappa split, interdepartmental rivalries, the loss of expertise, the scrap problem. There was a good deal of frustration around these issues. The following comment summed up some of the feeling:

The frustration is due to banging one's head against a brick wall. When you talk to people they look around the room and don't really listen. Even if they say it's a good idea nothing is ever done about it. Or they say they are too busy now, but will see you this afternoon, tomorrow, next week, but they never do. So you have to keep chasing them and never get any satisfaction.

Against that had to be set comments on the People Programme (in which at the time of the survey the small groups were still the dominant experience). About a quarter of the responses were quite negative; half were positive, and the remainder equivocal. But OK reported that the most significant outcome in general was said to be better communications:

> The people I talked to think that they themselves and other members have become more perceptive, more observant, more willing to listen to other people, more self-examining and less dogmatic. The sessions were seen as an opportunity for people to get to know each other and as a stimulus for better communications across departments. The groups are seen to have provided a beneficial environment for exchanging information and are said to have created a greater awareness of what is going on in Omicron and a greater willingness to check out information before accepting it.

Other reported effects of the group experience were that: it had given greater confidence to speak out; it had provided some insight into the operation and power of groups; it had brought to the forefront the issue of the supervisory role – resulting in some appropriate action; some people had been made more dissatisfied and critical; it had made the organization damagingly introspective; and it had caused a good deal of resentment among those excluded from the Programme.

Thirdly, and in some respects most interestingly, the survey report focused attention on the number of new problem-solving groups that had begun to emerge during the preceding six months. Most of them straddled conventional departmental and hierarchical boundaries. At least some of them were formed as a direct outcome of the People Programme, either at the initiative of a head of department (perhaps partly in response to pressures from his subordinates for greater involvement) or spontaneously among a group of colleagues.

An example of the latter was the Project Engineering Group (PEG), its aim being defined as 'to examine the structure of the department and the roles of individuals within it in order to be better able to meet the objectives of the department'. It was set up without the participation or even permission of more senior managers in the engineering department – a fact which rankled for a time. But PEG persisted in its weekly meetings, it invited AS to act as its consultant, and by the spring of 1976 – a year later – it was sponsoring a miniature People Programme of its own for some fifty engineering employees.

Let me return now to the decision by the Large Group to continue to meet on its own initiative after the initial programme of experiential learning had been completed. The mounting of the People Programme had relied heavily on the personal leadership of the general manager, who himself had participated as a member of the Programme through all its phases. By doing so, he had demonstrated the possibility of role-changes: the notion of superior and subordinate need not pervade all organizational relationships; it could be appropriate for some tasks and not for others. At the same time there were pressures on him, sometimes very powerful, to give up the role of fellow student and to provide instead a leadership on which they could depend. He had introduced Omicron to new ideas and methods, for which there was a fair degree of support, but there was the risk that it was more comfortable to go on following him – almost to the extent of going through the motions in order to please him – than to exercise one's own independent authority, with the attendant anxiety of actually re-examining safe assumptions about the superior–subordinate relationship. The spontaneous decision by the Large Group to continue its existence, which was followed by its appointment of a chairman and coordinating group, represented a belief in the possibility that leadership did not have to come only from the top. (The chairman was not a member of the senior management group and the coordinators came from different levels.) The Large Group became a forum in which such issues as the objectives of the company, the processes of management, the meaning of the managerial role and the whole question of industrial democracy and participation were explored. AS continued as its consultant. The coordinators successfully applied to the general manager for a small budget, part of which they spent on sending two of their number to a course on participation in industry, on which they reported back fully to the Large Group. One of the speakers on the course was Lord Brown (formerly Wilfred Brown, Chairman of the Glacier Metal Company and an authority on organization, especially the creation of representative systems in industry), and they invited him to present his ideas to the Large Group. Of the original 120 participants, about sixty were fairly frequent attenders at the regular weekly meetings, with the average attendance being about thirty. There was – and is – continuing uncertainty over whether participation in the Large Group should be seen as part of one's work role or as something of an indulgence, the 'real work' being elsewhere.

The Large Group was just one of the new forms which the People Programme took after May 1975. For the half-dozen members of the senior management group AS gave a series of weekly seminars on concepts relating to individual, group and organization. The high intellectual standard he set – which included reading and discussing journal articles from the psychoanalytic and organizational literature* – was fully justified by the response. He also acted as a consultant to them in regular 'state of the organization' meetings. Later he gave a similar series to the Large Group coordinators, to whom he was also a regular consultant. (Some of these found the material more difficult to grasp.) Several senior managers and a trade union convenor were financed to attend group relations training conferences run by the Tavistock Institute. AS continued as a consultant to PEG, to the Employee Consultative Group (ECG) and, from time to time, to other groups and individuals. And, of course, as this implies, the continuing commitment of Omicron to the People Programme – or at least the commitment of the general manager – was evidenced by continuing payment for the services of AS and OK, and of myself, from January

---

* Six papers were discussed in detail: Jacques (1970), Money Kyrle (1961), Menzies (1960), Rice (1969), Main (1975), and Hopper and Weyman (1975). The group also looked at work by Schein (1965), Rice (1965), Miller and Rice (1967), Bion (1961), and Etzioni (1964).

1975 onward, primarily in the role of external consultant to the internal consultants.

My picture of developments in Omicron is therefore derived from my regular discussions with AS and OK in this role, from their records and other documents, and from some documents from within the company – such as minutes of Large Group meetings. In our discussions, we worked on the proposition that the way in which the organization related to them might illuminate current dynamics within Omicron, such as underlying attitudes towards senior management and to the general manager in particular; and that their relationship to me was likely to reflect the relationship between the client system and themselves.

Undoubtedly, our dominant concern in the second half of 1975 was the continuing precariousness of the Programme – how far its survival was still dependent on the personal leadership of the general manager. He was a fairly regular attender of the Large Group, and we were struck by the frequency with which the group, when in difficulty, would mobilize him in the role of general manager instead of fellow member and therefore, in a sense, regress. There were subterranean rumours – which turned out to be well-founded – that he would be leaving before the end of the year. Associated with the rumours was an anxiety, explicit in AS's and OK's discussions with me, that if Omega replaced him with a new general manager, members of the organization would surrender their precarious assertion of authority, revert to dependency on the new leadership, and all traces of the People Programme would quickly disappear into the sand.

In the event he nominated Omicron's manufacturing manager as his successor; a little later a new manufacturing manager was appointed from outside; and, despite all the fears, the transitions occurred with scarcely a hiccup and indeed, in January–February 1976, the People Programme seemed to be more firmly entrenched than ever.

My impression at the time was that the departing general manager had presented his nominee to Omega management almost as a *fait accompli* which it would be difficult for them to resist. Certainly, Omicron was in a much stronger position than it had been a year previously in relation to Omega. Results for the recently ended financial year had shown a dramatic turn-around. Omicron was moving from a loss to a healthy profit in a period when many fellow-subsidiaries of Omega were moving in the reverse direction. But Omicron managers were becoming perceptibly more confident, buoyant and assertive in their transactions with Omega long before the figures had been added up and published – a phenomenon commented on by some Omega visitors to the site. Cause-and-effect relationships are notoriously difficult to establish within complex systems. It is not even clear whether confidence 'caused' profitability or profitability 'caused' confidence. *Prima facie*, however, the People Programme is likely to have been associated significantly with the increased confidence. The contribution of the Programme to profitability is not established; OK is currently seeking methods to explore the null hypothesis – i.e., that it had no effect.

The actual change of general managers, therefore, contradicted the mood of precariousness which AS and OK often (though not perpetually) communicated to me in our discussions. Their feeling came mainly from the experience of the Large Group. It was thus possible to speculate that the Large Group, including AS as its consultant, was a container into which managers were depositing some of their uncertainties and anxieties about the unknown future into which the Programme was taking them, while in their other roles, both within the established departments (where some organizational boundaries were being realigned) and within the newer working groups, they were tackling their tasks with greater energy and effectiveness. I am not suggesting that it functioned only as a container: it was certainly seen by at least some of its members as a crucible where new ideas and also new values were being forged and tested for application in their other roles. I am in no doubt, however, that an innovative developmental programme of this nature requires the formation of new and separate sub-institutions, such as the Large Group, which have a degree of insulation from the 'real work', in order to provide a legitimate forum not only for the debate of major issues, such as the forms of industrial democracy, but for the voicing of either 'crazy' ideas or doubts and anxieties which, if left unexpressed, get in the way of the 'real work'.

Throughout this period, direct participation in the Large Group and the People Programme generally was largely restricted to the 'management group' of about 120 people (though there had been some leavings and joinings), and the ECG remained the only forum for the rest of the organization. The ECG was kept informed of the Programme. Indeed a progress report by AS and OK from which I quoted earlier was prepared at the request of the ECG in August 1975 and urged the importance of extending the work done with the management group to include all members of the organization. The ECG discussed this but reached no conclusion. What it did, however, was to ask AS and OK to carry out a survey of the way in which the ECG was perceived within Omicron. They conducted interviews with all ECG representatives and deputy representatives (twenty in all) and a further forty with constituents selected at random. Additionally a stratified random sample of 184 employees received a questionnaire: on this there was a 60 per cent return. The findings were not comforting. Among the main points to emerge were:

1 There is considerable diversity of opinion within the ECG itself as to what its function is on site.
2 There is lack of information available for constituents to assess the performance of the ECG.
3 There appear to be gross failures of communication between the representatives and the constituents which makes it difficult for the representatives to fulfil the expectations of the constituents.
4 In some instances there is a clear divergence between the way the representative sees his role on the ECG and the way the constituents see the role of the ECG . . .
5 There appear to be certain omissions in the representational structure . . .
6 Correctly or not, many people are worried that representatives may use their position on the ECG to obtain privileges denied to others.

Thus the ECG was faced with basically re-examining its objectives and method of working. It proceeded to do this in a series of five special meetings between January and March 1976.

I have said that at this time the People Programme seemed more firmly entrenched than ever. However, this is not to be taken as implying that the Programme was static: on the contrary. Overall management of the company had for some time been vested in a group consisting of the general manager and five executive managers. This Executive Management Team (EMT) operated on the cabinet model of collective responsibility, the general manager being roughly equivalent to prime minister. Careful distinctions were drawn between actions taken by members on behalf of the EMT collectively, and actions taken in their departmental roles. Management of the People Programme was plainly in the former category. (Thus when PEG wanted to sponsor its own 'People Programme' for members of the Engineering Department, the negotiations were between PEG and EMT – as distinct from other possibilities, such as between PEG and the manufacturing manager or the personnel manager.) Probably, in fact, the confidence with which the new general manager and his EMT were operating made possible the surge of new developments that occurred between March and May 1976. Here I will only record the main events, without elaboration, in order to give a flavour of the internal life of Omicron at that time:

1 After the fourth meeting of the ECG, the stewards of the three major unions met as a Combined Trades Unions Select Committee (CTUSC) and resolved not to participate in the ECG in its present form; but they were prepared to take part in a form of participation with higher management.

2 The ECG decided to disband and to re-form, with the same membership but a different task, as an Employee Participation Discussion Group (EPDG), this being seen as a transitional body that would itself disband when an appropriate representative system had been created.

3 CTUSC was equivocal about taking part in the EPDG and began a direct dialogue with the EMT to discover senior management's view of participation. The EMT also agreed to a request from CTUSC for observers to attend EMT meetings 'as a learning experience'.

4   EPDG and CTUSC agreed to send out a joint document to all employees on participation. A document was drafted but not sent.

5   Representatives of the Large Group (LG) were invited to a CTUSC meeting and it was agreed to send out a joint letter to all employees on participation. A letter was drafted but not sent.

6   The LG established a separate Research Group. (An initial list of eleven potential research topics was prepared. Examples were: 'the nature of authority in a representative system of management'; 'what part does scrap play in the dynamics of the site?'; 'the place of myth in understanding the development of organization'; and, of most immediate concern, 'how to develop a representative system for participation at Omicron'.)

7   The LG, with some qualms, opened its membership to all employees on site. The half-dreaded, half-hoped-for inundation did not occur, but a few new faces appeared and two newcomers were drafted as Coordinators.

That list of events demonstrates the active search by various groupings in the company to find new ways of engaging with each other and with the site as a whole. It also illustrates the difficulty of risking change. However, it should be noted that amid this evident ferment, the 'real work' of Omicron was continuing unimpaired.

The consultants were not unaffected by the ferment. As the external consultant, I had experienced, from the previous autumn onwards, increasing difficulty in occupying an effective role in relation to the internal consultants. One interpretation of this was that there was increasing uncertainty about their role in relation to the client system. Who was the client? AS and OK were working with a variety of different groupings and saw themselves as actually, or at least potentially, consultants to the entire organization. From the outset they had seen this as the requisite position from which to help the people of Omicron to re-examine the implicit 'rules' that they had collectively adopted. On the other hand, an alternative view could be that the client was the departing general manager. It was he who had negotiated the original contract with them and who authorized the spending of money on the consultancy. (One can see that such a view would be comforting for those with doubts about committing themselves to the People Programme.) In this construction, the client system was certainly no broader than the senior management group – the EMT. Meanwhile, increasing demands were being made on the time of AS and OK; yet it was by no means clear whether the determination of priorities rested on their professional authority or on the EMT's managerial authority. In either case, what kinds of mechanism were required to sanction the authority? In my judgement it was therefore made extremely difficult to hold on to a notion of the organization as a whole and to interpret events and processes in the context of that overall dynamic. From the technical point of view, therefore, the consultants' role needed to be redefined in order to make that more possible. A further point was that there was a recognized need to develop some of Omicron's own staff to take on part-time consultant roles as a means of making the experience of the original management group of 120 more widely available. Who was to be responsible first for their training and subsequently for the work they did in the consultant role? For this quite distinct task it seemed more appropriate that their authority should be derived from membership – albeit temporary – of a professional group, rather than the management of the company.

In March 1976, we therefore proposed to the EMT that the consultancy resources currently available to Omicron for the People Programme – i.e. OK, AS and, on a part-time basis, myself – should be brought together as a quasi-independent Consulting Resource Group (CRG), separate from, but available to, the Omicron organization as a whole. One image used later was of the CRG as a man-made satellite of Omicron, thus potentially, at least, having a perspective on the company that would not be available from a consulting position within the boundary. We postulated that from the position outside we should be better able than we had been as Large Group consultants to help the organization to explore the interrelationship between the internal dynamics of Omicron and its transactions across the boundary with systems in its environment. Given that the CRG would be analogous to these external systems, we inferred that the behaviour of the organization towards CRG would reflect significant aspects of these other transactions across the boundary. This can perhaps be illuminated by reference back to Figure 1.3 (Chapter 1, p. 22). Assume that M represents Omicron, that m_1, m_2, m_3 . . . m_n represent sub-systems within the organization, and that C represents the CRG. We would expect the CRG's experience of its relationship to M to throw light on the $m_1 \leftrightarrow m_2$ relationship. But the dynamics would be more complex than in a conference, where M is a temporary group formed for the purpose of learning and C (the consultant) is the most significant system in its environment. In the model we were proposing, M (Omicron) was a system with its own established transactions with external systems, while C (the CRG) was to be a more temporary system, though in a special relationship to the client system. In this context we postulated that the relationship between M and C would shed light not only on $m_1 \leftrightarrow m_2$ relationships internal to M, but also on relationships between M and other systems in its environment (not marked in Figure 1.3). In this way, M could begin to study how, *as a system*, it managed its main boundaries with its environment.

This account must end with the EMT's acceptance of our proposal in May 1976. The following extract comes from the EMT's announcement of its decision:

> The People Programme at Omicron was set up in 1974. Its aim was to help all of us, as individuals and collectively, to broaden and deepen our understanding of this organization and our various relationships to it. By examining how the organization actually functions – more fully and openly than is normally done – we are well on the way to achieving not only enhanced business performance but also increased individual learning and personal growth.
>
> In normal day to day situations the opportunity to do this does not present itself very often. Yet without such opportunities, learning cannot take place.
>
> In order to pursue this aim further, the EMT has created the Consulting Resource Group. The CRG has, as its primary task, the creation of opportunities for learning which, if taken by the organization, will lead to a progressive and cumulative gain in the ability of employees to understand the processes which operate within the organization in terms of relations between individuals in their various roles at work, between groups, and between the organization and the outside world.

CONCLUDING COMMENTS

Perhaps a better heading for this closing section would be 'Interim Comments', since what has been reported is very much work in progress. And the direction of the 'progress' is unknown.

That open-endedness, however, is to me one of the most crucial features of this approach. In our role as consultants, we can give people an opportunity to extend their personal and conceptual understanding of relations between individuals, between groups and between systems. We can help them to reflect on what they are doing as they apply this understanding in their work-roles and relationships. We can draw their attention to assumptions they are making and to choices they may not have recognized, and in this way they can acquire greater consciousness of the organisation as a system and of their own actual and potential contributions to the shaping of that organization. We can offer them greater scope for managing themselves in their roles. But what we cannot do is to predetermine what use they will make of these opportunities. Perhaps one of our more important functions, as they set about their task of managing themselves, is simply to be available.

Open-endedness is often found frightening by managers (and also by some OD consultants) who therefore often seem to impose limits on the development of participative processes: thus far and no further. Part of managers' fear, I think, is that their competence will come under close scrutiny; part, too, is that if the managerial role and authority are called into question, this poses a threat to all the trappings of 'management' – the assumption of power, status, privileges, the sense of self-importance, and so on. Such fears are not without foundation. Unbridled participation certainly does invite scrutiny of the ways in which roles are performed. But what tends to get forgotten is that appraisal of superiors by subordinates does not originate with participation. Judgements are constantly being made; and corresponding patterns of behaviour are developed as a means of exploiting weaknesses or expressing contempt. Sometimes these take the form of adjustments to the work-role itself; sometimes the union role is used as the vehicle. Participative mechanisms, therefore, do not provoke appraisal of superiors as a new phenomenon; they are much more likely to sanction the overt expression of views that have hitherto been covert.

Notwithstanding the immense gulf between the affluent industrial worker in Western society and the Third World peasant living in squalor and poverty, the industrial worker in his relationship to his work-place has something in common with the underdeveloped or the handicapped, in that within his work-role as such he is frequently in a dependent and relatively impotent position. To be sure, he may invent devices to cope with his situation, but they do not basically alter the typical posture of inferiority and subordination. He often has to rely on union membership to redress the balance. Hence the union becomes the vehicle for expressing the 'fight' that in the work relation has to be suppressed. The People Programme at Omicron makes room for more than one set of roles and role-relationships within the work-setting. On some issues, such as the optimum product-mix, the general manager can properly be expected to proffer an expert opinion; but on others, such as the values that the organization of the company should be pursuing, the shop-floor worker and the general manager are fellow employees and it is difficult to argue that one should expect to impose his values on the other. Thus it is possible for the individual to take on more than one kind of role within the work-setting and in this way exercise greater control over his environment.

However, even in the work-role itself that the individual occupies within the task system, there is the possibility of exercising greater or lesser influence in relation to his environment. Every individual employee may be conceived as being a 'manager' in two senses. First, there is management of the boundary between person and role: the individual determines what skills, attitudes, feelings, etc. he will devote to the role and what he will withhold. Second, there is management of activities within the role and of transactions with other role-holders. These two elements are included in the term 'managing oneself in role'. In practice, therefore, the individual will act as a manager in these two senses: the issue is whether room will be made for him to do this in the service of the task of the organization or, alternatively, perhaps, to its detriment. The role that we more conventionally think of as managerial is located on the boundary of a system or sub-system and is concerned with regulating the linkages between the internal activities of the system and its external environment. The task of this type of managerial role can be defined as: 'To provide the boundary conditions within which members of the organization manage their roles and relationships in such a way as to produce effective performance of the task.' Thus the People Programme, by legitimating the notion of 'managing oneself in role', leads to that somewhat austere, task-oriented definition of managerial roles and calls into question other kinds of behaviour associated more with power and status than with task. These are no longer available as covers for incompetence in task performance.

If this kind of shift is threatening to some managers, it may also be threatening to trades unions, since the employee who is managing himself in role, and who is not tied to a posture of dependency in relation to superiors, has less need of the union to carry 'fight' on his behalf. But this in no way implies that unions become redundant, any more than managers cease to be necessary. What it does mean is that union leaders, like managers, have to adjust to the demands of more sophisticated constituents, who may be looking not for a body to conduct a vicarious fight against management at a basic assumption level, but for advice and support in negotiating opportunities for participation that make more space for individual development and responsibility.

In general, therefore, the approach I have been discussing assails established dependency relationships, between managers and managed and between union leaders and their constituents, as well as assailing 'fight' relationships between unions and management. Authority, by becoming detached from rank and status, and attached instead to task and role, is available to each member of the organization. Conflict partly moves out of the well-known channels into new and shifting configurations. Hence it is not only to managers and trades union representatives that open-endedness is frightening: its consequences affect everyone. When I speak, therefore, of the importance of consultants' availability, I have in mind their function of receiving some of the dislodged dependency during these transitions. Beyond that, they have the task of trying to interpret such shifts in the dependency structure as a further way of helping the client system to understand these internal processes.

To sum up: the essential feature of the People Programme at Omicron, in my view, is that it aims to give each employee, regardless of role or level, a greater opportunity to consider what is happening in the relationship between himself and the organization and, if he so wishes, to seek new or modified roles within which he can exercise his authority. By extension, the same opportunity is available to groups within the organization and to the organization as a collectivity in relation to its environment. The primary task of the consultants in this setting is to try to clarify, as rigorously and uncompromisingly as they can, processes as they occur, the proposition being that this is the best way of helping members of the client system to discover their own authority. Attempts either by company management or by consultants to pre-structure new roles and mechanisms, and to ordain who is entitled to discuss what issues and when, are a negation of participation. Just as my experience of rural development suggests that it is not enough for a community to gain greater control over its internal or local environment – such changes have to be accompanied also by acquisition of greater control over the external environment – so in the case of 'industrial democracy' or 'organizational development' I postulate that significant developments will not be sustained unless participants also extend their authority into management of the external boundary of the relevant client system, whether that is a primary work group, a production department or the enterprise as a whole.

12 INNOVATION IN A PSYCHIATRIC HOSPITAL

In 1971 a young sociologist, David Towell, joined the staff of the Tavistock Institute. For his doctorate, he had carried out research on nursing at Fulbourn Hospital, a well-known psychiatric hospital on the outskirts of Cambridge. In the process he had earned the respect and trust of many staff at all levels, and reciprocally he had gained a great deal of respect for their skill and their commitment to improving patient care. Thanks to its enthusiastic medical director, Dr David Clark, who had promoted and written about new approaches to social psychiatry (Clark, 1964), Fulbourn was more open than most hospitals to innovative ideas. Towell believed that even more could be done in mobilizing change from the bottom up – not casual or impulsive change, but planned innovation based on analysing and conceptualizing problems, devising and implementing possible solutions, and systematically monitoring and, as appropriate, modifying them in the light of further experience. In other words, he was advocating the scientific method. What was distinctive was that the scientists and experimenters were to be hospital staff themselves.

That was the birth of the 'Hospital Innovation Project' (HIP). The concept involved establishing the role of 'social research adviser' as a resource to groups of staff engaging in research and

---

This chapter consists of edited extracts from Miller, 1979a.

development projects. With support from inside the hospital we put forward the proposition to the Department of Health, which gave funding first for a feasibility study and then for a two-year experiment, with David Towell taking the 'adviser' role on a substantial part-time basis.

Outcomes were impressive. To take one example from the psycho-geriatric wards, the nurses installed an entirely new working pattern which showed positive benefits to patients, while, together with medical staff, they negotiated with the local social services department a radical set of admission procedures: authority for admission, instead of being the preserve of the consultant geriatricians, was extended so that in some circumstances nurses and external social workers could make direct admissions. During the first two years about twenty projects, large and small, were launched by groups of staff. They were the initiators; the research adviser was a resource to them.

The major reorganization of the National Health Service in 1974 was a setback: it abolished the Hospital Management Committee and in creating new roles both inside and outside the hospital it disrupted established relationships. The HIP nevertheless survived it. Temporary funding from the Department of Health enabled David Towell to continue a little longer while we helped the hospital to create an internal innovation forum as a transitional mechanism for continuing the programme without external help. Then funding was secured from another source to pay for a new adviser, Clive Harries, who, as senior nursing officer at Fulbourn, had been an active participant in HIP projects. Demonstration that the role could be filled by someone without a social science training indicated that HIP was an idea that could have wider dissemination.

Measured in time, my own contribution to the programme was relatively small – mainly ongoing consultancy to Towell and membership of a steering group of senior Fulbourn staff. My interest, however, was high. The issues it was addressing, of creating conditions through which people could move from dependency towards autonomy, had been central to much of my work, from residential institutions to group-relations conferences, and the Fulbourn experiment overlapped with my consultancy on the rural development programme in Mexico. Moreover, Towell and I were concerned to understand how such shifts could become built into a system and survive the departure of those who initiated it. Hence when Towell and Harries decided to assemble a book on HIP, I saw it as a good opportunity to pull some of my ideas together. The following text has been extracted from my own contribution, a chapter entitled 'Autonomy, dependency and organizational change' (Miller, 1979a).

Practically all my work, HIP included, relates to the problem that organizations have in using and developing the resources and potentialities of people. But it is people who make organizations. Hence I see my concerns in terms of helping individuals and groups to discover and use their authority. Thus a central – perhaps *the* central – message of HIP is that the group of staff actually working on a job have the requisite knowledge and authority themselves to examine it critically and to seek new and more effective ways of performing the task; and they may indeed question the accepted definition of the task itself.

One major theme of this chapter, therefore, is 'autonomy'. I shall be expanding on the meaning of that term; but for the moment let me express it in the form of a simple hypothesis:

> The greater the control that the worker himself exerts over the productive process, the greater his job satisfaction and the better his performance.

This is no new discovery and the evidence for it is overwhelming. Recently, for example, an American team analysed the findings of about 600 research studies conducted over the previous fifteen years on organizational factors affecting job satisfaction and productivity. To quote from their summary of findings:

> the theme of *autonomy* emerges as a significant organizational factor related to both satisfaction and productivity. The concept of autonomy appears as an important aspect of the work itself, the nature of superior–subordinate relations, and the organizational climate of work. (Srivastva *et al.*, 1975, p. xvi)

With proper scientific caution they point out that 'correlational results do not demonstrate causality', but nevertheless, 'the predominance of autonomy over many of the studies suggests that it is a potentially effective action lever for improving productivity and the quality of working life' (ibid.).

So we have here a conception that seems to have everything on its side. There is the immediate pragmatic argument: organizations that make better use of their human resources tend to carry out their tasks more effectively. There is the wider social justification: organizational misuse of people and consequent alienation incur a high social cost. And more generally this is in tune with contemporary values: people matter; human dignity and rights must be respected; older notions of boss–worker relations are exploitative. On this basis one might expect sweeping changes to be taking place in a whole range of organizations. Reality, however, as the reader will know, does not support that expectation. First, successful experiments like HIP are rare. Second, the changes achieved, notwithstanding their evident benefits, often remain precarious – and, in this, HIP is not exempt. Third, there seems to be immense difficulty in disseminating innovations.

Why should this be so? Why should this 'potentially effective action lever' be so little used? One factor is that it poses managers, whether in industry or in the health service, with a discomfiting paradox. Their wish, understandably, is to maximize their control over their subordinates' activities – for example, what the factory worker does to the product or what the nurse does to the patient. This leads to a mechanistic and hierarchical model of management, in which each action is precisely controlled and monitored. The idea that *loosening* of control may enhance performance seems to fly in the face of common sense. So even where there are signs of willingness to permit autonomy there is usually also a wish to limit its influence. Thus a question that I and fellow social scientists are often asked runs like this: 'How can the people under me be motivated to change their attitudes/behave more responsibly/ increase their productivity . . . ?' Nearly always there is an unspoken qualifying clause: ' . . . without my having to consider any changes in my own attitudes or behaviour.' My response is to try to help the enquirer examine the total system of behaviour, including his own contribution to it. If he persists in defending his own role as inviolable, I send him elsewhere.

So this is a second theme that I shall be considering in this chapter – the need to make a more rigorous analysis of existing systems than is usually undertaken. Local innovations can seldom, if ever, be sustained unless there are also consistent changes, structural and cultural, in the wider system. Let me give one illustration. A rehabilitative strategy for geriatric patients – as in the case of the psycho-geriatric ward at Fulbourn Hospital – leads to a questioning of comfortingly familiar routines and to a ward that does not live up to conventional standards of tidiness. Risks are also involved: a frail patient encouraged to walk may fall and break a limb, which can lead to complaints from relatives; if she is tucked dependently and safely into bed, there is no such danger. How many hospitals ostensibly pursue a strategy of rehabilitation and at the same time use tidy wards and absence of complaints as criteria of good nursing?

Inconsistencies of this kind in different parts of a system can be seen as reflecting ambivalence towards change. I have been emphasizing managers' hesitations about the consequences of 'autonomy' for conventional superior–subordinate relations; but the managed too may find such changes disconcerting. A particular aspect of organizational systems that needs examination is the way in which they cater for quite basic dependency needs of those involved. A system of activities set up to perform a task also provides a system of defences for those who perform it; and if, as in many health care systems, the task itself is painful, dependency relationships are a significant part of the defensive structure.

This leads then to my third theme. Since an innovation geared towards autonomy is highly likely to threaten established dependency structures, what steps can we take to look after the dependency that gets dislodged, as it were, during the transitional period, while both the task system and the defensive system are being re-formed? This problem is insufficiently appreciated; and I shall be suggesting that we have to think specifically about providing roles for this purpose during a process of change.

In the rest of this chapter, therefore, I shall first expand on the meaning of 'autonomy', drawing on experience from widely different contexts. I shall then discuss particular aspects of systems engaged in patient care which pose problems of securing and maintaining changes. Third, I shall say something about leadership and consultancy in change processes. I hope in this way to illuminate the conditions for success in sustaining the HIP and for approaches like this to be developed in other settings.

THE MEANING OF 'AUTONOMY'

A pioneering experiment in forming autonomous work groups was conducted in India by my late colleague, A.K. Rice, in 1953–54. This illustrates what is involved in redesigning systems of work organization and at the same time highlights difficulties that arise in trying to transfer an innovation.

The original experimental site was a textile company in Ahmedabad, where automatic looms had been introduced into a weaving shed. Output was much lower and damage much higher that had been hoped. Rice found that the weaving process had been broken down into component elements assigned to nine grades of workers, who were individually accountable to two shed supervisors. Rice proposed the idea of a group of workers taking responsibility for all the weaving tasks on a group of looms and having authority as a group to manage themselves. The nine grades would be reduced to three and a form of group payment introduced. Shed supervisors and workers grabbed the idea and spontaneously formed four experimental groups. These quickly reached a higher level of performance and new groups were formed with similar success. After six months, however, there was a sharp decline. Investigation showed that the groups had been faced with a combination of adverse factors – for example, an excessive range of different cloths in any one group and the induction of untrained workers – as a result of which they had regressed to individual modes of working. Once corrective measures had been taken, output and quality quickly recovered, and so also did job satisfaction; and the new high norms of performance were sustained over several years. An experiment on non-automatic looms achieved comparable success. Accounts of the experiments were published (Rice 1953, 1955a, 1955b, 1958, 1963) and became widely known, both locally and internationally. Locally, some other mills in Ahmedabad instituted similar forms of group working, but failed to achieve the expected results.

Much later, in 1970, another colleague and I returned to the original company to assess the long-term outcomes. We found that, even within the company, later attempts to extend the 'group system', as it was called, had either achieved only mediocre results or failed entirely. In one of the original experimental loom-sheds, the form of group working had remained unaltered over the sixteen years and performance was as high as ever; in the other, some degradation had occurred (Miller, 1975). One reason for lack of success in spreading this innovation was undoubtedly the fact that attempts were made to transplant the *form* of group working, without sufficient regard to the *processes* involved in the original experiments.

Essentially, Rice had put forward working hypotheses, indicating a possible alternative form of organization that would satisfy the needs of both task and people; workers and supervisors themselves, through experimentation and discussion, had played an active part in design and development of the group system. It was a process that recognized from the outset the *authority* of the workers to take such a role, and this in itself was a significant innovation in the hierarchical culture of Indian industrial organizations (and indeed of most work organizations elsewhere).

A second, related factor was that the conception of the form to be transplanted was almost certainly too narrow. Given that internal management of the system was now vested in the group of workers, the role of the supervisor had to be reconceptualized. It was no longer appropriate to think of him as telling individuals what to do and making sure that they did it. His job was to provide the *boundary conditions* within which the group could manage itself. That is to say, he had to ensure that the group was equipped with the necessary resources to perform its task: trained workers, spare parts for the looms, yarn in the right quality and quantity for weaving, and so on. Management of progressively wider systems was conceived in the same way. In such a conception, if performance declines and/or the group reverts to a more rigid internal division of labour, this is taken as presumptive evidence that the necessary boundary conditions are not being sustained. When such symptoms are observed, the sophisticated managerial response is to reduce the sources of disturbances imported across the boundary of the system – for example, poor quality or excessive variability of inputs – and to reinforce the internal resources of the system – for example, by attending to training of personnel and maintenance of machinery.

This is precisely what happened when the first experiment had been running for six months, and as a result of that regression and subsequent investigation it became possible to specify much more accurately the boundary conditions within which the groups could be expected to retain their resilience. When my colleague and I looked at the degradation that had occurred in this same loom-shed by 1970, it became apparent that the requisite boundary conditions had not been sustained – for example, sub-standard spare parts were being supplied – and also that the supervisory role had shifted. Instead of transmitting pressure through their superiors to the suppliers, the supervisors intervened within the groups to try to get individuals to work harder. By doing this, they further helped to destroy the resilience of the groups as self-managing systems and made it inevitable that norms of performance would drop (Miller, 1975). Paradoxical though it may seem, a wide range of discretion, as opposed to tight definition of roles in a mechanistic framework, is likely to *increase* the viability of the system and the predictability of outcomes: if the role is closely circumscribed, the individual is more likely to impose his own range of discretion on it and therefore act in 'illegitimate' ways.

Rice's early experiments therefore give some practical and operational meaning to the notion of autonomy and make it clear that a group of weavers (or, for that matter, a group of nurses) cannot extend their authority to manage themselves in their own roles without consequential changes for managerial roles in the wider system of which they are a part. Both structural and cultural changes are involved, each needing the other.

Turning now to experience of rural development in the Third World, my own observations and analysis of a number of cases in Mexico have led me to the tentative hypothesis that changes will not take root within a community unless they are also accompanied and reinforced by changes in the external relations of the community with the wider social, economic and political system. I am now arguing that the primary task of a development agency is to help its client system – the rural community – to acquire greater control in its relations with its external environment, and that the conventional development projects must be conceived not as ends in themselves but as means to that end (Miller, 1976d, 1977; see Chapter 10 in this volume).

This view fits with the conclusions that a colleague and I drew from a study – much nearer home – of residential institutions for the younger physically handicapped and chronic sick (Miller and Gwynne, 1972, 1973; see Chapter 3 in this volume). We found it useful to compare institutions in terms of the kinds of role that inmates occupied. Adults in ordinary life occupy many roles – in the family, at work, in leisure pursuits, and so on – and move from one to another. Some roles provide for the individual's needs to be dependent and looked after; others for his drives towards self-assertion and autonomy. Even within a single relationship, such as marriage, the individual shifts between varying 'sub-roles', as it were, in some of which he is more autonomous and in others more dependent.

In many of these residential establishments, however, the individual has only dependent roles open to him. The inevitability of a degree of physical and emotional dependency made it seem to us the more important to make room also for 'independent' roles which catered for drives towards autonomy. In this way, the inmate could come closer to the ordinary adult experience of moving between multiple roles. In the few institutions which provided these opportunities, inmates were characterized by a much greater aliveness, especially where they were involved in transactions across the boundary of the institution and so relating to the external environment. In this way, they were taking over responsibility for transactions normally handled by staff or 'management', and indeed the logical conclusion, which we helped one voluntary home to implement, was full inmate participation in management. Like the Mexican peasants, therefore, they were extending their control over their environment, instead of being passive victims of external forces.

THE LURE OF DEPENDENCY

Creation of multiple roles in residential institutions is a specific solution to a problem that has been arousing more and more public concern over the last decade: the problem of institutionalization, depersonalization and more overt ill-treatment in hospitals providing long-stay care for the old, the mentally ill and the mentally handicapped. Indeed, this concern dates back at least to the fifties and contributed to the passing of the 1959 Mental Health Act. My impression, however, is that Barbara Robb's *Sans Everything*, published in 1967, was significant in making it an issue for the public and not just for the professionals. Since then, we have had a succession of committees of inquiry, each evoking a new surge of public indignation. At first the emphasis was the neglect or sadism of individual nurses; this was then linked to gross under-provision of resources; and it is only in the reports of more recent inquiries, such as South Ockenden (Department of Health, 1974) and St Augustine's (South East Thames RHA, 1976), that – without denying deficiencies of individual staff and of resources – accountability has been more directly attributed to organizational and managerial shortcomings. In my terminology, the organs of hospital management stand accused of failing to provide the boundary conditions within which ward staff can properly manage their own roles.

To put it another way, the kind of role that Gwynne and I proposed for inmates and, more generally, the kind of treatment that it is now more widely felt should be accorded to long-stay patients, inescapably calls for a different role on the part of nurses and other caring staff. My argument would suggest that there is little possibility of nurses acquiring and sustaining such an alternative role unless there is also a change in their relationship with the wider system within which they operate, and which defines the task they are there to perform. Patients cannot exercise more autonomy unless nurses exercise more autonomy; but there are powerful forces holding patients in a dependency relationship on nurses and holding nurses in a similar relationship to doctors.

I will first examine dependency in the patient–nurse relationship. We can make a rough distinction between mature and immature dependency relationships. In the mature relationship, I as patient or client confer my authority on a professional, whom I judge to be competent, to take care of something on my behalf. It is a form of delegation which I continue to have authority to withdraw. In the immature relationship, this may still be the formal situation; but *de facto* I surrender my authority and the professional takes me over. This is closely akin to the 'basic assumption' behaviour in groups that was identified by Bion (1961). He observed that at times groups operate as if they are seeking dependency upon an omniscient and omnipotent leader, who will satisfy all the needs of every member. This can be seen as expressing a wish for return to the security of the womb or of early infancy. It is then very tempting for the leader to fall in with this demand and so to behave as if he is more knowledgeable and more powerful than he actually is; hence a reciprocal relationship is established which confirms the inadequacy of the one party and the superiority of the other.

Many of the residential institutions we visited in the course of our study exhibited this phenomenon in a striking way. The mothering, and thus the infantilization, of inmates by caring staff was not simply one aspect of a relationship that at other times made room for individuality and autonomy: it was the totality of the relationship. Inmates had in effect lost their boundaries as individuals and surrendered their ego functions to staff.

Now it is very easy to say that this should not happen, that it is antithetic to rehabilitative objectives or ordinary human dignity, and that nurses should be more mature; but it is by no means so easy to bring about a change. Exhortation is usually fruitless. More helpful may be an attempt to understand what it is about the system that sustains the culture of dependency. Thus, as we discovered in our study of residential care, it is only part of the reality to say that cripples are admitted to these institutions because they are too disabled to look after themselves or be looked after in the community. In fact they are no more handicapped, and sometimes less so, than many who remain outside. What those inside more significantly have in common is that they have been rejected. 'They have for the most part been rejected as individuals, in that their families are no longer willing or able to look after them. More importantly, by crossing the boundary into the institution, whether voluntarily or not, they fall into a rejected category of non-contributors to and non-participants in society' (Miller and Gwynne, 1972, p. 73; see Chapter 3 in this volume).

Goffman made a similar point about psychiatric hospitals: 'the society's official view is that inmates of mental hospitals are there primarily because they are suffering from mental illness', and this provides the rationale for staff behaviours; but, he asserts, 'mental patients distinctively suffer not from mental illness but from contingencies' (Goffman, 1961, p. 126). He analyses in some depth the processes of *extrusion* from family and community and the patient's corresponding experience of *betrayal*. Inmates of these residential institutions are unlikely ever to be rehabilitated: for most of them the prognosis is progressive deterioration and death. The realities of the disabilities, the rejection and the future are almost too painful to bear, either for staff or for inmates.

So what we came to call a 'warehousing' culture of dependency, with its infantilization and dehumanization, provided a redefinition of reality which was less intolerable for staff to cope with. Possibly it was less intolerable too for inmates to regress to a childlike position than to come to terms with depression at the loss of ordinary adult experience. Related to this, dependency serves a function in keeping at bay emotions of anger and aggression: instead of being directed outwards against, for example, staff, these emotions are turned inwards in destruction of the self. We have here, therefore, an example of what Isabel Menzies called 'the functioning of social systems as a defence against anxiety' (Menzies, 1960). By examining the dynamics in this way, one can grasp the obstacles to change in such a setting. It is highly improbable that staff would take steps to alter their posture without external support; and even if they did so, the inmates for their part, far from welcoming liberation, can be expected to suck staff back into the *status quo*.

A study that colleagues and I made of geriatric hospital care disclosed a slightly different dynamic (see Chapter 4 in this volume). Again, the manifest input into the system is an elderly person needing treatment. Arriving with the patient, however, are various and conflicting expectations from family and community. Indeed, the family's feelings are often ambivalent: it wants the hospital to cure, to rehabilitate and, at a less conscious level, to postpone death indefinitely, and it wants the hospital to take over the problems and provide terminal care. One way in which the hospital, as a system, may cope with this ambivalence is through an emotional division of labour. Both doctors and nurses respond to the family's rejection of the patient: the doctor, defending his limited beds from becoming clogged by long-stay patients, adopts a rigorous rehabilitative policy which compels the family or community 'to look after its own'; the nurse, empathizing with the rejected patient, responds to the pressures for dependency, wishing to become the good caring person whom the patient has lacked, and in doing so tacitly opts for custodial treatment, in opposition to the more austere regime that the doctor's rehabilitative strategy demands.

Obviously I have over-simplified. What I am concerned to illustrate, however, is the nature - and intransigence - of dependency in such health care systems. The geriatric example also further illustrates the point that change within the nurse–patient relationship is improbable unless there are also other changes, which must, in the hospital, minimally include a change in the relationship with the doctor.

Both patient and nurse invest much dependence in the doctor, especially the consultant. At least titularly, he is the leader of the treatment enterprise: he controls admissions and discharges; and he is also the carrier of the medical mystique. Notwithstanding my earlier comments, a degree of less than mature dependency in the relationship may be therapeutically necessary. With him I cannot be quite so objective about delegating my authority as I can, say, with a lawyer: faith that he can make me better may be an important ingredient in successful treatment. These little bits of faith are the building blocks of the massive dependency culture. It is epitomized in the ritual of the full-scale ward round, with the god-like consultant at the head, followed by his hierarchy of white-robed angels in descending order of rank. Most consultants are aware of the processes of deification and try to mitigate its worst effects; on the other hand, it is almost impossible to be the linchpin of a dependency structure without being seduced at times into illusions of omnipotence and omniscience.

One can put forward a number of hypotheses about nurses'

needs for defences which are satisfied by this type of dependency structure. Menzies did this in the case of general hospitals. She showed that responsibility for intimate care of sick and dying patients resonated painfully with the nurse's unconscious anxieties; this made her individual defences precarious; various mechanisms in the social system of the hospital could be seen as providing supplementary shared defences against these anxieties (Menzies, 1960). The phenomena that she described are widely prevalent in other types of hospital, though each may have certain specific characteristics as well. Thus one can postulate that, inasmuch as the geriatric hospital is tacitly asked to solve, or at least to bear, the insoluble problems of ageing, death and bereavement, nurses are subjected to a heavy burden of demands for dependency, some of which they then shift onto the shoulders of the consultant.

The power structures I have described may well appear to be intractable. Is there really any hope that nurses or patients can escape from the toils of dependency and acquire autonomy? Menzies suggests that defensive systems lead to less than optimum performance of the primary task of patient care; that this intensifies the use of the defensive systems, leading to further decline in task performance; and so on, in a deteriorating cycle. Perversely this offers a ray of hope: the situation may become so intolerable that something has to be done about it. And one thing that can be done, in my view, is to make more explicit the problems and processes of the kind that I have been discussing. The stress and pain of caring for the crippled, the old, the mad or the dying cannot be made to go away; but if they are articulated, then at least the burden can be distributed more widely. In this way the need for defensive structures, though not eliminated, may be reduced, and alternative systems may be found which, while catering for defensive needs, do so in a way that is less destructive of the autonomy of the parties concerned.

LEADERSHIP AND CONSULTANCY IN CHANGE

Let me first consider the role of the medical consultant in change. It is probably fair to say that most innovations in patient care in hospitals have come from the initiative of consultants. I have called the consultant the linchpin of the defensive dependency structure, and the metaphor is an apt one, because it is the linchpin that keeps the chariot-wheel on its axle. Unless he changes, it seems, nothing else can; but the positive side of this is that when he makes use of his charisma to introduce something new he is in a strong position to get it implemented within his system.

Paradoxically, however, while it is this charisma that makes change possible, it also makes it precarious. Although methods of working and even staff roles and relationships may have been altered, the new pattern continues to be sustained by the shared dependence of the system on the consultant. In other words, the basic dependency structure persists and indeed the dependence on him is likely to be magnified during the uncertainties of the transition; and the consequence is that the continuance of the pattern relies on his presence. All too often, then, such innovations evaporate when the initiating consultant departs; and even when he is absent for relatively short periods regression is often observable. As I have indicated, to occupy the apex of a dependency structure is a heady and seductive experience, so that the consultant needs rigorous and continuing self-discipline to distinguish between the authority that rightly belongs to his actual competence and the fantasied powers that are imputed to him. It is a rare consultant who does this thoroughly enough to enable the nurses and patients around him to acquire and retain their own individual authority. And, even if he does so, the chances are that his less conscientious and sophisticated successor will only remobilize the latent pull towards dependency.

From this it follows that sustained change in the direction of autonomy cannot be localized within the system most directly affected: changes must also be brought about in the relationship between the system and the environment in which it operates. Indian weavers could not sustain their new way of working without concomitant changes in the relationships with supervisors and managers. Mexican peasants cannot establish new agricultural techniques unless they also bypass exploitative middlemen and discover a new sense of potency in their external transactions. Crippled inmates of residential establishments cannot win independent roles only by striking a new bargain with caring staff; they need to express such roles through exercising authority in relationships across the boundary with the environment; and this development will not survive unless the roles and role-relationships of caring staff are also recast. And correspondingly, nurses in psychiatric, mental subnormality or geriatric hospitals cannot be expected to extricate themselves from immature dependency and to make room for the individuality of their patients unless they themselves not only acquire a new relationship with the consultant but also exercise greater authority across the boundaries of the system as a whole.

In order to achieve such transformations, one or preferably both of two conditions seem to be necessary. The first is the operation of a sanctioning authority which straddles both the system concerned and the relevant environment. The second I shall call 'consultancy'. These can be illustrated by going back over the examples I have used.

In the case of the weaving innovation, the boundary that I have identified as crucial was that between the new type of work group and the supervisor. Rice's description of the original experiment in 1953 and 1954 makes it plain that he was in effect acting in a consultancy relationship with a 'vertical slice' of the organization, from the company chairman and senior manufacturing management through to the weaving supervisor and operatives directly involved (Rice, 1958). The chairman was committed to the innovation and kept himself closely informed of progress; and in addition to the developments at shop-floor level, Rice and I helped with a wider management reorganization of the company, through which boundaries of organizational systems were re-drawn and a somewhat different conception of the managerial role – in line with my definition earlier in this chapter – began to be introduced (Rice, 1958, 1963). Hence the changes in management helped to reinforce the 'group system'; and, as is often the case, an element of organizational 'conscience' was vested in the consultancy role, so that even the intermittent presence of outside consultants over several years also reinforced both the group system and the reorganization of management. By 1960, the consultancy had ended; the chairman, now involved in direction of an expanded group of companies, was seldom seen inside the mill; and the new ethos of management, which had supported the autonomous work groups, was gradually eroded (Miller, 1975).

The rural development scene is much more complex. In the case of Mexico, for example, the Federal Government, in making large sums available for rural investment, aims to remedy a history of neglect and injustice. Thus it is providing an overall sanction for change, and it is making new resources available for the poorer peasants; but it is not intervening in local exploitative systems that perpetuate the poverty. Significant change does not therefore occur unless more local leadership/consultancy is available to help a client community acquire a greater control over its environment. As I have written elsewhere:

> There is a need to help them discover an identity as a client system. One approach is through political education: they learn that their condition is not the result of inherent inferiority but the consequence of perhaps generations of oppression and exploitation. Dependency gets transformed into fight. However, this needs to be accompanied by improved social and economic capability. A community that relies too much on fight as its basis of identity and organization is placed at risk not only by defeat but by victory. The other approach is the transfer of dependency to the benign leadership of the 'developer'. He guides his protégés along new paths of economic development and secures their commitment to new activities and methods. Here the risk is that the client system will not have been allowed to learn through making mistakes and it will have been protected from adjusting and developing its internal organization to cope with the changes. Hence, if the benign leadership disappears, the system is likely to collapse. Very few development efforts in Third World countries have been able to navigate a course between this Scylla and Charybdis. (Miller, 1977, pp. 41-2)

In the residential institution where my colleague and I had a consultancy role, leadership in change (which had originally been initiated by a small group of inmates) had been taken up by the chairman of the management committee, thus embracing a system that included both inmates and staff plus relevant elements of the environment. Our consultancy was with the three groups: inmates, staff and the committee itself. Our main function was to identify underlying issues and processes, so that they could become available for examination, and to provide help and support while the three parties struggled to reach agreement on a philosophy, policy and organization that legitimated inmates' participation in management. One thing we helped to do, for example, was to draft a job specification for the role of warden when it became vacant and to help devise mechanisms through which inmates took part in the selection procedure (Miller and Gwynne, 1972). The consultancy ended in 1967 and my evidence at the time of writing (1976) is that innovations that were controversial ten years ago have become firmly established as a taken-for-granted part of institutional life.

My conclusion from these and other experiences is that over and above the specific leadership towards innovation that may come from the sanctioning authority or the specific advice that may be given in the consultancy relationship, one or both of these roles has to have a major function as a receptacle for dependency. Although the culture of dependency and associated defensive structures are especially pervasive in 'people-processing institutions', such as hospitals, they are present in all organizations. The importance of this for the consultancy role in change was recognized by my Tavistock Institute colleagues twenty-five years ago:

> There was a shared recognition that both individuals and groups develop mechanisms to give meaning to their existence and to defend themselves from fear and uncertainty; that these defences, often unconscious and deeply rooted, are threatened by change; and that consequently it is an important aspect of the professional role to serve as a container during the 'working through' of change, so as to tackle not only the overt problem but also the underlying difficulties. (Miller, 1976c, p. 48; cf. Wilson, 1951)

Less recognition, however, has been given to the role of super-ordinate leadership as a repository for what I have called elsewhere 'dislodged dependency' during transactions (Miller, 1977). The kinds of transition we have been examining dislodge prevailing defensive structures not simply within the system (for example, a group of weavers) that is acquiring autonomy, but in at least one other system with which its relationship is changed. In organizations this is usually the next higher-order system within which it operates (for example, the weaving department). I would postulate that leadership that can give sanction and carry dependency is required at least at the level of the next wider system (for example, the factory or the company). My reasoning is that individuals and groups most directly affected by the change need temporarily to deposit dependency in a leadership that encompasses both the pre-change and post-change configurations. This is not to suggest that the super-ordinate leadership itself remains unchanged: in the shifts towards autonomy the operation of that role too will be subject to modification if the revised system is to survive. Insecurity at this level, however, should be less.

In the case of change through conflict, which I mentioned briefly in reference to rural development, an oppressed group usually receives consultancy/leadership from outside – from a political activist, for instance – to fight for a new deal that will give it greater autonomy. He has the same function of carrying the group's dependency during the transition.

I am not suggesting, therefore, that both internal sanctioning leadership and external consultancy are necessary. While, obviously, my own experience has been of the consultancy role, many transformations occur without such external help. I would expect to find in such cases, however, an internal leadership that has been strong enough and resilient enough to contain the dislodged dependency, and at the same time sophisticated enough to relinquish it again as the new system became established.

Some support of a consultancy type may also be drawn from an internally created group, such as the innovation forum which emerged at Fulbourn in the transitional phase. Such a body, however, is likely to be a weak container of dependency if, as in that instance, its membership is only very part-time: the pull of ongoing working relationships is correspondingly powerful. It would therefore thrive only in the context of the wider sanctioning mechanisms that would be provided by a fully developed and institutionally secure 'HIP'.

IMPLICATIONS FOR HIP

If in conclusion, then, we turn back to the emergence of HIP at Fulbourn, we can see that both conditions that I mentioned have been present. In relation to the specific projects undertaken, the

Steering Committee, which included the senior members of the nursing and administrative hierarchies and the most influential consultant in the hospital, has operated as a sanctioning authority above the level of the systems most directly affected by the changes; the social research adviser has provided the consultancy; both roles have carried dependency; and the Project as a whole has been successful in fostering an ethos of questioning past ways of doing things and of seeking more effective approaches.

One project in particular – in the psycho-geriatric ward – nicely illustrates my proposition that a significant and sustained change is unlikely to occur only within a system: reinforcing change is also required in the relationship between the system and its environment. In this particular case my hypothesis is that the new treatment strategy within the ward is reinforced by the enlarged role of the nurses in relation to the external Social Services Department, including some relocation of authority for admission. This innovation was greatly facilitated by the geriatric consultant, who, while recognizing the symbolic importance of his role, was alert to the negative aspects of the dependency culture and who therefore made ample room for the nurses to take authority in developing their new roles.

None the less, the success in that ward, as in HIP as a whole, remains precarious. A potentially major weakness – of which I was not fully aware until I put my thoughts together to write this chapter – is that the Steering Committee and the social research adviser have been primarily devoted to encouraging innovations rather than with sustaining them. The latter has been left to the discretion of individual Steering Committee members in their managerial roles. Now if a new method of working affects staff only within one discipline, such as nursing, then it is possible – and, given the present incumbent, quite probable – that the senior nursing officer who is a member of the HIP Steering Committee will also concern himself as a manager to safeguard the boundary conditions for sustaining the innovation. But in this he has no accountability to the Steering Committee. An innovation straddling disciplinary boundaries is even more vulnerable to the vagaries of a new nursing officer or a new consultant. As I have already mentioned earlier, the 1974 NHS reorganization has dispensed with the old Hospital Management Committee and left a vacuum at that level; and the disciplines in the hospital have still to come together and form an authoritative management group of their own. Such a body is required to confirm that the philosophy and concepts of self-management that are inherent in HIP are an integral part of hospital policy and to ensure that they are implemented and maintained. That body will also need to defend Fulbourn's innovations against the creeping bureaucratization of the NHS hierarchies. By my definition every employee is a manager and at least some of the staff at Fulbourn have acquired the requisite authority to manage themselves in their roles. The notion that groups of staff have the capability and authority to take initiatives and that it is the task of managers of wider systems to provide the boundary conditions within which nurses and other staff can perform their task more effectively seems, however, to be at odds with the culture of prescriptive superior–subordinate relationships that prevails in the NHS generally. Until, therefore, such a hospital management has come into being and taken on this task, the long-term future of HIP and of the specific innovations that have been introduced must remain in doubt.

PART FIVE:
SOCIETAL PROCESSES

INTRODUCTION

In 1975 I became one of the founders of an educational charity, for which I invented the name 'an Organization for Promoting Understanding of Society' – OPUS. (A few years later, when OPUS was registered as a company, the 'of' became 'in' – a slippage that I came to regret because it reduces the rigour implied by 'of'.) The idea behind OPUS came from the late Sir Charles Goodeve, FRS, who, already an eminent physicist, was one of the originators of operational research in World War II. Coming to the Tavistock Institute as a member of our Council, he became convinced that a major cause of conflict, particularly in industry, was a lack of understanding of socio-economic systems. As a result, people were pursuing incompatible goals. He set out to distil basic laws and principles derived from economics and other social sciences – equivalent to the laws of physics – and to disseminate these to politicians and to employers and employees in industry. OPUS was formed as a vehicle to take this forward. Sir Charles put together a booklet, *How Society Works*, which was distributed quite widely and used by several companies in employee education programmes. The next step was to be production of educational material for use in schools; but funding proved elusive, Sir Charles's health and energy were declining and OPUS became inactive.

Meanwhile I was becoming intrigued by the idea of trying to tap into unconscious processes in society. The 1970s had seen quite a growth in Leicester-type group-relations conferences both in

Britain and in the United States, where the A.K. Rice Institute was expanding under the leadership of Margaret Rioch. She and I were often aware of the emergence in conferences of dynamics that seemed to belong to the wider society (see Rioch, 1979). At the same time, the experiment in the manufacturing company, described in Chapter 11, pointed to a possible methodology. OPUS, with its commitment to helping individuals in their role of citizens to understand the society they lived in, seemed an appropriate vehicle. This interest was shared by several associates, mainly outside the Tavistock, and in 1980 one of them, Olya Khaleelee, who latterly had led the consulting resource group in the manufacturing company, was appointed director of OPUS to develop the approach. Though operating on a shoestring, the work has been maintained. During the 1980s twenty-nine issues of the OPUS *Bulletin* explored contemporary dynamics in British society and OPUS has continued to organize conferences and study days and to publish occasional papers on particular themes.

Chapter 13, jointly authored with Olya Khaleelee, describes the theoretical basis and methodology and the first two years of OPUS's experimental attempt to apply it. (It was written in 1981 but not published until 1985.) Chapter 14 consists of extracts from a published account of one of OPUS's intensive two-day conferences. Finally, Chapter 15, though it carries my name, draws heavily on the ideas developed with OPUS colleagues. Written in 1984, it expands on the themes of dependency and 'failed dependency' in British society that are outlined in Chapter 13 and looks tentatively at what 'post-dependency' might bring.

13 BEYOND THE SMALL GROUP: SOCIETY AS AN INTELLIGIBLE FIELD OF STUDY

INTRODUCTION

In his series of papers, 'Experiences in groups, I–VII', which appeared in *Human Relations* (Bion, 1948–51; reprinted in Bion, 1961), Bion put forward certain propositions about unconscious behaviour in small therapy groups, of up to a dozen members, in relation to him as therapist. Applications of psychoanalytic theory and insights to understanding of group processes were not novel, and Bion acknowledged his debt to Freud (1913, 1921); but Bion's own work both made a distinctive contribution to psychoanalytic theory and broke new ground in theories of group behaviour.

In contrast to earlier writers he emphasized the importance in group life of the 'sophisticated group' or 'work group', which corresponds to Freud's picture of the ego in individual functioning. The work group mobilizes internal resources and relates to external realities for performance of a task. Work group activity, however, interacts with, and is sometimes supported but often obstructed by, the unconscious processes of what he called the 'basic assumption group'. Bion offered convincing evidence for the operation in groups of three mutually exclusive basic assumptions: fight/flight (ba F), pairing (ba P), and dependency (ba D). In a further paper

---

A slightly shortened version of Khaleelee and Miller, 1985.

(Bion, 1952; also reprinted in Bion, 1961) he emphasized the primitiveness of the emotional states underlying the basic assumption phenomena: 'The basic assumptions now emerge as formations secondary to an extremely early primal scene worked out on a level of part objects' – for example, the fantasy that mother's breast or body might contain parts of father – and thus 'associated with psychotic anxiety and mechanisms of splitting and projective identification such as Melanie Klein has described as characteristic of the paranoid-schizoid and depressive positions' (Bion, 1961, p. 164; see Klein, 1928, 1946, 1959; Heimann, 1952). In general, therefore, 'basic assumption phenomena appear . . . to have the characteristics of defensive reactions to psychotic anxiety' (Bion, 1961, p. 189), and thus 'the attempt to make rational investigation of the dynamics of the group is . . . perturbed by fears, and mechanisms for dealing with them, that are characteristic of the paranoid-schizoid position' (p. 162).

Bion insisted that the behaviour observed in groups was not a product of groups as such but of the fact that 'the human being is a group animal'. 'No individual, however isolated in time and space, can be regarded as outside a group or lacking in active manifestations of group psychology' (1961, p. 132). The individual's very belief in independent existence of 'a group' was evidence of regression; and at one point Bion defined a group as 'an aggregate of individuals all in the same state of regression' (p. 142). We carry our groupishness with us all the time. Physical assembly of people into a group simply makes 'political' characteristics of human beings more easily demonstrable. Also, as a matter of practicality, 'It is important that the group should come together sufficiently closely for me to give an interpretation without having to shout it' (p. 132).

Bion's argument therefore was that, so far as the *existence* of group phenomena was concerned, the assembly of a group and the size of that assembly were irrelevant. He was concerned, however, about what constituted 'an intelligible field of study' (1961, p. 104). Studies of neurosis had been largely sterile so long as the focus was on the individual alone: Freud's shift to the two-person relationship and examination of the transference produced an intelligible field of study which generated many new understandings about the

individual. Our judgement today must be that Bion's further shift to
the small group demonstrated new phenomena and produced new
insights which justify it as another such intelligible field. He himself
was more cautious and also more ambitious. He thought the small
therapeutic group deserved further attention; but he wanted also
to shift to a wider field, partly because this might shed more light
on the small group and partly because he was impatient to uncover
wider societal processes: 'The small therapeutic group does not
produce evidence . . . fast enough for my purpose and does not
produce enough of it' (p. 105).

The evidence Bion was seeking at that moment was about
disease. His theory of proto-mental phenomena had led him into
what might be called psycho-epidemiology. The operating basic
assumption serves to suppress emotions associated with the other
two assumptions; these are confined within the proto-mental
system; and the proto-mental levels then provide the matrix of
'group diseases'. Drawing on Wittkower (1949), he had evidence
that tuberculosis, for example, was 'very sensitive to developments
in the psychology of a group', the incidence 'fluctuating in what
appears to be some kind of sympathy with changes in the mentality
of the group' (Bion, 1961, p. 107). Given that the prolonged
nursing, diet, etc. of tubercular patients associated to the mental
state of ba D, then one might expect a higher incidence of
tuberculosis in phases when ba F is the dominant basic assumption
and emotions associated with ba D are locked in the proto-mental
system. He wanted statistical evidence. Similarly, he wanted data to
test another of his speculations at the societal level about the
meaning of money: he postulated that money might carry different
and fluctuating psychological values depending on the prevailing
basic assumption and corresponding proto-mental state.

He recognized that in larger systems phenomena might be more
difficult to detect: 'The glaring difficulty is to state what assumption
is operating in a large group' (1961, p. 112). He nevertheless offered
stimulating suggestions. For example, in discussing his notion of
the 'dual of ba D' – that is, the phenomenon in which the leader has
failed to sustain and nourish the group, so the group takes on the
task of sustaining and nourishing the leader – he cited the phase in
ancient Egyptian history when the country was manifestly

exhausted by the building of the pyramids for the Pharaohs. He saw this as 'a group movement to allay the anxiety state of the leader of the group. The nature of that anxiety . . . appears to be centred on the death of the leader and the need to deny its reality' (p. 120).

In his 1952 paper, 'Group dynamics: a re-view' – again building on earlier speculations by Freud – he postulated that society hives off specialized work groups to deal on its behalf with basic assumption emotions that would otherwise obstruct the work group activity of the whole. The well-known examples he offered were church (dependency), army (fight/flight) and aristocracy (pairing).

Provocative though these ideas were, Bion did not elaborate on applications of basic assumption theory to wider society dynamics. In this last instance he seemed almost to back away from the society level and was at pains to point out that church, army and aristocracy were often identifiable as specialized sub-groups within the small therapy groups about which he could speak with less uncertainty. And after 1952 his interest turned away from groups and he applied his wisdom more specifically to the therapeutic process with individuals.

Both his theory and the role-model he developed have nevertheless continued to have a pervasive influence directly and indirectly. One stream of work stimulated by Bion's ideas is the Group Relations Training Programme (GRTP) at the Tavistock Institute. This began in 1957 with the first of a continuing series of 'Leicester Conferences'. In progressive developments since then, it has become possible to extend and build on the ideas and thus to find ways of studying unconscious processes not only in small groups, but in large groups, in inter-group relations and in a whole conference as an organization. Fed by and feeding into these conference developments have been some conceptual advances, and also advances in practice, particularly in consultancy to larger institutions.

Between 1974 and 1979, the authors (who had been and continue to be involved in the GRTP) were engaged in one such experimental application in an industrial enterprise, in which the focus of interpretation became the organization as a whole. More recently, in association with other colleagues in OPUS (an

Organization for Promoting Understanding in Society), we have been trying to develop one methodology for the study of societal dynamics. Our aim in the present paper is to describe this approach, which is still very much in the experimental stage: its achievements, limitations and difficulties. First, however, we shall try to trace the lineage back to Bion by outlining more recent conceptual developments in and around GRTP and by giving a brief account of our 1974–79 experiment.

GROUP RELATIONS TRAINING: DEVELOPMENTS IN THEORY AND PRACTICE

The most direct extensions of Bion's concepts were by Turquet and Rice. Turquet (1974), for example, began to elucidate the characteristic dynamics and myths of groups of different sizes: the pair, the triad, 5–6, 8–12+, 20–30, 50–80. He also proposed a fourth basic assumption to add to Bion's three: the 'basic assumption oneness' group, in which 'members seek to join in a powerful union with an omnipotent force, unobtainably high, to surrender self for passive participation, and thereby to feel existence, well-being and wholeness' (1974, p. 357). In a second paper, which carried the subtitle 'A study in the phenomenology of the individual's experience of changing membership status in the large group', Turquet (1975) pointed out that the consultant to such a group is present in a dual capacity, both in a defined role and as a person, and in the latter capacity shares inescapably in the difficulties and dilemmas of the individual member. In this identification with members, he was expressing the central objective of GTRP, which is to help the individual to understand and grapple with his 'groupishness' and to discover within himself authority for his own interpretations and actions. Turquet went on to argue that whereas in the small group the operant basic assumption makes it relatively easy to establish leader and member roles, 'no similar emcompassment seems to be immediately available or discoverable in the large group' (1975, p. 116). Larger numbers allow the individual more opportunities for projections, but correspondingly he finds himself fractionated into multiple parts; moreover:

the introjected vastness of his external world meets a similar internal experience [i.e, of an internal world that is unencompassable and boundless] and by their mutual reinforcement the level of the anxiety is raised, requiring a further projection into the outer large group of the now reinforced sense of vastness, only to increase the fantasied percept of the large group as now greater than ever before, not only vast but endless. (p. 118)

Turquet's paper also explores the large group's potential for violence – errant violence – the fears this evokes, and the defences that are mobilized. The hunt for a victim can feel implacable and – though he does not make this point so explicitly – at times this can test to destruction the consultant's capacity to manage the boundary between interpretation and control.

Rice (1969) applied the system theory of organization (see Miller and Rice, 1967) to individual and group behaviour. Bion, as we saw earlier, had spoken of the 'glaring difficulty' of determining what basic assumption was operating in a large group (and for Bion 'large' could describe a society, not merely the fifty to eighty members of a conference 'large group'). Rice felt that Bion's concepts described 'special cases which are most easily observable in small groups, because they are large enough to give power to an alternative leadership, and yet not so large as to provide support for more than one kind of powerful alternative leadership at any one time' (1969, p. 40). He argued that task performance (of the work group) uses only parts of group members. If the members find a commonality in the unused parts and invest sentience in it they may then overtly or covertly be agreeing on a role that is irrelevant, and perhaps antagonistic, to the work task. If conscious, this may lead to revolt; if unconscious, to a shared basic assumption opposed to task performance. The larger the group, the greater the threat that such agreement would pose, but the greater the difficulty in agreeing.

Implicit in the design of the conferences is the proposition that the phenomena – often seemingly psychotic – experienced and observed in the relatively unstructured temporary groups, with their task of studying their own behaviour in the here-and-now, are likely to be present in all such groups of equivalent size; but in everyday life – say, in work organizations – structures and conventions will overlay these phenomena. Most of the time they are less visible, and when they do obtrude they appear all the more irrational and dangerous. Menzies (1960), building on Jaques (1955), argued that the structures themselves, though ostensibly created for task performance, are a defence against persecutory and depressive anxiety, and she showed how the specific anxieties of hospital nursing can produce defensive structures which actually reduce the effectiveness of task performance. The resultant increase in anxiety erects further defences, and so on in a deteriorating cycle.

This concept has proved fruitful in analysis of various types of organization: see, for example, Chapters 2 and 3 in this volume. Published material, however, is disappointingly scarce. A recent book entitled *The Psychoanalysis of Organizations* (de Board, 1978) offers few examples.

Perhaps we should not be surprised by this. Given that Western man tends to pride himself on his invention of organization as a rational means of performing large-scale and complex tasks and given too the difficulty of providing scientific proof of the kinds of insights that Jaques and Menzies offered, we can hardly expect such interpretations to be greeted with enthusiasm. And even if clients accept such interpretations of organizational defences – which tend to have a static, structural, 'this-is-the-way-things-are' quality – there is the question of how to help them use the understanding dynamically and effectively. This is a critical problem for members leaving group relations training conferences and returning to their own institutions (Miller, 1980). So the applications of Bion's theories and of psychoanalysis generally to organizational consultancy have tended to be unintegrated. Thus we have theoretical contributions on the experience of work (e.g., Pederson-Krag, 1951, on mass production) and the defensive use of structures (e.g., Jaques, 1955); we have much evidence of consultants using their experience of the transference and countertransference to garner insights into the dynamics of the client system (see Rice, 1963; Sofer, 1961; Miller and Gwynne, 1972; Miller, 1976b, 1977); we have individual members of organizations enlarging their understanding of unconscious processes through attending group relations conferences (and in exceptional cases a significant number of employees being exposed to this type of training as an

instrument of organizational development: see Menninger, 1972);
and where a consultant has worked with a client group in
elucidating unrecognized and unconscious organizational processes, it generally turns out that the group is only a small
sub-system, usually a management body, within the larger client
system – thus leading to ethical and political questions about the
consultant's role in reinforcing the *status quo*. Moreover, in these
cases it has been almost unknown for the consultant to preserve in
relation to such a client group the austere role of, say, a Freudian
analyst. (Writing of his Indian work, for instance, Rice recorded:
'My clients and their families became my close friends' (1963, p. 9).
This may well be appropriate or at least unavoidable in organizational consultancy; but it clearly reduces the consultant's availability as a projective receptacle). The only case we are aware of in
which the action research team consciously tried both to maintain
some distance and to collaborate with the total organization as the
client system was the early Tavistock Institute study at the Glacier
Metal Company (Jaques, 1951).

An Experimental Intervention in a Manufacturing Company

Between 1976 and 1979 the authors had an opportunity to take this
approach further. The earlier stages of this intervention have been
described elsewhere (Miller, 1977; Chapter 11 in this volume) and
we shall merely outline them here.

The client was a manufacturing business with its main factory
and head office in the Home Counties and a small plant in the
Midlands. It was part of a large international group. When help was
sought in 1973, the presenting problems were low output, a high
scrap-rate, poor morale and imperviousness to attempts to increase
efficiency. It teetered between making a marginal profit and losing
money. It transpired that the main factory had belonged to a
company that the group acquired a few years previously. The
Midlands site was the remains of the group's own former subsidiary
producing a similar product: it had been decided to amalgamate the
two businesses – previously competitors – and concentrate production mainly at the southern site, where a two-shift operation was

introduced. This had led to a damaging loss of female labour and thus of production expertise. Selling had been removed from the acquired company and incorporated in the group's separate sales organization. A questionnaire administered to all employees – approaching 1000 – revealed responses to these changes. There were notable internal splits cutting across one another – between management and workers, between employees from the two amalgamated enterprises, and between departments. Identification with the organization was notably lacking: the boundaries had been fractured and had to some extent disintegrated; and employees had fallen back onto their individual boundaries in a culture of survival.

The understanding of the consultants was that the fragmented boundaries of the organization needed to be reconstructed at three levels at least – between individuals, between groups and between the organization and the outside world – in order that a more integrated sense of identity could be developed. Based on the diagnosis, the consultants initiated what came to be called the 'People Programme'. Its main feature was an extended, non-residential version of a Leicester Conference, comprising small study groups, inter-group events, and a large group, which fitted precisely the need to work at the three levels: the individual in interpersonal relations; the department and other groupings in their inter-group context; and the organization as a whole in relation to its environment. One hundred and twenty employees took part in the programme which extended over a period of eight months.

Outcomes over the next year were impressive. The People Programme, having been run by the consultants, was taken over by the participants and the training extended to other echelons of employees; weekly meetings of the 'Large Group' continued for three years; spontaneous task groups arose at various levels – including engineers and apprentices – to tackle pressing work issues; internal coordination improved; a noticeable new air of purposefulness, competence and self-confidence appeared in transactions across the main boundary with group headquarters; and there was a surge in manufacturing performance and profits.

The next innovation – and this is the one we are concerned with here – was the formation in mid-1976 of a quasi-independent Consulting Resource Group, comprising initially the three consultants though later including seconded employees. Up to that time consultancy had been provided, on request, to various internal groups. This the CRG would continue. But in addition it took on a new task, which was to try to elucidate the underlying dynamics of the organization and to interpret them to the whole organization as client. One analogy was of CRG as a man-made satellite which, from its orbit, would have a perspective on the organization not available from the surface of the planet. To be more specific, our proposition was that in taking a consulting position outside the boundary, we would be better able to help the organization explore the interrelatedness between its internal dynamics and its transactions across the boundary with systems in its environment; the transference to the CRG would reflect significant aspects of these other transactions.

We had to devise a technique to get round the problem posed by Bion of being able 'to give an interpretation without having to shout it'. Each week, therefore, members of the CRG held a one-and-a-half hour 'private' meeting, at which we would review our experience of the week, think out loud, and begin to formulate working hypotheses – i.e., interpretations. But this 'private' meeting was held in public: any member of the organization could attend. It was immediately followed by an open meeting, at which those present could question our interpretations, confirm or modify them with evidence from their own experience, and bring forward other preoccupations. In this way we provided participants with a new role – as 'citizens of the organization' perhaps – from which they could examine their experience in their other roles as members of work groups and of trades unions. It was as if the organization as a whole was the analysand; and we always tried to perceive these visitors' inputs as expressing something on behalf of the whole organization in relation to us. Our aim in doing this was to help them to recognize how much they might be caught up in the underlying organizational dynamics.

Attendance at these sessions was variable and never higher than 2 per cent of the total personnel. (It was realistically very difficult for most employees to be released from their jobs, particularly on the production lines.) However, our working hypotheses were also used directly and indirectly in our regular consultations and meetings with sub-groupings, and we had evidence that our voice was being 'heard' – albeit sometimes distorted – by at least a quarter of the organization. That sounds unimpressive until one remembers one's frequent experience as a small group consultant that not more than one or two members out of the dozen are hearing what one has to say.

As in work with small groups and individuals too, it was difficult to be sure of any cause–effect relationship between interpretation and subsequent action. The most overt evidence was in the growing number of individuals able to perceive organizational processes in which they were implicated and able also to act on their understanding by taking greater personal authority in their other roles. Other evidence that we were heard was the strength of the organizational defences that were mobilized to throw the satellite out of orbit. It was either to be brought down to earth – by absorbing the CRG into the organization as just another depart-ment – or it was to be dispatched into outer space. At times the CRG was internally split, part being drawn right inside, and part extruded so far out as to lose sight of the dynamics. Another device was to mobilize a split between the (usually good, caring, participative, creative) CRG and the (usually bad, neglectful, authoritarian) management group. Or again, the CRG would be converted into prophets and priests of a new religious group: for worshippers it was enough to listen to the evangelists and attend the rituals; the rest of their work-place lives could remain unaffected. Sometimes we were totally ignored; yet there were also indications of considerable concern that the rituals should continue even if there was no congregation. Dependency, fight/flight and – rarely – pairing were therefore observable at the organizational level, and could be used to elucidate both the shifting internal dynamics – for example, splitting and projection between departments, with one department carrying for a time all the negativity – and the changing postures towards the external world, particularly towards group headquarters.

We should have foreseen that the client's success would be the undoing of the People Programme. Its transition from the bottom of the league-table to the top in terms of profit aroused envy in other companies in the group and put them under pressure to improve performance; and at group headquarters pleasure that this sick patient had recovered radiant health began to be overlain by anxiety about the shift from compliance to assertiveness, which seemed tantamount to insubordination. Group headquarters therefore applied various sanctions on the client organization's management to get rid of CRG, which was perceived – not inaccurately – as a core of dissidence. Sanctions ranged from withholding managerial promotions to, eventually, installing a new general manager to re-impose compliance. A sharp trade recession and pressure for redundancies gave him added power in reinstalling a more familiar authoritarian regime. The belief developed, with some substantiation, that 'friends of CRG' were particularly vulnerable. With official and personal support withdrawn, the intervention came to an end.

In this sense, the intervention failed. Members of the client system did not acquire enough authority to manage their collective future. Their new insights had to be privatized or denied. Technically, however, it showed that methods could be devised to detect and interpret unconscious processes in sizeable systems. (See Lawrence, 1980, for a report of another related method.) This provided encouragement for the more ambitious experiment described in the final section.

SOCIETY AS AN INTELLIGIBLE FIELD OF STUDY: AN EXPERIMENT

We saw earlier that Bion properly recognized that the small group of ten to twelve is an 'intelligible field of study'. Experiences with the Leicester Conferences suggested that the large group (from forty to fifty up to eighty) mobilizes a sufficiently distinctive set of dynamics to be classed, at least provisionally, as another such intelligible field. This applies both to the 'large group event' as such, in which numerous members meet with (say) four consultants to study their own behaviour, and to the 'institutional event', which explores the relatedness of the membership with the total staff group, in their managerial, consultative and administrative roles. In terms of dynamics, the main observable differences between the two arise from the greater structuring of the latter – membership formation into self-chosen sub-groups; differentiation of role among staff – which crystallizes and give quasi-permanence to the more shifting splitting processes of the large group event. Perhaps because of this, the phenomenon of mirroring is much easier to see in the institutional event. For example, one sub-group of members may precisely mirror the composition of the staff group in overall numbers and in numbers of men, women, ethnic groups etc.; or different fantasied aspects of the staff group may be clearly expressed by the different sub-groups into which the membership divides. These unconscious representations may be potentially present in the small group – and indeed, as we saw earlier, Bion was sometimes able to identify church, army and aristocracy in small groups – but the fact that the larger group of fifty upwards throws them so much more sharply into focus justifies the argument that somewhere around this size a frame-change occurs and another intelligible field of study has been identified.

The question that now arises is whether with our manufacturing company, with nearly 1000 members, we had advanced to another field. Our provisional answer to this is 'No'. Technically, to be sure, we had to invent new ways of communicating to a group that was beyond shouting distance; but working at this level did not seem to elicit phenomena distinctively different from those we have observed in groups of fifty to eighty. 'Society', therefore, may well be the next higher intelligible field.

However, before discussing our attempts to interpret at the societal level we want to examine the appearance in lower level systems of dynamics belonging to a higher level. Our tentative proposition is that number as such is not the determining factor. In other words, groups that are small in size may express phenomena that do not belong to the small group in itself but are manifestations of the large group, or even of society. Thus, in our work with the manufacturing company, organizational dynamics were readily apparent in the shifting groupings of ten or fewer that we met each week, while the dynamics that one would expect to see in the small group were much more elusive. There is other supporting evidence. For example, colleagues conducting therapy groups have reported the occasional experience of working with a group depleted to two members or even one; and there have been similar occurrences in GRTP conferences. In such instances the transaction with the 'group of one' is markedly different from, say, individual therapy. What happens is that the absent group held in the minds of both parties to the transaction has a profound influence on the unconscious dynamics that are mobilized: in Bion's terms it is the 'groupishness' of the individual that comes to the fore. Another way of explaining this is through the concept of 'role'. A psychologist observing the behaviour in a small group of ten people and using the individual as his interpretive focus will not 'see' small group phenomena. Conversely, the consultant to the small group as a system sees the individual's behaviour wholly or primarily as a contribution to group processes (see Miller, 1976b). The perceived role and role-relationship tend to determine those aspects of himself that the individual consciously and unconsciously brings forward, while other aspects are suppressed or repressed (Rice, 1969). Hence if the consultant addresses a solo individual as a representative of a group whose other members are absent, it is the 'groupish' role that will be mobilized. Our method of working in the manufacturing company used and validated this proposition.

There is, however, one further complication: because the larger group is always potentially present in the smaller, at times the larger group phenomena break through. For example, the individual at times may experience in a very small group of six people the same problems of holding on to his skin as he might experience in a crowd: the six have become a crowd. This can be put to constructive use. For example, the group-relations methodology has proved a valuable tool in identifying organizational cultures: a group composed of people from the same organization will display often unrecognized elements of the culture, in particular by mobilizing them as part of their defence against pursuing the primary task of 'here-and-now' study. At a broader level we have increasingly become aware of the influence of societal phenomena on GRTP conferences, particularly in the large group but also more generally in the defences adopted. Indeed, the conference is often called, not inaccurately, a microcosm of society. As Rioch (1979, p. 56) puts it, discussing the American scene:

> It is now expected not only that local issues that affect the institutional affiliations of members will show up in conferences, but often, even more strongly, that the tone or preoccupation of a nation will appear.

[For example,] in one conference in 1973 the dominant theme . . . seemed to stem from concentration camps: not to let oneself be noticed. Fascism and terror . . . were casting a dark shadow, as if the membership were already responding with a concentration camp mentality to such things as the use of the Internal Revenue Service as a weapon against political enemies. In the first half of 1974 corruption, deception and lack of trust in management were important themes.

She notes that after 1968–69 memberships were less prone to violent revolt and less able to mobilize effective leadership of the whole. Parallel changes had been noted in the British conferences. The myth that the group is a creative matrix has been progressively submerged by the countervailing myth that groups and institutions are dangerous and destructive. Correspondingly, there has been a withdrawal of commitment to groups, an increasing reluctance (noted also by Rioch) to use the conference setting for experiment and play (in the Winnicottian sense), and a tendency for the individual to put up protective boundaries against group influences or to seek security as an isolate or in a pair.

Up to now, identification of such societal dynamics has been a byproduct of GRTP conferences. Since mid-1980 the group of staff associated with OPUS (many of whom have been actively involved in the conferences) have been trying more directly to tease out these dynamics. OPUS works on the proposition that if the individual citizen has a fuller understanding of the processes operating in the society of which he is a part then he will learn to manage himself in his own roles with greater maturity: its aim in other words is that of the GRTP writ large. The method used so far has been simple. Every three months the staff of OPUS, who come from all over Britain, meet for a day and attempt to distil, from their experiences in their various roles and institutional settings, current themes and preoccupations in society. A written version of this discussion is offered in a following meeting to the OPUS Forum. This, in contrast to the staff group, which is comprised mainly of middle-class professionals, is a group selected for its diversity of backgrounds – a more genuine microcosm of society perhaps than a staff group. The Forum reviews the staff's distillations and its members offer evidence, confirming or otherwise, from their own experience. As a next step, OPUS is beginning to build up a number of 'listening posts' in different parts of the country. These will be groups of a dozen or so people, also meeting quarterly to share their preoccupations, which will then enlarge the input into staff meetings. So far the only voice, outside Forum meetings, that OPUS has devised to 'shout' its interpretations to society is its quarterly *Bulletin*, which publishes an account of the staff and Forum transactions (OPUS 1980–1).

One way of looking at this approach is that OPUS staff are formulating a role of 'consultant' in relation to society as client and from this position are able, however crudely, to identify and interpret societal dynamics. This would seem to be a natural extension from the analyst/consultant working at the transference in the analytic pair, the small group and the large group, and from the role of the Consulting Resource Group in our manufacturing company. But in these other cases the client gives at least some degree of sanction to the consultant role. And it is the consultant's boundary position, pulled inside and pushed outside, that generates the data for interpretation. However, as we shall argue below, if the putative client is society there is no outside: the Forum is only a representation of society-as-client; and moreover the consultant role is self-defined. This poses a technical difficulty for staff. As we write this paper, we and our colleagues are in the process of examining whether the task boundary and the institutional boundary of OPUS are sufficient to contain the diversity and the chaotic and violent feelings that staff as societal members find they are bringing into it. It seems that each staff member at times is frightened and angry to discover such feelings in himself or herself.

A theoretical difficulty is that OPUS's approach is premissed on society being an intelligible field of study; hence there is a risk familiar to physicists that the phenomena observed are a function of the measuring instrument used. This argument could equally be used against Bion's small therapeutic groups but was in fact controverted by the quality of the evidence and the theory that he was able to adduce. We shall return to this point after presenting our own evidence so far.

At the time of writing (1981), the cycle of Associate Staff and Forum meetings has been repeated five times. Here we briefly review the emerging themes and offer some interim comments on the experience to date.

Summer 1980

A pervasive motif of everything falling apart, impending dissolution and disaster. Falling apart linked to fall-out and the bomb. A theme of waiting helplessly, impotently – waiting for the end, the bomb. A tentative hypothesis: anxiety about the bomb/doom/destruction is a defence against a deeper fear of anarchy. The bomb is fantasied as an uncontrollable retribution for mankind's hubris; whereas anarchy is a consequence of the individual's greed and irresponsibility, which he could do something about, but the action is unpalatable. The unemployed and the blacks represent the threat of anarchy and are seen as contaminating. The price paid for trying to avoid contamination is isolation, lack of meaningful intercourse. Perhaps the ultimate terror is the blackness/anarchy/uselessness/ nothingness inside.

> The current government is seen to mirror these processes, partly because it represents an ideology of *survival of the fittest* in economic terms . . . and also because it came to power on a platform of *law and order* and therefore was a response to anxiety about anarchy. But the more you provoke a belief in the survival of the fittest – self-seeking, individuation, greed – the greater the fear of a 'Lord of the Flies' situation . . . Greater inequalities . . . increase the anxieties of the winners and survivors about protecting their gains against the attacks of those impoverished by the process. The process is escalating; anxiety is mounting; the demand for law and order is intensified . . . The demand for control from outside is a response to failure in exercising personal authority, which relates to feeling valueless, and therefore powerless. But powerlessness is a myth which leaves the individual exonerated from personal responsibility. (OPUS, October 1980: 12–13)

One further theme that emerged in the Forum meeting was loss of ideology, which makes freedom frightening, because we cannot imagine what to do with it: in the current environment freedom means survival of the fittest, which does not mean survival of the majority. Loss of ideology was equated with loss of meaning and therefore with anarchy. Linked to this the Forum also noted that the organization had lost credibility.

> The notion that one was actually part of several sub-systems was not felt to be evident in British society at the moment. The tension between individual and organization which provides dynamism and a force for change seems to be missing. It is either individual or society. Where is Organization? (ibid., p. 18)

Autumn 1980

Withdrawal from organization comes up again in both meetings as part of the dominant theme of retreat: retreat as temporary withdrawal to re-engage better with reality, and retreat as flight from reality, flight for survival. Retreat is from feelings of impotence, of being locked into a situation. Holidays were a retreat into sanity; returning to normal life is a return to madness. Television has been offering a crop of period-pieces: when the future is frightening, there is a reassurance and comfort in looking back. There is a demand for teaching, a search for 'the word', as opposed to thinking for oneself, a wish to go back to old knowledge and received thinking (cf. the Conservative government's monetary doctrines), to a fundamentalist position. Tradition may be a defence against finding alternative modes of being, relating and organizing oneself to lead through the future. The retreat is also flight from violence: non-involvement, lack of courage, self-preservation at the expense of others. The redundant – victims of an enforced retreat – are again seen as an embarrassment, a source of contamination.

It seemed that at this time flight was a defence against fight – which is not quite in accord with Bion's view of this basic assumption in the small group context, where he saw flight and fight as readily interchangeable and as having the function of containing within the proto-mental system emotions associated with the other two basic assumptions. At the time of these meetings, however, fight was unthinkable: there was no external enemy, so it would have to be civil war or – still more likely – anarchic violence. A speculation we made then was that to keep this possibility at bay British society had created the Thatcher/Foot split – the Conservative right wing and the Labour left wing – so that fight could be projected into the familiar, and therefore 'safe', class war. A second speculation was that the myth of a shared national economic crisis and the myth of the threat of nuclear holocaust were both being invoked so as to preserve the social structure and keep order: they offer a justification for feeling impotent; they restrain impulses to burst out in violent protest.

One proposition put forward in the Forum meeting was that there was almost a wish for a holocaust: 'The problems of the world call for changes that we as a society recognize we are incapable of making: they can be tackled only if most of it is destroyed and the survivors can begin afresh' (OPUS, January 1981: 23). But the individual had to see himself as surviving: 'Each one of us is going to be Noah.'

Early 1981

The recurrent theme in meetings of both Associate Staff and Forum was failed dependency. Individuals feel increasingly let down by the institutions to which they look to meet their needs. Institutions seem to be engaged in a search for a 'clean' model of the world: it is becoming more difficult to put the work and the being together. So the person I am and the aspirations I have are not being recognized and met in the way that they were; there is a gap between what I think I am and what I get. Institutions do not make space inside them for people; they are constructs of power, antagonistic to humans, concerned with cleaning things out. Or alternatively, as one staff member experienced when his wife was hospitalized, they may seem too human, ordinary and casual, when 'what you really want is reassurance and tight guidelines and a consultant dressed in a white coat'. But having responded in this human way they do inhuman things to us. (The telling examples given were mastectomy and orchidectomy.) And since they no longer meet our dependent needs, there is a hope and wish to be taken care of, to be rescued, to be saved from one's own feelings and the situations one finds oneself in.

> It is no longer clear what feelings belong to whom. We project our inhumanity into institutions – prisons, hospitals, bureaucracies – in order to remain human ourselves.

The problem is that institutions are the only way society has found to . . . enable people to cope with primitive feelings like dependence, hate and rage. We have developed a pattern of projective receptacles. In the analysis of organizations we have a rational picture of a person in a role in an institution. But implicitly we are describing a process through which we can get rid of bits of ourselves that we want to disown. Those are the bits that the person transmits into the 'containers' of 'role' and 'organization'. So at present institutions are failing us either by becoming more humane and more like us, or they fail us by becoming more extreme and inhumane. If they are too humane, they can't carry things we'd like them to hold for us, but if they're really extreme they become persecutory and frightening.

The reality of unemployment means that, in the absence of alternative mechanisms, we have to come face to face with the feelings that we put into organizations. We have to take them back inside ourselves and put them to creative use. We have to hold on to hope, while giving up childish fantasies of having all our wishes fulfilled (OPUS, April 1981: 12).

We are ashamed when we discover the dependency we have invested in institutions and frightened when we have to take it back. External changes rub up against parts of oneself that were not available before. One feels exposed, vulnerable, uncertain. People still employed feel increasingly unsure about the worthwhileness of the work they do – hence the demands for reassurance and rescue. They envy the freedom of self-employment – breaking through the employment barrier, risking the abyss of no structure – but not its risks and anxieties. ('You have to create it: you don't know what it will be till you get there. You just have to hope it will work out OK.')

The question of where to put one's hopes was taken up by the Forum. Religion, education and political parties have failed us in turn. Perhaps the attraction of the new Social Democratic Party lies not in its policies but in the offer of an alternative hope. (And the prospective royal wedding suggested that aristocracy was living up to the role that Bion assigned to it.) Union solidarity is crumbling; the role of shop steward is unenviable and hard to fill; different levels in the union hierarchy state contradictory opinions. It was also suggested in the Forum that:

People are no longer sure of what is the optimum number of people to join forces with. There's a contradiction between the needs for survival and the needs for achieving something. To survive, I'm forced back on myself and my family. If I'm not employed, I'm safe in the sense that I can't be made redundant; but I can only do so much as a loner: to achieve I have to be connected into the society. And if I've previously accepted the dependent position – that the state should provide employment – when that dependency fails me I can survive only by being angry, against the Government, against the unions (ibid., p. 18).

The government is increasingly perceived as being highly insensitive, uninterested in the people it purports to represent and pursuing an obsessional preoccupation of its own. Staff suggested that as our other institutions, especially employing institutions, decline and crumble, some of the negative feelings normally carried by them are displaced into government instead. The final question that summed up both meetings was: 'Where can we put our trust?'

Spring 1981

The Forum meeting was characterized by two sharply different interpretations of what is happening in society: that there is no real change and what we are experiencing are slightly different manifestations of the same patterns; and that there is actually a massive change in society which is leading to an experience of disillusion and disconnectedness for the individual. A third perspective was that the onus is now on the individual, whether inside or outside institutions, to produce solutions for himself and others.

Interestingly, this had followed a meeting of staff in which a dominant theme had been splitting – the emergence of a strong sense of differentiation and clear splits in individual, group and organizational life.

Rules are increasingly being invoked in organizations. Role and status differentiations are also expressed more sharply – for example, in psychiatric hospitals between patients and staff, sick and well, and among professional groups; and in schools between teachers and pupils, between acceptable and unacceptable children. Splitting comes from a sense of being beleaguered. Amidst turbulence, rules give certainty and professional role boundaries are defended to confer a sense of identity; but it means that people are much less able to act with personal authority. They huddle in smaller and smaller groups, with mounting anxiety about what is going on outside, fearful of power and ruthlessness. Society is preoccupied with structure, not content. If you lose your role, you are nothing. Redundant people disappear into an unknown underworld. Your mates deny the pain by expunging the memory that you were ever there: open mourning is impermissible. In this way the rest of us stay on top, but insecurely.

This is linked to another major theme: deception, betrayal, treason. To quote from the record of the Forum meeting:

> Once you're out of a job, as well as coping with the feeling of being hopeless, you've got to hold inside envy and jealousy of colleagues who are doing the work you'd like to do. Holding these feelings inside yourself corrodes you – you feel betrayed (OPUS, July 1981: 10).

You deal with your aggressive feelings not by attacking the manager who has told you that you are redundant but by displacing all the anger into faceless management, a non-caring institution. But if you protect yourself by splitting in this way, your feelings never get worked through. The Forum persisted with the theme of being locked in, locking yourself in, locking things inside yourself, and its connection with splitting. For example, people who know their job is the only thing they can do – those who work to live rather than live to work – cope with being locked in by splitting themselves: they do their work automatically and meanwhile travel elsewhere in their fantasy life. But the staff meeting was more preoccupied with betrayal. Where there are redundancies, as an employee you either get rid of yourself or you collude with the process that gets rid of other people. You may feel betrayed by your institution; but not supporting and not speaking up are also betrayals. In that sense we all betray part of ourselves. Yet by acting on what you believe in and being true to yourself you can still be seen by others as betrayers – for example, the MPs who transferred to the Social Democratic Party. Treason in the Establishment is in the news, following publication of Chapman Pincher's book. Although the alleged betrayals occurred thirty years ago, they strike a contemporary chord. In one sense,

> the individual's sense of betrayal is based on fantasy . . . In childhood
> you believed in all the rules . . . absolutely and were appalled when
> people broke them . . . But around us is real betrayal. So . . . we feel that
> perhaps it is the version [of history] we've been using that has betrayed
> us. We are at present in a situation which history does not explain, so
> there's an urgent need to rewrite history. It's as if 30 years ago there was
> a fall or betrayal and we search for a myth to explain how we have got
> to where we are now (ibid., pp. 16–17).

Politicians, for example, are betraying us today by treating us like
dependent children, so we are prevented from coming to terms
with the reality that, say, full employment is a myth. We are
being betrayed by failures of institutions: trade unions, religious
institutions.

In turn we as adults are betraying and sacrificing the youth of
today. But this was only one side of an ambivalence about the
young: on the one hand, the older generation feels that it has failed
them, so we deserve to be punished by them for our sins of omission
and commission; and on the other hand, we expunge them and
push them out, into unemployment, into detention centres. Parents
are not providing secure boundaries any more against which the
young can find out who they are; and we refuse to accept our
responsibility for their plight. No wonder we are frightened of their
violence. Maybe they are going to act out *my* destructive impulses,
do the thing *I* do not have the guts to do.

Summer 1981

Fear of violence and experience of actual violence provided the
dominant theme for this next staff meeting, which took place just
a few days before the new round of inner-city rioting in Toxteth,
Moss Side, etc. Splitting was still around, but the sense was that it
would no longer hold as a defence. Forum members – meeting after
the riots had subsided and also after the royal wedding – advocated
action by OPUS; but it was difficult to design actions based on

thought and reason that might effectively combat mindless, violent action.

It is convenient to apportion thought and action between old and young. A staff member saw a youth trying to break into a flat and expected him to run off. 'He didn't; he came at me [with a knife]: "What is it to you?" he said. Shook me rigid. I had a real sense of this not being fair. All I was doing was to warn him that he'd been seen. Then he'd run away: those are the rules. I didn't expect him to threaten to cut me up.' Yet the older also see the need to break through conventions that no longer work. They envy the young. Perhaps there is a demand for psychopathic leadership. A quotation from Norman Mailer: 'Only psychopaths can save us.' Disturbing echoes of Germany in the 1930s. An older man has been terrified to recognize his own violent fantasies: a suicidal impulse to play Russian roulette; a murderous impulse towards a baby grand-daughter. He finds he is transferring commitment from society to his family; but perhaps the cost of doing this is that you have to bring back into the family violent feelings that have been projected outside. Anti-Thatcher feelings are an important social phenomenon. People have to look elsewhere for humanity, for ideas about the future. Anger and rebelliousness are becoming much more overt. Felt hopelessness of the future is the kind of vacuum that psychopathic leadership is sucked in to fill. Desperation creates ready-made victims for exploitation and fraud. You have only to offer hope. For example, a new factory in a new town is opened with much fanfare and the fact that the same company has closed a much larger factory elsewhere, making many people redundant, is irrelevant. People cope by splitting: at one level they know it is a fraud; at another level they deny it and cling to the hope.

As the staff saw it, on the one hand there was violence, real or close to the surface, coming out of feelings of being defrauded and exploited, and on the other hand a wish for a way through. One positive model, put forward in the Forum, was simply of performing one's own roles more effectively and more responsibly. But is that enough, asked the staff. How do you engage at the societal level? If society is split and psychotic, how do you communicate? People have to believe in linear progress and not hear scepticism; so they are ripe for totalitarianism.

Into this climate came the royal wedding, offering hope, renewal, involvement – at least for the day. For most it was a unifying experience: one felt a greater belonging to family and country. Besides being comforting and uplifting, re-evocation of the hierarchies of church and state also brought out the negative: 'Lord of the Manor' feelings are still around – the envy and anger alongside respect and submission – but ceremony and ritual were important in sustaining a sense of belonging and keeping negative feelings at bay. Rituals have been destroyed in our society. (Whatever happened to the harvest festival? A Forum member's daughter brought home a message from school: teachers do not want vegetables or fruit for this year's festival – they go off – so bring something like a packet of tea instead.) We allow contemporary institutions to impose their values on us; so perhaps instead of rituals that have meaning we have observance of bureaucratic rules and conventions. Can we manage without them? One encouraging snippet: During a recent power-cut which shut off the traffic lights in Winchester the traffic moved more freely. So at least motorists could manage themselves. But is that expandable?

> Our educational institutions are engaged in disseminating 'acceptable meanings' – established ways of understanding the world – which are becoming discredited; whereas it is OPUS's job to disseminate 'unacceptable meanings'. But the question then is: How can we pursue that role in a divided split society? (OPUS, October 1981: 24).

What we have offered above are summaries of summaries – over twenty hours of meetings condensed into a few pages. Moreover it is an account of the earliest stages of an experiment. However, it allows us to offer some tentative conclusions, first about society as an intelligible field and second about the role of consultant.

To begin with we can state with confidence that 'society' has been a significant construct in all these meetings. We mean by this that the individual apparently needs to have a picture of something beyond institutions or organizations in order to explain his experience of relatedness (or non-relatedness). 'Society' as used in these discussions is clearly not synonymous with 'nation' or 'state'. It is a more formless notion, though occasionally given a boundary by being equated with 'country'. The stronger evidence that it is an intelligible field is the way in which society is used as a projective container. Bits of the self are projected into bits of society; yet at the same time the individual acknowledges that he is part of society. It seems to us that it is the inexorableness of societal membership that gives rise to distinctive dynamics. One can opt out of a role in an organization – for example, a particular job, membership of a union, a marital relationship – and, with perhaps greater difficulty, one can opt out of participation in a whole institution – for example, the institution of employment or the institution of marriage. But, as Bion so correctly observed, not even the hermit can escape an ultimate relatedness to a group; and the inescapable group is society. If I become a disenchanted émigré, my use of projective containers may change, but I am still only shifting my relatedness from one society to another.

It further seems to us that the nature and quality of the projections are different. Splitting and projection manifestly occur in the 'conference-sized' large group and in the larger manufacturing business described earlier, and they serve to provide the individual with some confirmation of role and identity; but the projection in these cases is into identifiable sub-groups. Even though the large group at times feels boundless and even though the boundaries of the sub-groups may in some instances be blurred – for instance, 'workers' or 'management' – there is in every case a nucleus of perceived sub-group members who are known to the individual by direct contact and many more who are known by sight. So there is a sense that when the individual employee in a factory is projecting on to 'management' or on to 'workers' he can feel that he knows whom he is talking about; and reciprocally at least some of the people in his mind will accept his label, even though they may regard the projections as unjustified. At least potentially, therefore, projections in groups up to this size are discussable, examinable, negotiable and even capable of resolution. More often there is a collusive interplay of projections between these groupings and this in itself confers on the organization some structure of predictability and therefore stability – which gets sustained even though overtly no one is comfortable with it.

In society, the combination of size and physical dispersion

permits projection into whole categories of people – the young, blacks, Jews, the disabled – or whole institutions – the church, big business, the unions – and their common characteristic for the individual is that he is personally acquainted with only a minuscule sample from them. Paradoxically he may regard these as exceptions; but the paradox disappears if we realize that a satisfactory societal container for negative projections has to be distant and anonymous. In this way a potentially problematic personal relationship that crosses these projective categories can be kept positive, often through an extension into, say, inter-ethnic relationships, of the joking relationships that anthropologists have identified in kinship systems. Thus 'nigger' and 'whitey', which used publicly are taken as insults, become the accepted expression of affection and intimacy in a black–white friendship. We can suggest further that the use of societal containers for negative projections may have a function in enabling organizations to hold together despite deep internal conflicts. Splits can be limited by projection into an ultimate societal 'them' – head office, left-wing agitators, the government, the Japanese, or even an abstraction such as 'the recession' or 'changing society'.

Without attempting to state this in psychoanalytic terms, which is beyond our competence, we would surmise that the need to use 'society' in this way for a different order of projections, beyond the known environment into the unknown, is itself a product of increased societal size and complexity. Starting from what seems to be the universal infantile experience of a polarized world, we can identify some primitive societies, such as the Nuer, whose social structure neatly reproduces a set of nesting good/bad, us/them relationships in an ascending order of sub-systems, systems and supra-systems (Evans-Pritchard, 1940); and in relatively modern societies, infinitely larger and more diversified, there have been long periods of relative institutional stability, in which status and values have been unambiguous; but even the very young child today has to manage his way through multiple cross-cutting us/them relationships, with uncertain values that can flick friend to enemy and back again. (How can Mummy be good and Daddy be good if they're divorced and each tells me the other is bad?) We tentatively postulate that what gets projected into the various anonymous categories that comprise 'society' for us is our rage at the contradictions we have to manage closer to home. Our extreme destructive feelings have to be projected as far away as possible to make our day-to-day relationships tolerable: that is the advantage of the common enemy; but Britain has been deprived of that outlet for thirty-six years.

To continue for a moment with one possible interpretation of British society over the last forty to fifty years, we can see Chamberlain's flight leadership of 1938–39 succeeded by Churchill's fight leadership, and then in 1945 an abrupt transition to a dependency culture. This was foreshadowed by Beveridge, implemented by the first Labour government and continued into the 1970s by governments of both complexions. In addition to the welfare state as such, with its provisions for education, health care, pensions, unemployment benefit, supplementary benefit and so on, there has been an experience of economic prosperity based on Keynesian growth and high employment and of political stability in the two-party system. Moreover, the dependency culture has been reinforced by the formation of very large employing organizations, public and private (the ratio of large to small businesses being significantly higher in Britain than in other European countries), with large trade unions ostensibly engaging in fight but essentially also fulfilling dependency needs. In this process welfare functions have increasingly been removed from the family to the state and there has been an effective reduction in familial and individual autonomy and self-reliance. This has been disguised by the pseudo-autonomy of the consumer role, within which, during a period of a steady rise in real incomes, the individual could experience himself as exercising greater choice and therefore having greater autonomy. In a very short period of time, all this has been turned on its head: zero or negative growth, the collapse of manufacturing industry, an unabated escalation of unemployment, reductions in real income, political polarization and instability, and a welfare state that is a diminishingly reliable breast. Moreover, thirty years of an economically orientated dependency culture have effectively eroded alternative institutions, such as the church and the family, that might have provided the fall-back for dependency needs.

There is no doubt, therefore, that what we are picking up in our OPUS meetings during 1980–81 are the dynamics of the relatedness of the individual to society during a phase of failed dependency. Hitherto safe institutional structures have become unreliable: not only are they no longer to be relied upon as sources of employment and prosperity, but they are also too fragile to cope with the force of our negative projections. These have to be taken back by the individual, whose props to identity are already undermined either by unemployment or uncertainty of employment, and re-projected on to 'society'. The force of projection required to defend the individual against the experience of internal chaos aggravates the fear of retribution from the projective receptacles, or, in more ordinary language, the fear of anarchy and violence.

Comparing this with Bion's and Turquet's observations of small group behaviour, we can liken this phase of failed dependency to a typical interregnum, when one basic assumption culture and leadership has become discredited and another has yet to be installed. But whereas in small group life such an interregnum usually lasts only for minutes or at most for a session or two, here at the societal level we have a phase that has already continued for at least two years and shows no sign of early resolution.

If it is granted that the phenomena are part of a societal dynamic and do confirm society as an intelligible field of study, then we have to ask whether our observations merely reflect random or idiosyncratic aspects of a *state* of failed dependency, displaying itself in different guises, or whether the observed differences which emerged in the successive meetings reflect actual short-term changes and developments in the societal dynamic (leaving aside the issue of whether such changes may turn out to be cyclical or linear). If the latter, then one could contemplate development of a method of analysis and forecasting of societal processes analogous to those attempted by several schools of economists. Our tentative view is that we have been observing such changes, albeit perhaps crudely. The reader may or may not agree with us that a significant progression can be traced from the experience of disintegration in summer 1980 to retreat (flight) in autumn 1980, followed by the mixture of anger and impotence at failed dependency in early 1981. Then came splitting, and the mounting sense of betrayal, in spring

1981, and the powerful foreboding of violence in the summer 1981 staff meeting, immediately before the major inner-city riots. After the brief interlude of basic assumption pairing, we were thrown back on the need to act individually – but how? – with the threat of psychopathic leadership hanging over us as the only apparent alternative.*

Earlier in this paper we suggested that OPUS staff are developing a role of consultant in relation to society as client in order to identify and interpret societal dynamics. We also discussed Turquet's picture of the large group consultant as being present in a dual capacity, in a defined role and as a person, in the latter capacity sharing inevitably in the difficulties and dilemmas of the individual member. It follows that OPUS staff in their roles of trying to understand what is happening in society are even more inescapably present as persons – as members of society. Indeed, that is their defined role. What perhaps distinguishes us from other persons is simply that we offer a model of trying to understand and communicate our experience as members of a 'psychotic' society as well as enacting our societal roles.

Thus our evidence suggests that by defining a task boundary, it is possible to evoke, experience and observe societal dynamics in a group of ten to twelve. Society is present in the group; society and the group are present in the individual.

---

*   We did not know then that less than a year later the British Prime Minister was to declare war on Argentina.

14 SOCIETY IN MICROCOSM

*Out of my much longer report on an OPUS weekend conference,
I have selected three extracts: a Prologue, which sets the scene and
discusses the rationale of these conferences; an account of the
opening session on the Saturday morning; and a further account
of a plenary session twenty-four hours later, after members had
reported on their work in smaller groups on the previous evening.
The theme of this conference was 'After 1984: New Directions?';
the date was 28–29 September 1985.*

PROLOGUE

This was the first OPUS conference. Thirty-nine people assembled
on a Saturday morning for two days of deliberation. Two or three
had warned that they'd be delayed; all the rest were accounted for.
Marginally more women than men; age-range from mid-twenties to
mid-sixties. All white, and mostly middle-class professionals, drawn
from the so-called 'helping professions' – education, social work,
consultancy, psychotherapy, the Church, and so on.

The building was in Bloomsbury Square. On that sunny Saturday
it was a traditional quiet London square, paved in the middle, grass
and trees round the edge, and benches for the public. It is not at all

From Miller, 1985.

obvious that it is also the roof of a big car-park, which spirals deep down into the ground below.

On Sunday morning it was still the same on the surface. The sun was still shining, the trees had shed no leaves. Yet it felt very different. Overnight a riot had erupted in Brixton – violence, arson, looting. One conference member – the woman who ran the organization whose premises we were using – arrived very early. She lived in Brixton. Her house had been vandalized and she'd had to stay elsewhere. Other members brought their own Brixtons, the heavy headlines and photographs on the front of every Sunday newspaper. It was as though the surface of the square had fractured, and we could see and smell the ugliness – our ugliness – underneath.

An OPUS Conference itself is designed to operate at two levels. On the surface, it brings together a set of serious, intelligent, concerned citizens who want to contribute to an understanding of what is happening in British society and perhaps to use that understanding to influence future directions. 'The task of the Conference' (says the advance information) 'is to draw on our own individual experience in our various social roles, including our experience of working together in the Conference itself, in order to try to identify underlying themes and processes in contemporary society; and beyond that to explore possible actions, individually and perhaps jointly.' To carry out that task, a provisional structure is offered. After an introductory plenary session, members are allocated to work in sub-groups, each intended to be as heterogeneous as possible. Another plenary, and then self-selected groups to explore emerging themes. The second morning again involves work in the total group – 'Where have we got to?'. The Conference finishes with work in new self-selected sub-groups to explore possible actions, and a plenary on the theme of: 'What do I/we do now?'

It is a design that makes for intensive, in-depth discussion. Given the problems of our society – all the social, economic and political changes and uncertainties – this kind of 'think-tank' is all too rare. There's too much doing and not enough reflection.

That is the intellectual level. But, like Bloomsbury Square, the Conference also has a life at a second, subterranean level. This is hinted at in the phrase, 'including our experience of working together in the Conference itself.' *The Conference itself is a microcosm of society.*

That may well sound an extravagant, far-fetched claim. How can a bunch of mainly middle-class professionals represent 'society'? Practically all are employed or self-employed and have comfortable incomes. Where are the poor, the ethnic minorities, the young? Or the City, the Government, the police?

Mostly, when people gather for a meeting or a conference, they are held together by an organizational structure of chairperson, speakers, discussants and so on. Periods of question and answer, or of reporting from sub-groups to plenaries, are relatively tightly controlled. Sometimes questions from the floor even have to be submitted in writing. This structure provides a boundary which defines the permissible roles and the way in which people are to behave in them. The implication, of course, is that without such a structure there would be chaos. Rephrasing that, one might say that without the structure the assembly would be more like the society from which its participants are drawn.

In an OPUS conference, much of that structural paraphernalia is discarded. The Director of OPUS opens it, as a convenor, gets assent to the proposed programme, and thereafter becomes (or tries to be allowed to become) a participant. Other OPUS staff present try to keep notes of what is happening, but they too are co-participants (and there is an inverse correlation between their involvement and the quality of their record). The timetable provides a minimal structure: the sessions have labels, but within them the role of chairperson lies with each individual. The combination of the subject matter and the paucity of structural conventions means that the boundary between inside and outside becomes highly permeable. So on the Sunday morning, Brixton *was* in the room – frighteningly so.

But can we really say that the resulting processes are actually a reflection or microcosm of the wider society, as against processes that might happen in any fairly large unstructured group, no matter where or when? And what about the poor, the blacks and the young?

One answer to that rests on theory. I have a picture of 'society' in my head. It is not at all a coherent picture. It is made up of the meanings I give to and feelings I have about all sorts of groupings which I believe to exist out there. My experience of those groupings is fragmentary, even nil; and the notion that they *are* groupings may be a function much more of my imaginings and stereotypes than a feeling that would actually be shared by the people I think I am talking about. With some of these groupings I may identify – 'people like us'. Many others, however, are important to me because I see them as different from me along some dimension or other – aspects of me, perhaps, that I would rather disown. It is through this sum of perceived samenesses and differences that I am able to locate myself, to establish my identity. But it is not a stable configuration. Things I see, hear or read may shift my picture. Or my own position may change – I may move house, get married, become a parent, lose my job, get a new job – as a result of which I have to reconstruct my identity.

That's just me; but everyone is doing it. Through my relations with others and through the media I may feel myself to be part of a particular grouping – an 'us' – over and against a particular 'them'. Of course, I'm not part of just one 'us', but of many overlapping and even contradictory 'us's'. Some are deep-rooted, others more fleeting. And negative pictures of 'them' have a habit of becoming self-confirming: if I believe that police are violent and I pick up a weapon to protect myself against being attacked by them, then I'm all too likely to prove that I was right. That happens with positive projections too. Thus in 1984 a substantial part of the population was identified with the striking miners as fighting Mrs Thatcher on their behalf; and the miners gained strength from this to fight the harder.

That same example can be used to illustrate the ways in which these societal dynamics shift. Egged on in their fight by the vicarious involvement of so many others, the miners took up a more and more extreme and intransigent position and perhaps acted more violently; and in doing so began to become increasingly unsatisfactory figures for others to identify with. There was thus a progressive shift in individual and shared configurations.

So we can come back to the theory behind the Conference itself. If we create a setting which refrains from providing the security of a temporary structure, and especially if in that setting people are defined as citizens of the wider society, then they will import into it their internal pictures of society and impose them on that setting. They need to do that to hold on to their identities, to feel sane. If in society at large there is a prevailing image of a significant split between a law-abiding majority and a dissident minority, then the mini-society of the Conference will contrive to produce that split – even though, on the face of it, the actual spectrum of degrees of law-abidingness among the members might appear to be very narrow. In that way, if the poor and the blacks and the young are significant in the wider context they will find representation within the Conference. The dilemma in designing an event of this kind is that if there is too much structure these processes and phenomena are not allowed to appear, while if there is too little we simply live out the processes and we lose our capacity to notice what is happening to us and to think about what it means – the function that some psychologists have called 'the observing ego'.

That then is the theoretical argument that the Conference can be a microcosm. The other argument rests on people's experience of what actually happens – in particular, getting caught up in positions and quite powerful feelings that are unexpected: they are pushed and pulled into taking up roles that are latent somewhere inside them and that the group of participants evidently wants from them. For example, one member, a psychotherapist, reported that the weekend 'catalysed and reanimated my political voice that had got somewhat buried over the years'; and another commented (about the opening phase of the Conference): 'I found myself collusionally and powerfully caught up in the whole psychodrama . . .'

Other examples will come out in the account of the Conference itself. This attempts the awkward task of bringing together both process and content. It draws on notes taken at the time by OPUS staff and on comments sent in afterwards by a number of the participants. Of course, this can't be a definitive publication of 'the Proceedings', as in a scientific conference. Every one of the thirty-nine participants will have had a unique experience, and correspondingly there could be thirty-nine reports, all different and all equally valid. All we can hope is that those who were there will recognize this as an account of the same weekend and that those who were not will gain at least some small new insight into what is happening in British society today.

SATURDAY: THE BEGINNING

First, the arrival. Much anxiety around. Not acknowledged at that stage, but visible in cautious entries, in the almost exaggerated relief when old acquaintances were discovered, and also in worried looking around: 'Where's so-and-so?' (Perhaps she isn't coming; perhaps I should have stayed away too.) Acknowledged later: 'Standing outside the front door I felt really frightened' – but there were people inside who would know she'd chickened out. Though the building itself felt welcoming – newly decorated, wall-to-wall carpeting – and that helped a bit. (Not, however, to everyone: 'My experience on first entering the house [was] of being funnelled along the narrow entrance and then blocked by the desk across the hallway whilst I was registered. I may well have wondered then about what might be born for me!')

Then the opening plenary sessions. One participant recorded:

> As first member to arrive I was able to observe the formation of the opening plenary. The first to register came in and clustered near the open window of the end opposite to the fireplace, in the centre of which the Director of OPUS had clearly marked her own chair. With two exceptions this group grew from its edges round towards the Director's seat, which was eventually left isolated with empty chairs, one on each side.

(Chairs were arranged in roughly a hollow square, double except at the fireplace end.)

The dependency was palpable. The tacit demand was for a leader who would dispel the anxiety. The dependency was also a means of helping her to cope with her anxiety – her own and that of OPUS as the sponsoring body: was this going to be a disaster? So acceptance of the roles of leader and followers relieved the tension for everyone – at least for the present.

From that point of view it was a relatively conventional opening plenary. The Director rehearsed the origins and history of OPUS ('the scriptures' as one person commented later), with emphasis on the role of the founder, the late Sir Charles Goodeve (and, asked the same person, by implication 'offering us the role of "Good-Eve", the facilitating mother, providing the boundaries of dependency and the source of nurture?'). She described the current way in which OPUS operates and then introduced the Conference itself – its task and the proposed structure. Was this structure acceptable? No discussion; a consensus of nods.

The timetable provided for the opening to last from 10.00 to 10.45, with sub-groups to start work at 11.15. It was now almost 10.30. No questions, no discussion – a strong collective pressure to end the plenary session at that point, while the structure of dependency still held. 'So what do we do now?' asked an OPUS staff member. One option would have been to continue that session until 10.45 – the schedule that had been agreed a minute before – but if that option was in anyone's head, it was not voiced. Everyone, apparently, was relieved when the Director proposed going straight for coffee and resuming at 11.00, 'to give more time in the sub-groups before lunch'. Rapid flight to the basement.

It seems a simple enough process: obvious, hardly worth recording. Yet the consequences reverberated over the next twenty-four hours and told us something about our society. Privately, over coffee, and later more publicly, it emerged that some individuals *had* spotted the option. They were angry with the Director for having overridden the timetable that had just been agreed; they were angry with themselves for colluding with it and saying nothing; and this made them doubly furious with 'the leader'. So there it all was: the anxious society; the retreat into dependency; the pressure for a leader to meet the dependent needs; the relief when she does so; her offer that people should take responsibility for decision-making; their tacit confirmation; her further proposal for action, responding to their anxiety and to her own; again the tacit acceptance; and then the rage at her for having done exactly what they were collusively asking her to do and knowingly let her do. Good-Eve becomes Bad-Eve. That Thatcher dynamic was to recur. (As one participant wrote later: 'In the opening minutes of the conference, at an extraordinarily powerful and fast-moving pace, some of the most fundamental dynamics of current British political and social culture were re-enacted.')

SUNDAY, 11.30 - 12.45: PLENARY: 'WHERE HAVE WE GOT TO?'

The 10.00–11.00 session on Sunday, designed for reports from the Theme Groups, had started off compliantly, as if to preserve the established order; but as it went on the intervening discussions that the reports triggered became longer and more acrimonious, while the feedback itself was briefer and more fragmentary, until the spokesman for the fifth group only just managed to grab two minutes of airspace at the end. One woman was becoming increasingly irritated at the interchanges. Work had been started the previous evening, but only bits of it were being picked up and instead of being heard and built on it was being used for a competitive, self-indulgent process of coming up with the next metaphor, arguing about language, making the next delicious interpretation – a game of jumping on other people's sand-castles. Another woman felt increasingly upset and stifled.

The fear was of 'letting yesterday go', of 'letting go of the past without knowing the shape of the future', 'the terror of the unknown'. Yesterday's symbols in preference to the real life of today. Everyone knew of the Brixton riot, and some were aware that the house of the member who lived there – and lived there *because* she believed in a multi-ethnic community – had been vandalized overnight. Twice Brixton was mentioned and immediately dropped. It was more difficult to ignore when she herself brought it up – that her vision of Brixton had been shattered yet again. And she had no time for the pusillanimity of the so-called 'Action Group': if you live in Brixton it's only too plain that it just needs one or two people who feel strongly about things to get together . . . Even so, there was a last-minute attempt to get back to yesterday's structure – the final group's report.

That large group – that miniature version of society – was becoming an increasingly threatening place and 'Where have we got to?' an increasingly threatening question. During the coffee break one member had fled to a bench in the square for solitude; there was a marked reluctance to reconvene; and when we did so there was an immediate proposal to move into small groups for 'more fruitful interchange'. Yes, I would like to move into 'a more concrete project' in smaller groups. Yes, I would like to be on our family's narrow boat (incidentally named *OPUS*) on a canal. Far from the madding crowd. No, we should stay *here*: *here* is what's relevant. Here, where individuals are spurting out their anger. Here, where individuals get scapegoated. Here, where we're divided between those interested in the process, in dreams, and those wanting to do something. Yes, 'I'm more interested in citizenship of this temporary society.' More anger: Brixton is right here. Why are we conspiring to stay quiet on our feelings about it? We're fiddling while Brixton burns. So much for the people who wanted to flee to 'their little suburban wombs' in small groups, opting out of the struggle to be citizens of the whole of society.

The Director of OPUS voiced her rage. 'What wasn't talked about here yesterday was acted out in Brixton.' (Today she was working from another seat in the back row, and being much less directive.) She was furious at her experience of having, as she'd thought, offered leadership and facilitation and then being put into a role in which she got sadistically attacked. 'You are doing to me what we are doing to Thatcher!' She'd come to feel hard, contemptuous. No wonder Mrs Thatcher is seen as – and has perhaps become – uncaring.

In contrast, a young English priest said he could feel nothing: he was only functioning from the eyes up, like an observer, feeling redundant, as if there were no mediating role for a priest in Brixton.

Exasperation from the Brixton woman: 'Does this Conference understand or have any connection with what happens in Brixton?' An interchange in a different mood. Priest: 'After yesterday, I felt last night I could almost have voted Tory.' Another man: 'I voted Tory last time and will again.' A woman: 'It's brave of you to say so in here!' Exasperation again: 'We're not talking about sand-castles: Brixton is reality.' The Brixton woman describes young middle-class kids there talking about where to buy guns, so as to kill Thatcher. 'I said downstairs at coffee that if I hear any more about "process" I'll pick up a gun . . . Why I am shaking with rage at this conversation? What can I do with my anger?' 'Use anger to fuel action . . .' 'I'm angry with Thatcher who doesn't care.' 'Thatcher *does* care.'

'We *want* there to be riots in Brixton: when I heard the news I felt glee.' The Brixton woman agreed: 'I felt glee when I saw

Barclays Bank smashed this morning: they'd got the right targets for once.' A plea for reflection, overridden: 'The real world *is* dangerous: two weeks ago my son and his wife were threatened with a knife . . .' 'My daughter was shot at.'

Another plea for reflection: 'How can we use being here to think about Brixton – the different positions we have? How can we intervene in the anger that ends up with daggers drawn?' What's needed is middle ground. In these times we're living as if there were no middle ground, as if notions of faith, forgiveness and peace don't have meaning any more. 'We have to find another position.' A man recalled his shifts in identification as he'd read the *Observer* that morning – which had resonated with his shifts in mood during Saturday: first, identification with the rioters (a sense of outrage, feeling attacked, done down); then with the police (besieged in the police station, the situation out of control); and finally with the people caught up in it, the commuters pulled out of their cars and knocked about.

A tearful and passionate intervention, protesting at sogginess of 'the middle ground' and the arrogance of white priests. 'We all keep this thin blue line between the haves and the have-nots.' Recently in Birmingham a policeman shot a child out of fear; yesterday in Brixton, a white policeman nearly killed a black mother out of fear. 'They're frightened and angry; we're frightened and angry.' We're not sharing what we have to share – food, safety, warmth. The frustration is that we can see it, talk about it, but can't *do* it. 'I felt so irrelevant here yesterday'; and this is how the Cabinet and Parliament react – fiddling around. No, said someone else, yesterday was hideously relevant; the question is what to do about it. *Is* 'middle ground' a fantasy? The Scot broke his long silence to say that not only was he not in touch with a middle ground, but he felt so polarized that middle ground was the last place he wanted to get into. The behaviour of the Metropolitan Police was deplorable – they do it all too often – yet there were people here who might actually re-elect a Tory government . . .

Leadership from the Irish priest for another line of enquiry: 'What have *I* done here to push the Director in the Tory position? I have to take responsibility for that. As citizens, *we* have to take responsibility for the negative sides of people that emerge when they're in authority roles.' 'Guilt gets in the way.' 'We have to work on our own inner apartheid . . .' 'The origins are in us . . .' We deny our blackness, so that blacks and the have-nots act it out for us: 'We feel the rage and do sod-all.' Then we're devastated: 'Just when something positive was beginning to take place in Brixton . . . It will take years . . .' 'You're grasping for a world where accidents don't happen . . . '

Violence flares again: 'Bullshit!' 'I don't accept that the shooting was an accident.' 'It's no accident that the police have guns without a safety-catch.' And, icily: 'Metal doesn't have a natural and compulsive attraction towards human flesh. A gun has to be loaded and aimed, and a trigger has to be squeezed . . .' So the man who'd mentioned accident was faced with a veritable firing-squad!

One man *could* empathize with the policeman: 'You're shit-scared, you tense, you jump, you shoot.' He went on to speak poignantly of his own mini-Brixton. Fifteen years ago he and his wife – for whatever middle-class reasons, collective guilt – adopted a black baby boy. Despite all their efforts, they had been faced throughout with deep, unfathomable anger, things being smashed and stolen . . . Brixton is a macrocosm of that . . . We brought them here, we invited them to do menial jobs, we treated them accordingly . . . And now we can't afford to pay them to clean up our shit any more . . .

But the last thing the blacks in Brixton (or the adolescent boy, or other enraged minorities) want is that their behaviour should be 'understood' – the white middle-class professional line. If you try to explain away powerful feelings, you conjure up an even more violent reaction . . . Why, asked the adoptive father, do professionals pretend to be at one remove, cling on to the myth of being cut off? We *are* involved, said another man: 'My daughter's had a West Indian boyfriend for the last six months . . .' And there is intense vicarious involvement: 'When I saw that sign in the tube station – "Due to civil disturbance, Brixton and Vauxhall are closed" – I felt excited and relieved. In a way I'd been hoping for it. So long as they do it, I don't have to. I have a vested interest in seeing it and perpetuating it and keeping them there – the Blacks, Asians, Irish, women – understanding what they're doing – and disowning it . . .'

15 POWER, AUTHORITY, DEPENDENCY AND CULTURAL CHANGE

This chapter explores current shifts in Britain in the relatedness of individual to organization and to society and their implications for the distribution of power and exercise of authority. It draws on my experience in consulting, research, and educational roles, working with a wide variety of groups and organizations, ranging from community groups to multinational corporations. The Tavistock Institute's Group Relations Training Programme, which I have worked with for twenty-five years and directed for the last fifteen, has enacted, in the temporary institutions formed in its conferences, contemporary versions of power and authority prevailing in the society outside. And specifically over the last four to five years I have been involved with a group of people in OPUS (an Organization for Promoting Understanding in Society). We have been talking about our own and other people's changing feelings, preoccupations, concerns, anxieties, and ways of coping with their lives, and trying to tease out underlying patterns or trends, conscious and unconscious, in society as a whole (see OPUS *Bulletin*, vols 1–15, 1980–84). The primary objective of OPUS is educational: to provide citizens, as individuals, with a set of observations, questions, and occasionally hypotheses that make up our understanding of what is going on in society and to encourage

This paper was initially prepared for an international symposium on executive power at Case Western Reserve University, and published under the title of 'Making room for individual autonomy' (Miller, 1986).

them to think about and examine their own involvement in their various roles and accordingly to exercise their own authority within them. Insofar as OPUS also has a research objective, its methodology is a crude form of interactive research. Correspondingly, this chapter also builds on my own experiences in the role of citizen. Beyond this, of course, I have drawn on ideas and concepts of many other people. Where I can, I acknowledge names and give references, but there are many influences of which I am not aware, and I doubt whether anything I have to say could be called original.

My main proposition runs along these lines: Between the end of World War II and the late 1970s, British society generally and its employment institutions in particular were dominated by a dependency culture, in which the individual's relatedness to the state and the organization was dynamically similar to that of infant to mother. This was associated at the organizational level with a consistent and persistent pattern of power and authority and at the individual level with certain common coping and defence mechanisms. These underlying patterns were remarkably resistant to the importation by behavioural scientists and others of newer 'liberal', 'democratic' values and associated forms of work organization. Since 1979, which saw the installation of the Thatcher government and mounting unemployment, especially in the manufacturing sector, various symptoms of 'failed dependency' have appeared in the UK. The welfare state and employing organizations have in reality become less reliable in meeting dependency needs, and the exercise of power and domination has become more overt. The unemployed – who, in losing their jobs, have lost crucial props to their identity – are merely the more obvious and dramatic cases of a far more widespread societal phenomenon, symptomized by psychological withdrawal from organizations, retreat into the past and fantasy, expressions of impotence in face of nuclear annihilation, displacement of aggression onto social sub-groups, and a paranoid search for an enemy.

Paradoxically, the unemployed also are pointing the way to a positive alternative to the dependency culture. While widespread demoralization has prevented the unemployed from forming a critical mass politically, and the economic gap between employed and unemployed, the haves and the have-nots, is perceptibly widening, the presence of a significant minority surviving outside employment begins to undermine the Protestant work ethic. So there are signs that the employee is renegotiating the basis of his identity and shifting the nature of his relationship to the organization. (As noted later, although women are not immune to the crises described in this chapter, it is the male role and self-image that are the more threatened.) As instrumental values and more conscious compliance take over as the mode of relating to the organization, authority becomes personal authority to be exercised more outside employment than within it. Hence, a challenge for employing organizations – to which only a few are beginning to respond – is to find ways of reconnecting personal authority to the task of the enterprise.

The Dependency Culture

Post-war social policy in Britain was shaped by the widely acclaimed publication in 1942 of the Beveridge report, which essentially held out the promise of the welfare state as a reward for enduring the rigours of the war and winning it. Warriors could return to be suckled by the bountiful national breast. And the bounties were many: free education for all; free health care; child allowances; pensions for the old and disabled; subsidized housing; dole for the unemployed; supplementary benefits to ensure that no one fell through holes in the safety net; and a host of other provisions, from maternity benefits to funeral grants. Along with this, Britain embarked on a thirty-year period of economic stability and rising prosperity, based on Keynesian growth and high employment, and also of political stability, with government alternating between the two major parties, whose policies – after a short flurry of nationalization, denationalization, and renationalization – became more marked in their similarities than their differences. By the mid-1970s, many people came to feel that – apart from minor recessions – this state of affairs could be regarded as normal and would continue indefinitely.

A further important characteristic of these thirty years was a growing reliance on large organizations. This was a product partly of the welfare state (for example, the National Health Service, besides catering to our medical needs, became a vast employer) and partly of nationalization; but, in addition, a series of mergers and takeovers in industry meant that large companies accounted for a higher proportion of total employment than in any other European country. Medium-sized and small firms were relatively fewer. Correspondingly, a small number of powerful unions claimed the membership of most of the work-force.

Nationalization, it must be remembered, particularly of industries such as coal and steel, was introduced as a safeguard against any recurrence of the exploitation and bitterness of the inter-war years. Almost by definition, the nationalized enterprises provided security of employment comparable to the civil service and local government service, and this came to be expected of other major employers also; and by and large the rate of economic growth enabled it to be provided. Legislation furnished progressively greater protection of employees, and the unions were strong enough to keep the employers in line: if mother showed signs of being less than generous with the breast, father could be relied upon to step in to keep the milk flowing.

In many respects – economically, socio-politically, and even to some extent psychologically – this was a satisfactory set of arrangements for all concerned. Economically, although return on investment was held down by relatively low productivity, overall growth generally kept profits at a level sufficient to satisfy shareholders while, despite inflation, wages steadily rose in real terms. When goods began to return to the shops after post-war shortages, there was money to buy them: 'You've never had it so good,' Mr Macmillan was to tell us. Consumerism rapidly established itself. Also, wages actually grew faster then salaries over the period as a whole, and this, coupled with heavy taxation on higher incomes, brought about some reductions in inequalities of wealth. In monetary terms at least, the historical blue-collar/white-collar, working-class/middle-class distinctions were significantly blurred.

As Bott (1957) noted thirty years ago, two models of class system operate in British society: the prestige model, which postulates three or more classes and scope for upward mobility into all but the highest; and the two-class power model, which fosters solidarity of the working class through the shared belief that the route to greater individual prosperity is through the collective power of workers to gain a larger return for their labour – a bigger share of the 'national cake'. Sociologists in the 1960s were preoccupied with the phenomenon of embourgeoisement, which is essentially a shift from the two-class model and its associated values toward the prestige model; but if it was occurring at all, which some contested (see Goldthorpe *et al.*, 1967), it was a process that made most headway in southeast England and much less in the main centres of heavy industry in northern England, South Wales, and southern Scotland. Unions after all could justify their claim that they were securing a higher standard of living for their members, and reminders of the 1930s could serve to encourage waverers to hold on to their working-class identity.

Persistence of strong unions, enacting the power model, was also convenient for the other, 'management', side of the boundary. I put the term in quotation marks because top managers in the employing organizations were faced with the problem of securing the motivation and commitment of a wide range and growing proportion of supervisors, specialists, and other staff who did not necessarily have the title of 'manager' and whose earnings were becoming relatively and even absolutely lower than higher-paid 'workers'. The solution to this problem lay in perpetuating a myth that they had been made members of an exclusive club called 'management' and that through diligence and loyalty they could progressively gain access to the club's inner sanctums and to the power that went with it. (To put it another way, the organizational breast was on offer, but regulated by top management – in this case 'father' – which demanded deferred gratification.) This promise of access to the club's inner sanctums implies the need for competitiveness and rivalry for promotion. Perpetuation of a perceived conflict with the unions could therefore mobilize what Bion (1961) called 'basic assumption fight/flight' as a means of cohering an otherwise internally disparate and rivalrous 'management' and differentiating it from 'workers'.

Therefore, the collusive fight between the supposedly exploitative management and the supposedly greedy and idle workers helped the unions maintain working-class solidarity and diminished the threat of embourgeoisement. Not until the late 1960s and early 1970s did significant numbers of the junior corps of 'management' begin to defect and join unions themselves. Overtly, these employees were resentful at being excluded from significant management–union negotiations (often hearing about the outcomes from their subordinates rather than from their superiors); perhaps less consciously, they recognized – especially when expansion and therefore promotion opportunities slowed down – that the notion of club membership was indeed a myth designed to preserve the overriding power of top management. They were, however, subject to strong pressures to remain 'loyal to the company', with the result that they neither left 'management' nor fully joined the union, and their officials in particular were subjected to a good deal of role-conflict and stress.

Psychologically, too, this set of arrangements was satisfactory, at least superficially. The employing organization, with its hierarchical structure, provided security and met dependency needs. The job, however unsatisfying the content, gave the individual a role in a production system and a social grouping. At the same time, resentment at dependency – the other side of the ambivalence – and the need to find outlets for expressing aggression and experiencing potency were also accommodated. For those on the 'management' side of the boundary, peer rivalry in the struggle for promotion fulfilled this function. (Their interorganizational mobility, incidentally, was far lower than in the United States.) The others had their union to act it out on their behalf. Here, however, there was an added complexity. The level at which the union fought its battles with management was often so remote that the individual member's dependent relationship within the union hierarchy seemed to him not very different from his dependency within the work structure. For these reasons greater power became vested in shop stewards, who being somewhat closer to the individual, were more satisfactory carriers of his needs to feel potent. Particularly in those companies where the price to be paid for dependency was exceptionally mindless work content or an authoritarian mode of management and supervision, union members tended to elect shop stewards whose relatively extreme left-wing views, advocating the overthrow of capitalism, more adequately reflected the rage experienced by members in their employee roles. In fact, the left-wing extremists implicitly played a significant role in the collusive maintenance of the equilibrium. Union officials and employers' negotiators were united by their paranoia about the disruptive influence of extremists on the labour force, and this led, during the 1960s and early 1970s, to many agreements on wages and manning that employers, at least, have since had cause to regret.

Before concluding, however, that those thirty years of the dependency culture were an only slightly tarnished golden age, we need to look a little more closely at what was happening at the level of the individual. Alienation remains as valid a description of the work experience of many employees as it was one hundred years ago; if anything, it is magnified by the greater size of employing organizations. The individual feels forced to do something that gives him no satisfaction by someone else who has coercive powers and steals most of the fruits of his labour. Talking to groups of manual workers and junior clerical staff in 1979 at a factory that was part of a large industrial group, I was struck by the coexistence of rationality and fantasy. At the rational level, these employees could give a clear and accurate account of the way in which their company worked: the market for their products; the relations between costs, prices, profits, and investment. Yet not far below the surface was a fantasy that all the profit went to the factory general manager, who took home a bag of gold at the end of the week. Articulating such a fantasy, they could laugh at its absurdity yet acknowledge that it was there. The coercive hold that the organization has over the individual, whether 'manager' or 'worker', is that it satisfies his dependent needs and his infantile greed, though it does so indirectly by offering him the pseudoautonomy of the consumer role. As a consumer, to be sure, he has choices; but it is pseudoautonomy in that the orchestrated pressure to spend and consume is itself a secondary coercion that reinforces dependence on an employing organization, which is to be placated through passivity and compliance. (Correspondingly, I postulate that, at least in Britain, embourgeoisement has been associated with only pseudoinstrumentality; that is, consumption patterns and class

identification may shift, but the underlying organizational relatedness of dependency and coercion remains.)

The individual's rage and his wishes – not always unconscious –
to destroy the organization have to be split off and suppressed or
repressed. Psychoanalytic theories of splitting and projection
illuminate this process. In the language of Klein (1952, 1959), there
is re-evoked in the individual the primitive 'paranoid-schizoid
position', which is the phase when the young infant cannot yet
distinguish between his impulses and their effects. His fantasy is
that the objects he wishes to attack and destroy – notably the 'bad',
uncaring breast of the mother – are actually damaged and will take
revenge on him with equal destructiveness. Hence, the dominant
anxiety in that phase is paranoid, and the dominant defence to cope
with that anxiety is schizoid: unconsciously splitting the 'good
object' (gratifying breast, mother) from the 'bad object' (depriving
breast, mother), even when there is conscious recognition that they
are one and the same. In the adult this can lead to formation of a
compliant 'pseudo self' (Fromm, 1960) or 'false self' (Winnicott,
1960, 1971), which, as Fromm put it, 'is only an agent who actually
represents the role a person is supposed to play but who does so
under the name of self' (Fromm, 1960, p. 177). Split off from this
and repressed is a private self, which may be what Winnicott calls
the real self, the creative potential; but it is held incommunicado,
locked in an unconscious world of infantile omnipotent fantasy. By
means of this splitting, any questioning of the institutional roles that
the false self enacts, almost ritually, is inhibited. Winnicott was
discussing this defence as a form of individual psychopathology,
but over fifty years ago Fromm was already perceiving it as a
phenomenon of a society that increasingly 'automatizes' the
individual ([1941] 1960, p. 178); and work that I and others did in
British industrial organizations during the 1970s suggested that
employees had increasingly taken up a position of schizoid
withdrawal (Lawrence, 1982; Lawrence and Miller, 1982), which
affected all their social relations, not only those of the work-place.
And, indeed, Winnicott's description of the individual operating
with a high degree of 'false self defence' is all too apposite to the
observed life experience of a large sector of our population:

In the healthy individual who has a compliant aspect of the self . . . and who is a creative and spontaneous being, there is at the same time a capacity for the use of symbols. In other words, health here is closely bound up with the capacity of the individual to live in an area that is intermediate between the dream and the reality, that which is called the cultural life . . . By contrast, where there is a high degree of split between the true self and the false self which hides the true self, there is found a poor capacity for using symbols, and a poverty of social living. *Instead of cultural pursuits, one observes in such persons extreme restlessness, an inability to concentrate, and a need to collect impingements from external reality so that the living time of the individual can be filled by reactions to these impingements.* (Winnicott, 1960, p. 150; emphasis added.)

Television and video-recorders have provided a rich source of such impingements.

It may be added that this set of structural arrangements and individual defences serves to maintain a particular conception of authority as concerned with superordination and subordination. Insofar as conflict is split off into union–management relations, the work organization is maintained as a hierarchy of dependency and compliance. The alternative conception of authority – exercise of capacity to contribute to performance of the task – cannot flourish in such a culture. Authority based on competence is always a threat to an organization that defines authority as based on position (if it is exercised by a subordinate, it is treated by the superior as insubordination), and so the imperative to maintain the dependency structure takes precedence over effective task performance. Hence, there is a collusive myth that the hierarchies of status and competence coincide. (Suggestion schemes are an ingenious but seldom very successful device for preserving that myth, in that first, they imply that the subordinate's capacity to contribute to improved performance is an exception, almost an aberration; and second, they reconfirm that the authority to implement improvements has to come from above. In addition, of course, they are an almost explicit acknowledgement that if the suggestion were made directly within the hierarchy, the immediate superior would experience this as a threat to his or her position and either suppress the idea or steal it for him- or herself.)

These structures and defences proved remarkably tenacious and resistant to change. I have discussed elsewhere the processes whereby employment institutions 'give a few selected individuals a monopoly on creativity and offer work – without creativity – to the majority, the so-called "working class"' (Miller, 1983, p. 10); and I am far from the only person to be concerned not just with the waste of people's talents in organizations but, more generally, with the damaging effects of alienation on the individual and on society. There has been widespread awareness of the growing dissonance between the constraints on the individual in his role as employee and his relative autonomy in the role of consumer, between the authoritarian values of the work-place and the democratic values of the wider society. In the Tavistock Institute, for example, this has been the focus of much of our work ever since the late 1940s. Formulation of the concept of the socio-technical system in the early 1950s opened up a whole new approach to work organization and stimulated many experimental innovations in places as far apart as Scandinavia, India, and North America. And one can list a long series of approaches/concepts/philosophies of intervention by behavioural scientists and others to try to do something about that dissonance: OD, democratization of the work-place, job enrichment, job enlargement, participation, industrial democracy, quality of working life – to mention but a few. The Case Western study, *Job Satisfaction and Productivity*, carried out in 1973–75, analysed some 600 cases and showed conclusively that autonomy, as an 'important aspect of the work itself, the nature of superior–subordinate relations, and the organizational climate of work', is a 'significant organizational factor related to both satisfaction and productivity' and hence a potentially effective action lever for improving productivity and the quality of working life (Srivastva *et al.*, 1975, p. xvi). As I have noted elsewhere, on the basis of this evidence 'one might expect sweeping changes to be taking place in a whole range of organizations. Reality, however, . . . does not support that expectation . . . Successful experiments are rare; . . . the changes achieved, notwithstanding their evident benefits, often remain precarious; . . . and there seems to be immense difficulty in disseminating innovations' (Miller, 1979a, p. 173; Chapter 12 in this volume).

One explanation is that such innovations are, almost by definition, a threat to existing power holders in the organization. So we see self-styled democratic and participative managers seeking to bestow autonomy without surrendering one iota of control; or the top management that can afford to profess advanced, even radical, views because middle management and supervisors can be relied upon to take the obstructive roles. Then there is the manifestly successful experiment that somehow fails to be replicated; or the innovation is transferred in such a way that success is improbable, since the requisite boundary conditions are not sustained. For example, Rice's original experiments in the work organization of weaving (Rice, 1958) remained effective over a long time period (one being still almost unchanged fifteen years later), and the method was introduced in other loom-sheds. What was not transferred, however, was the crucial shift in the role of the supervisor (supervisors had no training in how to work with semi-autonomous work groups, as distinct from individual workers); as a result, the potential benefits of the changes were vitiated (Miller, 1975). So there is much evidence to suggest the 'Speakers' Corner' syndrome: power holders accommodate radical or dissenting views by providing a limited, legitimate outlet for their expression – thereby encapsulating the threat to their power and, as a bonus, demonstrating their liberality.

Unions as established power holders may also obstruct such innovations. Here the position is more complex. They can argue persuasively that management's motivation in introducing innovations in the work organization is not entirely altruistic, that management simply wants to screw more effort out of workers. Moreover, it is more difficult for unions to command the loyalty of workers with high job satisfaction. Whether or not diminution of union power is an overt intention of management in endorsing these developments, it is often a consequence. It is a common belief on both sides of the boundary that less power for the unions means more power for management. The notion that it is the workers actually involved in a programme of, say, job enlargement who gain in power may be given lip service but is not always borne out behaviourally. Our own experience of interventions has been that unions' anxieties about losing power are often voiced in the negotiation of a project, and they sometimes succeed in blocking it by limiting their members' participation.

However, the resistance has not been located only in the union. Managers contemplating an experimental change that might involve greater exercise of authority and discretion by subordinates are seldom unambivalent. Given the available management–union split, differences of views within management tend to get suppressed, and unvoiced doubts and objections can be and are projected onto the unions – the 'common enemy' syndrome.

Our experience further suggests that, as an intervention goes forward and shows signs of 'success' in the sense that employees are operating with greater authority, it is management rather than the union that is anxious about a threat to its power. In one instance, colleagues and I worked over a period of five years with a subsidiary company of a larger group. (For a fuller account of this intervention, see Miller, 1977 and Khaleelee and Miller, 1985: Chapters 11 and 13 in this volume.) Within eighteen months outcomes were impressive: internal coordination improved; chronic problems got solved; there was a general increase in self-confidence and purposefulness, especially in transactions across the boundary of the organization with group headquarters; and, more concretely, there was a surge in manufacturing output and profits. In addition to providing consultancy and training for a range of internal groups, including the executive management team and a joint trade union committee, we had some success in creating a 'space' in which people in the organization, regardless of level, could take up what we called a 'third role' – not as members of a work group or as union members but as 'citizens' of the organization as a community, from which they could reconsider their actions and attitudes in their other two roles. This 'space' approximated what Winnicott (1960, p. 150), in the passage quoted earlier, described as 'an area that is intermediate between the dream and the reality' – an area of play, of the use of symbols, of emergent creativity. (With the schizoid defence, no such space is available between external conformity to normative reality and internal flight into infantile fantasy.) Progressively more employees became involved in the programme, and it was evident that we helped many people recognize that they could use their authority to influence the operation of the organization and their own roles in it in creative ways. Financial results continued to be impressive; and, in relation to the larger group of companies, having started out at the bottom of the league in terms of profits, our client was now at or near the top. What my colleagues and I had not sufficiently taken into account was that this achievement was a threat, both to other subsidiaries in the group, whose managers were being pressed for higher performance, and, more importantly, to group management. Our client organization was guilty of cultural deviance. Elsewhere in the group, the dependency culture of compliance and conformity prevailed; here it was one of exercising authority and taking initiatives. Headquarters perceived this as insubordination, since the assertion of competence undermined the hierarchy of status. The fact that effective decisions were being made was less important than who was making them. Group management applied various forms of pressure on the management of the subsidiary to close down the programme, and so consultancy came to an end.

It is therefore extremely tempting to interpret this outcome and others like it solely in terms of the threat to executive power and to postulate that if we, as consultants, had been politically more astute we would have acted to co-opt group management in supporting the programme: 'Organizational development cannot be effective without also being a political activity, involving changes in the distribution of power' (Miller, 1979b, p. 231). My proposition here, however, is that this threat, though a major part of the story, is not the whole of it. Members of our client organization were not just innocent victims of a coercive top management. Even the staunchest supporters of the programme were not without ambivalence, and when headquarters closed it down, their response of shock and dismay carried undertones of relief.

Elsewhere, Lawrence (1979) has reported on another project in which he and I were involved – in this case the design of a new factory based on semi-autonomous work groups. Again, it had all the appearance of a success story. The new work groups fully demonstrated the influence of autonomy on productivity and satisfaction, and they were progressively enlarging their range of activities. In this case management terminated the project, saying explicitly that it had 'gone far enough'. Indeed, at various times some managers had voiced anxieties that the project might put them out of a job. Again, therefore, it seemed that the threat to managerial power was the stumbling block. But in this case, too, our interpretation was that there was something more. As Lawrence put it:

> The other reason probably lies with the workers. On what journey was this project to take them? While they could and did express a high degree of satisfaction with conditions in the new factory, it may be that the demands were too high . . . My hypothesis is . . . that the project and its new work experiences put into disarray the taken-for-granted assumptions made by most workers about the relatedness between themselves and management [– management in its meanings] both as a status and political aggregate and as a process. (1979, p. 246)

These two cases are not atypical. At one level management, as what Lawrence calls a 'political aggregate', was undoubtedly concerned to protect its power and status. But at another level, there was also collusion to maintain management at the apex of a dependent hierarchy. As I have written elsewhere about the former case:

> Opportunities [for employees] to reflect, to question, and to innovate are exciting; but they are also a threat to primitive needs for security and dependency. Those needs lie in all of us and are met by stable institutional structures and cultures. Upsetting those structures raises anxiety [in employees] that their schizoid defences will break down and their destructive impulses will erupt into violence and chaos. Reassertion of control by headquarters served to patch up the defences. (Miller, 1983, p. 17)

One further point needs to be made. It can be argued, perhaps, that workers' resistance to innovations of the kinds discussed here results not from the schizoid defence but from the operation of much more straightforward instrumental values. That is to say, workers seek to minimize their involvement in the work-place because their interests, satisfactions, and indeed their identity are invested in their lives outside. This would be the embourgeoisement thesis. I can certainly think of examples, but my impression is that they are a minority. Supportive evidence for the wide prevalence of the schizoid defence comes from studies of what happens to people when they lose their jobs. If instrumental values predominated, the main problem posed by unemployment would be reduction of income. But a study in which I recently took part in West Yorkshire (Khaleelee and Miller, 1984) confirmed the findings of other research that money is, though a problem, not the major one. Over and over again, people equated employment with respect (self-respect and respect of others) and unemployment with worthlessness. Depression, diminished mental functioning, impotence, mental illness, marital breakdown – these well-documented consequences of unemployment are not consistent with the instrumental theory, which posits an identity securely placed outside the world of employment. The other significant concern demonstrated in the West Yorkshire study, as in others, is that employment is equated with order, while unemployment is equated with anarchy. Couple this evidence with the frequent observation on the behaviour of unemployed men – that they shut their front doors, watch television, and never come out except to collect their dole – and it appears that the hypothesis of the schizoid defence is only too well confirmed.

My argument in this section, therefore, is that between the late 1940s and the late 1970s Britain in general and employing organizations in particular were characterized by a pervasive and collusive dependency culture. (And it may well be that the shifting values in society, especially during the 1960s, which generated uncertainty and left the individual less secure about his or her own identity, actually increased the implicit demand that work organizations should meet needs for dependency and security.) The dependency culture was sustained in two ways: structurally, through the almost ritualized split between unions and management, which provided a safe outlet for destructive impulses that might otherwise have imperilled the hierarchical structure; and intrapersonally, through the schizoid defence, which also protected the structure by passive, compliant conformity – to the employing organization or to the union, as the immediate circumstances demanded. In total, there was an integrated defensive system in the classical sense (Jaques, 1955; Menzies, 1960), and it is hardly surprising that interventions based on 'autonomy' values should be difficult to sustain.

FAILED DEPENDENCY

High employment was a major element in the culture of dependency. Until the early 1970s, the rate of unemployment was typically below 3 per cent, which meant that, even though the size of the labour force was increasing by nearly 0.5 per cent per annum (and for women at a much faster rate), virtually everyone seeking a job could get one; and the numbers of long-term unemployed, those out of work for over a year, were considerably below 1 per cent of the labour force. (Given such a low rate of unemployment, the low level of job mobility at all levels is telling evidence of a dependency culture.) Between 1974 and 1976, unemployment doubled (from 2.6 to 5.4 per cent) and it remained at just over 5 per cent until 1979. This was felt to be immorally high. Moreover, the rate of inflation was escalating; the country's competitiveness overseas was declining; the manufacturing industry was in particular difficulty; and there was widespread recognition that Britain's economy was in a mess.

In electing the first Thatcher government in 1979, after the Labour party had been in power for eleven of the previous fifteen years, the voters were almost explicitly asking to be punished for their infantile greed. Margaret Thatcher had warned that productivity was too low and wages too high and that she was going to make the country live within its means. There was much talk of having to take nasty medicine. Few people foresaw, however, how nasty the deepening recession would make it. In 1979 registered unemployment stood at just under 1.3 million; by the beginning of 1983, it passed 3.2 million (13.5 per cent) though most economists put the true figure nearer 4 million – about one-sixth of the work force. Employment in manufacturing had fallen dramatically. Within three years it had shed one-fifth of its remaining labour – nearly 1.5 million people. Long-term unemployment had risen to over 1 million, more than one-third of the jobless total; and, despite the big expenditure on youth training and other schemes for young people, more than a quarter of this number were under twenty-five.

The nasty medicine had other side effects. Cuts in education expenditure, ending of free school meals for children from low-income families, greatly increased prescription charges in the Health Service, and a host of other measures combined to suggest that the welfare state was being eroded (see Stern, 1982). Nor did it pass unnoticed that such measures impinged most heavily on those with the lowest incomes, while changes in the structure of taxation made people in the higher income brackets not only relatively but also in real terms far better off.

Since 1980 OPUS has been attempting to identify underlying preoccupations, concerns, and processes in society, using a fairly crude methodology. Associate staff, who are based in different parts of the country, meet every three months to pool their observations and experiences; their shared perceptions and emerging hypotheses are reviewed by a forum consisting of a cross-section of people from very different walks of life; data are amplified through meetings of other linked groups; and the results are published in a quarterly *Bulletin*, which is intended to offer readers a reference point – OPUS's understanding of what is happening – against which they can begin to think about their own part in processes of which they may not be fully aware. Here I will describe briefly a few, mostly recurrent, themes that appear to be responses to failed dependency. (I am drawing heavily on Khaleelee and Miller, 1983.)

One continuing theme has been withdrawal and retreat – hiding from reality. This is manifested in all sorts of ways. The world of entertainment has always played into nostalgia for a fantasied Golden Age, but this appears to have been accentuated since 1980. Television, for example, has produced a crop of plays and other programmes set in the eighteenth and nineteenth centuries. Cinema has offered escape to a supernatural or idealized future (*Star Wars, The Empire Strikes Back, The Alien, Close Encounters, E.T.*) or to a mythical and magical past (*The Sword and the Sorcerer, Excalibur, The Dark Crystal*) – films that present in an extravagant way the archetypal struggle between good and evil. Best-selling books have had a similar quality. Architecture, interior decoration (for example, of pubs), and even gardens have gone back to the 1930s or to Victorian fashions. In organizations, too, the phenomenon of withdrawal has been pronounced. I shall come back to this point later.

A second dominant theme has been fear of the nuclear holocaust and people's impotence in face of it. For a minority the peace movement and the Campaign for Nuclear Disarmament (CND) have provided the reassurance of togetherness and the release of action to mitigate the anxiety; and the sisterhood of the Greenham Common women, sustaining continuous protest at the US Cruise missile base, has supplied a model of potency that cannot be ignored. But for most the Bomb remains a diffuse threat, sometimes acknowledged, often repressed – a sword of Damocles under which they somehow have to go on living. This allows the individual to feel, or to behave, as if there is no point in doing anything himself as a citizen because it is all futile: a dreadful uncontrollable force may wipe him out. Voicing of the fear and support for the CND seem to be closely correlated with the increase in unemployment and the linked fear of the employed that they will be made redundant. So there are grounds for postulating that the individual's sense of impotence in relation to British society and indeed to the rest of the world is being projected onto the nuclear threat. The real threat is also a vivid symbol.

Third, society's anger and fear have been split off to be carried selectively by the young and the blacks. Aggression and nihilism in the wider society have been expressed through punk culture, skinheads, or the National Front. The 1981 riots in parts of Liverpool and London (with 'copycat' disturbances elsewhere) were more concentrated expressions of anger and rage. There was a mounting fear that violence could sweep out of the inner-city ghettoes into the middle-class dormitories. The convenient familiar myth is that the young and the blacks are intrinsically unstable and violent. The fact that society has so arranged its affairs as to impose the brunt of increased unemployment on to these groups, and therefore deserves retribution, obviously generates fears of spreading violence but is seldom explicitly acknowledged. (See Note, pp. 314-5.) By a similar process of splitting, Northern Ireland continues to serve the rest of Britain as a repository of violence, and this is not perceived as having any connection with a level of urban unemployment that has long been the highest in the UK.

A fourth theme has been the identification of a 'real' enemy against whom the population could enact its anger. The crisis over the Falklands was a convenient vehicle. Because of the war, for example, dock workers decided to refrain from striking; but once the fighting with the Argentinians was over, the industrial disputes at home resumed. So the apparent collusion with Argentina to fight over the Falklands provided the governments of both countries with short-term palliatives for domestic dissatisfaction and disintegration. Momentarily, the British knew who they were again. When the excitement died down, the old feelings and problems returned: impotence, worthlessness, apathy.

The phenomena just outlined – withdrawal and retreat, impotence in the face of nuclear annihilation, displacement of aggression into social sub-groups, and creation of an external enemy – can be interpreted as societal defence mechanisms developed to cope with the anxiety, fear, and anger generated by the experience of failed dependency. The state, the institution of employment, and the trade unions have all three displayed themselves as unreliable in meeting needs for dependency and security. Church and family – the other institutions with the traditional function of catering for dependency – are, respectively, discredited and beleaguered. And the fundamentalist religious movements, which have been burgeoning in many parts of the world and which serve to sweep away uncertainty and to confer on the individual a clear-cut set of meanings, have so far gained little ground in Britain.

Returning now to look specifically at the phenomenon of withdrawal and retreat in relation to employment institutions, we can see that there was, of course, an immense amount of involuntary withdrawal. Whole departments and even whole factories were closed down, with massive redundancies, or layoffs. 'Reducing head count', 'shedding labour', and – a particularly telling *double entendre* – 'demanning' were the terminology of the times. In some large organizations, including some nationalized enterprises and also universities, an attempt was made to manage the process with kid gloves. A major chemical company, for example, spent large sums to find highly paid jobs in the Middle East for surplus employees. Also, such organizations set up generous and costly schemes for early retirement and voluntary resignations. What surprised many personnel managers, particularly at the beginning of the recession, was the eagerness with which these offers were taken up: there was a rush for the door. Doubtless many volunteers were bemused and seduced by the size of the offers (if take-home pay, after tax and other deductions, is £100 a week or less, £20,000 tax free seems like a fortune), but this was the first indication that at least some people regarded employment as less of a privilege or even necessity than employers may have imagined. In other organizations, large and small, dismissals were much more arbitrary and the terms much less generous. Instead of the caring family model in employment, we were back to the military model with a vengeance: casualties are inevitable; people have to be thrown out of the boat so that it can continue to float. Some managements quite openly enjoyed the opportunity to reassert their power *vis-à-vis* the unions. (Excessive power of the unions had, of course, been one of the planks on which the Conservative government had been elected in 1979, thereby undermining the Bullock report, which two years previously had proposed a significant shift toward industrial democracy in British industry ([Bullock Report], 1977). However, even among overtly more circumspect and generous employers, the high price they were prepared to pay to shed labour suggested that they were at least as much concerned with assertion of power as with restoring economic viability.

Apart from the involuntary and voluntary leavers, withdrawal was also manifested by those who remained in employment. 'Don't stick your neck out'; 'keep your head down'; 'keep your nose clean'; 'cover your arse': those were the prescriptions for survival, expressed in stark physical terms, as if one's own body were at risk. This also became manifest in the Tavistock Institute's group relations conferences: preoccupation with learning the 'rules', the 'right' ways of behaving, so as to 'get by'; distrust of groups and a search for safety in secret pairs and trios; privatization of learning generated at the conference and a strong resistance to the idea of applying it to roles at work. Correspondingly, in these outside roles, a consistent theme has been a withdrawal of identification with the outer boundary of the organization and a falling back onto smaller groupings to support the individual's identity and need for meaning. The notion of loyalty to the firm gets eroded when a person fears that he himself may be the next for the axe; yet he also has to deny his vulnerability. One widely observed phenomenon has been the severance of contact with the victims of redundancy – a tendency among those remaining to obliterate the fact of their existence. The groups left behind close their boundaries even more tightly. 'Enclave' became a word of the times. Such 'survivor' groups may also cross the boundaries of the organization. Survival, however, is not the only connecting link. It is sometimes reported that such groups, almost conspiratorially, experience a regeneration of creativity, which had been blocked in the larger structure. Members of such groups gain a new confirmation of their individual identity. More commonly, however, survivors seek to derive their identity negatively from their position of 'non-unemployment'; besides seeking increased material rewards, which will further differentiate them economically from those (including ex-colleagues) who are on the dole, they are inclined to adopt that set of values which defines 'the unemployed' collectively as inadequate, lazy, and shiftless: 'They could get a job if they tried.' The fact that they themselves have jobs can then be attributed to their own merit and virtue.

POST-DEPENDENCY AND EMPLOYMENT INSTITUTIONS

Failed dependency may be thought of in terms of the predicament of an infant being abandoned or even assaulted by hitherto dependable parents, yet also aware that this is a fate he has brought upon himself by his own greed and destructiveness. He is outraged and terrified, angry and depressed, and in a state of shock does not know what to do with his conflicting feelings. How to survive? The aspect I am particularly concerned with here is the loss of well-established meanings and ways of coping. Failed dependency may be seen as a transitional phase, in which that loss is being dealt with and acceptable new meanings and coping mechanisms begin to emerge. I postulate that a post-dependency culture is just beginning to take shape in British society. The most recent (1985) evidence, mainly from the soundings of OPUS, indicates that, although the crisis is far from over, new models may be coming forward; and these new models have profound implications for the relatedness of the individual to the employing organization.

Executive power and authority, as they have been conventionally conceived and exercised, are called into question.

A first observation is that the nostalgic element of withdrawal and retreat is moving into living memory, instead of lying in a prenatal past. Britain's most popular TV serial, *The Jewel in the Crown*, was set in the 1940s. So also were the extraordinary celebrations of the fortieth anniversary of the invasion of Normandy: whatever the political motivations of the national leaders, the immense media coverage beforehand indicated that a popular chord was being touched. Undoubtedly, there was a big element of harking back to the days when Britain could boast an empire and win a war. But *The Jewel* also portrayed the less creditable aspects of the British in India – racial discrimination, oppression, and torture; and the Normandy celebrations underlined Britain's dependence on its Western allies in defeating Germany. A possible hypothesis, therefore, is that, alongside an escapist flight to largely imaginary past glories, there is emerging a need to incorporate the past into the present. The 1983 Beatles revival, followed by a growing preoccupation with the meaning of the 1960s, supports the hypothesis.

The major strike of the National Union of Mineworkers against the National Coal Board in 1984 seemed to suggest that splitting, polarization, and fight were alive and well. It was an up-to-date conflict with archetypal overtones, a struggle between good and evil; unlike the *Star Wars* films, however, the strike enabled onlookers to choose for themselves which was good and which was evil. Was the hero Arthur Scargill, the mine workers' leader, who was defending a major industry and the workers in it from a government determined to destroy the mines and miners and using police brutality as an instrument of repression? Or was the hero/heroine Ian MacGregor/Margaret Thatcher (mainly the latter), who was introducing economic rationality at last and reasserting law and order against the use of violence by the miners' pickets? The fight continued so long because it offered the public such splendid opportunities for the vicarious experience of potency: either Scargill or Thatcher could be used as the bad object, to be blamed for all sorts of felt grievances that had nothing to do with coal. And perhaps also it was a last plea for continuing dependency culture. If my parents are divorcing, I have to pin my hopes on one of them: was it to be mother (Thatcher) or father (Scargill)?

On the other hand, in parallel with this pattern of splitting, action, and confrontation, which is seen as the 'male' mode, there is evidence of an upsurge in the 'female' mode, which is orientated more towards process; toleration of uncertainty; integration and synthesis; and also a longer-term perspective, a preparedness to wait, to make do. There is a high correlation between the two modes and the two genders. (Thatcher is a frequently cited exception – variously admired, hated, and envied because she out-males the men.) Certainly there are signs that women are becoming contemptuous of men's posturing, of the seriousness with which they take their little games. Greenham Common is a continuous reminder that women can manage without men. Employment institutions have told a great many men that they are not needed; now men are beginning to get the same message from women.

All this, I suggest, has a bearing on the basis of individual identity, particularly male identity, and on the relatedness of the individual to the organization. The schizoid defence was part of the collusive preservation of a belief in the dependability of the employing organization, or at least of the institution of employment, as a satisfier, or satisficer, of multiple needs: for structure and order, for affirmation, and for money. The work-role embedded in a hierarchy met dependency needs; the role of union member offered the experience of solidarity, power, and a vehicle for expressing fight. But the costs were high – alienation from the work itself; the experience of coercion – and the defence was a necessary coping mechanism to sustain the system. Widespread experience of unemployment has shown all too vividly the centrality of employment in conferring on the individual from outside a sense of identity, self-worth, and potency. (During the West Yorkshire study, one refrain of many women was 'A man's not a real man unless he's got a job.') Correspondingly, it confirmed the operation of the schizoid defence by showing how many individuals evidently lacked an identity built around inner resources. A great many unemployed men (and here I am explicitly discussing men, not women) want only to get back into a job and can envisage no other way of being.

Massive unemployment, however, has also exploded the myth of the dependability of work organizations. Those men who do get back into a job are conscious of its precariousness and tend to adopt the 'heads-down' strategy of survival described earlier. In addition, there is evidence that a growing number of people can and do survive without employment. Alternative role-models are multiplying. Here I identify five.

Least salubrious of these models is that of passing the time, of existing without purpose. Being without doing can be a difficult and challenging process of self-examination and self-development; but the pattern I am identifying here is one of drifting from day to day. The followers of this way of life include many long-term unemployed men, especially in towns that industries have deserted, and a large set of young people. They are the casualties of failed dependency, not valued by society, not valuing themselves, surviving on state benefits and, often, petty crime. Among the younger of these lost generations, the hedonistic search for pleasure and excitement increasingly leads to drugs.

However, the remaining four role-models all reflect real and positive alternatives to the conventional concept of employment.

Self-employment – selling one's skills directly – is the obvious alternative. For some accustomed to the dependency of employment, the shift to independence and self-management is too big to make, but those who achieve it tend to report that they work harder while experiencing much greater satisfaction. The spouse is often at least partly involved; and Asian and other immigrants have displayed the success of family businesses in the full sense of the term.

The third model is not tied to a specific profession or trade but to making a livelihood through a mix of activities, part planned, part opportunistic. Often, though not always, this mixture of activities falls within the 'black economy'; state benefits provide the basic income.

Whereas these latter two are both economic models in that the primary concern is to make money, in the fourth model it is what one does that is primary. Its proponents are devoted to an activity, a cause, a set of values: making music, getting further education, doing voluntary work, campaigning for clean air. If such activities do not generate income, these individuals get by on the dole or through part-time or occasional earnings.

Finally, the fifth is the mixed model – that is, adopting different models at different phases of one's life: a period in full-time employment, a spell pursuing a chosen activity, another phase in a part-time job, and so on. If this model sounds familiar, that is because it has been a common model among women (the intervening 'activity', of course, being child rearing); and its availability has partly cushioned them from the demoralizing effects of unemployment. Only now is it beginning to be perceived as a viable option for men too.

All this may well imply, as many people said during the West Yorkshire study, that the Protestant work ethic is breaking down, that we are in the throes of the much-heralded paradigm shift. (For an important discussion of this, see Emery, 1982.) However, I am more immediately concerned with the growing evidence that it is the employment ethic – the notion that the normal and proper thing for a man to do is to devote his life to full-time paid employment – that is breaking down. The separability of 'work' and 'employment' is beginning to be recognised. For example, the West Yorkshire study (Khaleelee and Miller, 1984) exposed 'a feeling that much of what is done in "employment" . . . isn't "work" in the sense of doing something that you can feel is creative, or even useful' (p. 28), along with acknowledgement that 'a great deal of work which is useful or indeed essential to society is done outside employment' (p. 29) – child rearing being an obvious example.

For the individual, this paradigm shift means reconstructing his or her identity on different bases – forming a new integration of past and present, inside and outside, and even 'male' and 'female'. Undoubtedly, the collapse of the dependency culture, by undermining the schizoid defence, has produced many casualties. These are people who had invested their 'false selves' in enactment of organizational roles; and when these roles are removed, their other selves are trapped in an autistic inner world. There are nevertheless signs that many others are moving toward a fresh and constructive integration.

Essentially, high unemployment is producing a much more penetrating questioning of taken-for-granted assumptions about the institution of employment, not just by academics but by employees themselves, at various levels, struggling to cope with their day-to-day experience. I postulate that one significant outcome of their experience of the last five years is the demolition of the myth of authority. My argument runs as follows: Social order in the work organization has been sustained through legitimation of a hierarchy of managerial authority, with a consonant structure of status and rewards. Supervisors and junior managers in the lower reaches of the hierarchy, where there were some discrepancies between remuneration and authority, have been co-opted, as we have seen, through admission to the management 'club' and the implied promise of promotion within it. Continued economic growth until the early 1970s and beyond produced enough actual evidence of promotion to make this implied promise credible. It could be believed that competence would be recognized and rewarded and that by and large there was a correlation between level of competence and level of authority. Evident cases of noncorrelation could be accepted as exceptions and aberrations from the norm; basically, cream would rise to the top. With the shift to zero growth and then retrenchment, first there was a reduction in upward mobility and then many managers discovered that club membership made them no less vulnerable than workers to the exigencies of redundancy. Not merely individuals but whole levels of management were eliminated; and many others at the lower levels justifiably felt insecure. Moreover, the processes through which some managed to secure their positions while others were extruded have displayed that competence is often a less important factor than influence and patronage. Surviving junior and middle managers, with diminished scope for promotion themselves, therefore become much more conscious of the discrepancies between competence and authority; and, as the underlying relationships of power and domination become more obvious, the myth of legitimated authority is eroded. The underlying master–servant model is uncovered – and they, too, are servants.

Disillusionment, therefore, may be almost as prevalent among those who remain in organizations as among those who have been made redundant. Whereas the relatedness of the worker to the organization (and 'worker' here includes many technical and administrative staff) had tended to be one of passive compliance along with schizoid withdrawal, the self-perception of the line manager more typically resided in his exercise of authority and his place in a structure of authority and status, which it was his duty and in his interest to defend. Now there is as much pressure on him as there has been on the rest to be compliant in order to survive, except that he also has to go beyond that and display energy, enthusiasm, and commitment that he does not necessarily feel.

Among employees at all levels, there is a continuing attempt to hold on to accustomed defences and myths, but in the face of the palpable shifts both outside and inside the organization, these are becoming more difficult to sustain. To survive as a person (as distinct from simply avoiding losing one's job), there is a need to create a new set of meanings around which to reconstruct one's identity. These meanings, to be viable, cannot afford to rest at all heavily on the organizational role; they have to be built on a new integration of internal resources and external affiliations. The consequent relatedness to the organization is much more consciously and genuinely instrumental. And it is sustained by an internal conviction that the individual could survive and make a sufficient livelihood outside that organization and possibly outside any organization.

To the extent that the individual is able to dispense with organizational position as a prop to his identity, he is in a position of strength, from which real choices can be made. He is able in a fuller sense exercise his personal authority. (I conceptualize 'personal authority' as a function of managing oneself in relation to role and task performance, while 'power' is concerned with maintenance and enhancement of status and with control over other people.) In doing so, because his personal functioning is less keyed into defensive use of the structure and culture provided by the social system, he is less constrained by unconscious anxieties and dependent needs. On the one hand, he can choose calculated compliance: to support the objectives and norms of the organization only insofar as is necessary to serve his own, externally orientated, objectives. On the other hand, he can choose to exercise his authority in the service of the task of the organization and derive ego satisfaction from pursuing competence and excellence in role performance. This is the more risky option, since commitment to task does not necessarily mean, and indeed is unlikely to mean, commitment to the prevailing power structure or to the established ways of doing things. Although he does not set out to tilt against the system (my ideal type corresponds rather to Winnicott's description, quoted earlier, of 'the healthy individual who has a compliant aspect of the self . . . and who is a creative and spontaneous being'), he will often be taking a critical stance and his behaviour may well be perceived as insubordinate.

Commitment to task is sorely needed by the managements of today's organizations. Given the complexity of the problems to be tackled and the adaptive capability that is required, they cannot afford to go on giving a monopoly of creativity only to a few selected individuals (see Miller, 1983). In the past, when British managements have talked of the need for commitment to task, they have tended to behave as if the qualities they were really looking for were loyalty and obedience to themselves. Particularly in the newer technologies, with the knowledge base increasingly dispersed, the myth of omniscience at the top of the hierarchy is untenable; hence, obedience is the kiss of organizational death.

The idea (or ideal) of the individual exercising authority to manage himself in his role is far from new. For example, it has been the mainspring of the Tavistock Institute's Group Relations Training Programme since the 1960s and has guided much of the Institute's organizational consultancy (see Miller and Rice, 1967; Lawrence and Miller, 1976; Miller, 1977; Lawrence, 1979). It is also consistent with Maslow's (1970) conception of self-actualization. This orientation lay behind the innovative forms of work organization, such as semi-autonomous work groups, which have proved so difficult to sustain. The question is whether now, in what appears to be a rather different social and economic environment, there will be greater acceptance of a culture in which authority derived from task performance carries more weight than superordination/ subordination.

Schwartz (1983), in a recent review of Maslow's theories, takes a pessimistic stance: 'One might even hypothesize that those organizations that most require persons at the self-actualized level are least likely to tolerate them, since organizations whose myths are in danger of collapsing, who most need clear perception and creativity, are likely to feel most threatened by it' (p. 952). Dickson (1983) draws attention to one of the central myths: *'Managers believe they are the cause of subordinates' behaviour* at the same time [as] they believe in equality and democracy as a principle of life in society' (p. 927; emphasis added). A great superstructure of 'motivation theory' has been erected on this rather shaky premiss. 'Participation', on the face of it, recognizes and values the potential contribution of all employees to ways of improving performance of the task; but in practice it is often operated as a 'velvet-glove' strategy to obtain employees' acceptance of managerial decisions that have already been made. The persistence of the managerial behaviour that reflects these myths and assumptions, despite the efforts of many change agents and management educators, would therefore seem to justify Schwartz's pessimism.

Moreover, as we have also seen, many British managements seized the economic recession as an opportunity to reduce union power and exercise tighter control over the work-force. Far from encouraging employees to use their own authority, they were demanding greater compliance.

However, there is another, slightly more optimistic, perspective. Managerial behaviour is not a product simply of the kinds of people who occupy managerial roles, or of past processes of education, training, and socialization to which they have been subjected; it occurs in the context of a social system. The structure and culture of that system must be consonant with the behaviour and even reinforce it; otherwise, it could not be sustained. I argued earlier that, although 'resistance to change' can be attributed to managements' defence of power and status, the perceived 'beneficiaries' of changes – subordinates gaining more authority and discretion – are often ambivalent. In other words, there is a collusion, largely unconscious, to maintain the *status quo*, with its hierarchy of power and privilege. This is central to the dependency culture: there has to be the parental figure to receive the projections of love/hate, responsibility, and blame. If I am correct in postulating that British industry and society generally are moving out of that dependency culture, through a phase of failed dependency and toward 'post-dependency', and that an increasing number of employees are shifting into a more genuinely instrumental, 'take-it-or-leave-it' relatedness to the employing organization, then that collusion is beginning to be undermined. Exercise of personal authority should become less ambivalent and more legitimate.

Although gross economic and socio-political changes have occurred in Britain in the last five years, changes in culture and attitudes move much more slowly. I certainly do not predict a sweeping, rapid change. As Schwartz indicates, many managements are likely to cling fatally long to patterns of the dependency culture. Many employees, too, will be reluctant to surrender their dependency. But, as the pressures of the collusion diminish, a growing number of managers will be freer to recognize that the people working with them are not quite the same animals as ten years ago, that the belief that they are 'the cause of subordinates' behaviour' is not quite so tenable, and that conventional theories of motivation and indeed of organization seem less and less appropriate. The new technologies do not of themselves make hierarchies dispensable, but they certainly flatten them, by calling into question the function of middle-management layers.

This process will be at times a turbulent one. Genuine empowerment is not something that can be given by management in controlled doses; it is taken by individuals who use their own authority to speak out, without necessarily waiting for permission. The leadership required of management is to define the task and to equip groups and individuals with the requisite resources so that they can manage themselves to perform it. If in that way the task itself becomes the leader, hallowed concepts such as subordination, obedience, and personal loyalty become outmoded and are replaced by negotiation between adults responsible for managing the boundaries of their respective systems and sub-systems. This is not the familiar labour relations negotiation about pay and conditions; it is negotiation among people in their work-roles about performance of the task. It is the task, and their competence in relation to it, that confers their authority on them.

It may well be, therefore, that a steadily increasing proportion of those now in employment, at all levels, will be perceiving themselves and expecting to be treated as, in effect, professionals. There is already a growing use of self-employed individuals and groups to undertake on a contractual basis work previously done by employees; and that trend may call into question existing assumptions about ways in which employees are managed. More conventional types of industrial and commercial organizations might usefully look for alternative models in those organizations that use large number of professionals – for example, universities and medical institutions, in which executive power tends to be more problematic.

Although the obvious need to experiment with new forms of work organization and management will understandably raise the anxiety of many managers, it may be comforting to realize that they are not moving into entirely unexplored territory. The kinds of innovation that, despite their apparent success, met resistance in the 1960s and 1970s are no less relevant today, and they should fare much better with the decline of the dependency culture. And I believe that the pay-offs from reconnecting personal authority to the task of the enterprise can be very substantial.

NOTE

In the West Yorkshire study referred to earlier, the governmental Manpower Services Commission (MSC), which runs the major youth programmes, proved to be a universal scapegoat: 'The MSC is blamed if it provides realistic work experience and blamed if it doesn't; it's blamed if it offers training and blamed if it doesn't.' We concluded: 'Evidently the parental generation has ambivalent feelings towards the school-leaving generation: it wants the kids to have a decent future but sees them as a threat to adult jobs. That's hard to acknowledge: it's easier to put the blame on MSC' (Khaleelee and Miller, 1984, p. 16). In this context, it is hardly surprising that a comparative study of British and American students, carried out in 1982–83, showed the British as more cynical and as having significantly less belief in the responsiveness of the political system to the individual as an active participant. 'Above all, [the British students] appear to regard present political institutions and their incumbents as lacking in legitimacy' (Ranade and Norris, 1984,

p. 56). The British sample was shown to be distributed around the borderline between 'protest participant' (those who believed that they could affect their situation) and 'disgruntled apathetic' (those who believed that they could not).

PUBLICATIONS OF ERIC MILLER (EXCLUDING MINOR ARTICLES AND REVIEWS)

Place of publication is London unless otherwise indicated.

(1950) 'Dead, disposal of the'; 'Headhunting'; 'India: anthropology' (sections). *Chambers Encyclopaedia.* George Newnes.

(1954) 'Caste and territory in Malabar', *American Anthropologist* 56:410–20.

(1955) 'Village structure in North Kerala', in M.N. Srinivas, ed. *India's Villages.* Calcutta: West Bengal Government Press, pp. 39–50. Second (revised) edition: Asia Publishing House, 1960.

(1959) 'Technology, territory and time: the internal differentiation of complex production systems', *Human Relations* 12:243–72. Reprinted in H.E. Frank, ed. *Organization Structuring.* McGraw-Hill, 1971, pp. 81–115. Also in F. Baker, ed. *Organizational Systems: General Systems Approaches to Complex Organizations.* Homewood, IL: Irwin, 1973, pp. 261–94. Also in W.A. Pasmore and J.J. Sherwood, eds *Sociotechnical Systems: A Sourcebook.* La Jolla, CA.: University Associates, 1978, pp. 96–119. Edited version in E. Trist and H. Murray, eds *The Social Engagement of Social Science: A Tavistock Anthology*, vol. 2, *The Socio-Technical Perspective.* Philadelphia, PA: University of Pennsylvania Press, 1993, pp. 385–404. Abridged version, 'A socio-technical conceptual scheme', in P.A. Lawrence *et al.*, eds *Organizational Behaviour and Administration.* Homewood, IL: Dorsey Press, 1961, pp. 560–69.

(1963) Bridger, H., Miller, E.J. and O'Dwyer, J.J. *The Doctor and Sister in Industry: A Study of Change.* Macmillan (Journals) Ltd, 1964. Reprinted from *Occupational Health*, 1963, 15, 1: 235–50, 2: 293–308.

(1964) 'Social factors in setting up new works', in *Association of British Chemical Manufacturers, Proceedings of Joint Conference on Human Factors and Productivity, Brighton 1964.* ABCM, pp. 15–35.

(1966) Miller, E.J. and Armstrong, D. 'The influence of advanced technology on the structure of management organization', in J. Stieber, ed. *Employment Problems of Automation and Advanced Technology: An International Perspective.* Proceedings of a conference held at Geneva by the International Institute for Labour Studies, 19–24 July, 1964. Macmillan, pp. 318–31.

(1967) Miller, E.J. and Rice, A.K. *Systems of Organization: Task and Sentient Systems and their Boundary Control.* Tavistock. Social Science Paperback edition, 1970, 1973. Introduction and Chapters 1–3, in A.D. Colman and W.H. Bexton, eds *Group Relations Reader.* Sausalito, CA: GREX, 1975, pp. 43–68. Chapters 9–10 reproduced (1988) as 'The family business in contemporary society', *Family Business Review* 1, 2:193–210. Chapters 20–21, in E. Trist and H. Murray, eds *The Social Engagement of Social Science: A Tavistock Anthology,* vol. 1, *The Socio-Psychological Perspective.* Philadelphia, PA: University of Pennsylvania Press/Free Association Books, 1990, pp. 259–71. See this vol., ch. 2, 'Task and organization in an airline', pp. 32–66.

(1971) Miller, E.J. and Gwynne, G.V. 'Facing up to our own problems', *Townswoman* 38:136–8. Reprinted (1974) by The European Centre for Leisure and Education, in *Society and Leisure* 1:203–14.

(1972) Miller, E.J. and Gwynne, G.V. *A Life Apart: A Pilot Study of Residential Institutions for the Physically Handicapped and the Young Chronic Sick.* Tavistock. Social Science Paperback edition, 1974. Translated into Norwegian as *A leve i institusjon.* Oslo: Gyldendal Norsk Forlag, 1974. Translated into Japanese, Tokyo: Sen Shobo, 1985. Extract in R. McLennan, *Managing Organizational Change.* Englewood Cliffs, NJ: Prentice-Hall, 1989, pp. 350–60.

(1973) Miller, E.J. and Gwynne, G.V. 'Dependence, independence and counter-dependence in residential institutions for incurables', in R.H. Gosling, ed. *Support, Innovation and Autonomy.* Tavistock, pp. 133–49. This vol. ch. 3, pp. 67–81.

(1973) Bridger, H., Mars, G., Miller, E.J., Scott, S. and Towell, D. *An Exploratory Study of the RCN Membership Structure.* Royal College of Nursing and National Council of Nurses of the United Kingdom.

(1975) 'Socio-technical systems in weaving, 1953–1970: a follow-up study', *Human Relations* 28:349–86. Also in W.A. Pasmore and J.J. Sherwood, eds *Socio-Technical Systems: A Sourcebook.* La Jolla, CA: University Associates, 1978, pp. 271–90. Revised version, 'The Ahmedabad experiment revisited: work organization in weaving, 1953–70', in C. Crouch and F. Heller, eds *International Yearbook of Organizational Democracy,* vol. 1, *Organizational Democracy and Political Processes.* Chichester: Wiley, 1983, pp. 155–79. Revised version, 'The Ahmedabad experiment revisited: work organization in weaving, 1953–70', in E. Trist and H. Murray, eds *The Social Engagement of Social Science: A Tavistock Anthology,* vol 2, *The Socio-Technical Perspective*. Philadelphia, PA. University of Pennsylvania Press, 1993, pp. 130-56.

(1975) 'Demands and problems of face-to-face work with people', in *Open University, A Post-experience Course, The Handicapped Person in the Community, Units 9-10. Block 3, Part I. Providing Supportive Services*. Milton Keynes: Open University Press, pp. 57-90.

(1976) Miller, E.J. ed. *Task and Organization*. Chichester: Wiley.

(1976) 'Role perspectives and the understanding of organizational behaviour', in E.J. Miller, ed. *Task and Organization*, pp. 1-18.

(1976) 'The open-system approach to organizational analysis, with special reference to the work of A.K. Rice', in G. Hofstede and M. Sami Kassem, eds *European Contributions to Organization Theory*. Assen/Amsterdam: Van Gorcum, pp. 43-61. See this vol., ch. 1, 'Values and concepts', pp. 3-23.

(1976) *Desarrollo Integral del Medio Rural: Un Experimento en Mexico* (Integrated Rural Development: A Mexican Experiment). Mexico DF: Fondo de Cultura Económica. Second impression, 1985.

(1977) 'Towards a model for integrated rural development in Latin America', *Linkage*, 2:8-9.

(1977) Dartington, T. and Miller, E.J. 'A brave face for the handicapped?', *Social Work Today* 9:9-10, 8 November.

(1977) 'Organizational development and industrial democracy: a current case-study', in C. Cooper, ed. *Organizational Development in the UK and USA: A Joint Evaluation*. Macmillan, pp. 31-63. Also in A.D. Colman and M.H. Geller, eds *Group Relations Reader 2*. Washington DC: A.K. Rice Institute, 1985, pp. 243-71. Extracts in R. McLennan, *Managing Organizational Change*. Englewood Cliffs, NJ: Prentice-Hall, 1989, pp. 91-92, 547-8, 549. See this vol., ch. 1, 'Values and concepts', pp. 3-23; ch. 11, 'An intervention in a manufacturing company', pp. 195-216.

(1978) 'Some reflections on the role of the diplomatic wife.' *Diplomatic Service Wives' Association Newsletter* Spring 1978: 13-27. This vol., ch. 7, pp. 132-45.

(1979) 'Autonomy, dependency and organizational change', in D. Towell and C. Harries, eds *Innovation in Patient Care: An Action Research Study of Change in a Psychiatric Hospital*. Croom Helm, pp. 172-90. See this vol., ch. 12, 'Innovation in a psychiatric hospital', pp. 217-37.

(1979) 'Open systems revisited: a proposition about development and change', in W.G. Lawrence, ed. *Exploring Individual and Organizational Boundaries: A Tavistock Open Systems Approach*. Chichester: Wiley, pp. 271-33. Edited version published as 'A "negotiating model" in integrated rural development projects', *Development Digest*, 9, 1, January 1981:66–76.

(1979) 'Conditions for development and change', *Studies in Environment Therapy* 3:17–24.

(1980) 'The politics of involvement', *Journal of Personality and Social Systems*, vol 2, nos 2–3:37–50. Also in A.D. Colman and M.H. Geller, eds *Group Relations Readers 2*. Washington DC: A.K. Rice Institute, 1985, pp. 383–98.

(1980) Lawrence, W.G. and Miller, E.J. 'Psychic and political constraints on the growth of industrial democracies'. Paper presented at the Seventh International Congress of Group Psychotherapy, Copenhagen, 3–8 August 1980; in M. Pines and L. Rafaelsen, eds *The Individual and the Group: Boundaries and Interrelations*. vol. 1, *Theory*. New York: Plenum, 1982, pp. 399–403.

(1980) Miller, E.J. and Norris, M.E. 'Planning processes for medical education and the health services in London', *Lancet* no. 8199, pp. 846–9. 18 October.

(1981) 'The role of the wife of Head of Mission, *Diplomatic Service Wives' Association Magazine*, Spring 1981: 13–27.

(1981) Dartington, T., Miller, E.J. and Gwynne, G. *A Life Together: The Distribution of Attitudes Around the Disabled*. Tavistock.

(1982) Aguilar Amilpa, E., Garduño Velasco, H. and Miller, E.J. 'Algunas tendencias en el manejo de sistemas hidráulicos en grandes urbes' ('Some trends in water management in large cities'), in G. Guerrero Villalobos, A. Moreno Fernandez, A. and H. Garduño Velasco, eds *El Sistema Hidráulico del Distrito Federal: Un Servicio Publico en Transición*. Mexico: Departamento del Distrito Federal, pp. 16.1–16.18.

(1983) Miller, E.J., Broadbent, J., Day, A., Khaleelee, O. and Pym, D. *Psychotherapists and the Process of Profession-Building*. OPUS.

(1983) *Work and Creativity*. Occasional Paper no. 6. Tavistock Institute of Human Relations.

(1984) Khaleelee, O. and Miller, E.J. *The Future of Work: A Report of the West Yorkshire Talkabout, July–November 1983*. Work & Society.

(1984) Khaleelee, O. and Miller, E.J. 'The decline of the protestant employment ethic', *The Modern Churchman* 27, 1:3–9.

(1985) Khaleelee, O. and Miller, E.J. 'Beyond the small group: society as an intelligible field of study', in M. Pines, ed. *Bion and Group Psychotherapy*. Routledge & Kegan Paul, pp. 353–83. This vol., ch. 13, pp. 243–72.

(1985) 'The human element', in *New Technology in Water Services*. Proceedings of a symposium organized by the Institute of Civil Engineers in London, 20–21 February 1985. Thomas Telford, pp. 129–38.

(1985) 'OPUS Conference Report: "After 1984: New Directions", September 28–29, 1985', OPUS *Bulletin* no 20–21, Part II. See this vol., ch. 14, 'Society in microcosm', pp. 273–80.

(1986) 'Making room for individual autonomy' in S. Srivastra and Associates, *Executive Power*. San Francisco, CA: Jossey-Bass, pp. 257–88. See this vol., ch. 15, 'Power, authority, dependency and cultural change', pp. 284–315.

(1986) 'OPUS Conference Report: "Society and the Inner City", March 8–9, 1986', *Bulletin* no 22–23, Part II. OPUS.

(1986) *Conflict and Reconciliation: The Newham Experiment*. Occasional Paper no. 9. Tavistock Institute of Human Relations.

(1987) 'Le "Conferenze di Leicester" del Tavistock Institute', in G. Contessa, et al. *T-Group: Storia e Teoria della 'Piu Significativa Invenzione Sociale del Secola'*. Milan: Clup, pp. 29–41.

(1987) Miller, E.J., contributor. Panel on Organizational Consultation. In J. Krantz, ed. *Irrationality in Social and Organizational Life: Proceedings of the Eighth A.K. Rice Scientific Meeting*. Washington DC: A.K. Rice Institute, pp. 32–5.

(1988) 'The study of organizational dynamics', in M. Aveline and W. Dryden, *Group Therapy in Britain*. Milton Keynes: Open University Press, pp. 208–32.

(1988) *Support For Self-help: the Origins and Development of the Self-Help Alliance*. COVAS Occasional Paper no. 1. Tavistock Institute of Human Relations.

(1988) Miller, E.J. and Webb, B. *The Nature of Effective Self-help Support in Difference Contexts*. COVAS Occasional Paper no. 2. Tavistock Institute of Human Relations.

(1989) 'Leicester Conferences after thirty years' (opening address), in *Contributions to Social and Political Science: Proceedings of the First International Symposium on Group Relations, Keble College, Oxford, 15–18 July 1988*. Washington DC: A.K. Rice Institute.

(1989) *The 'Leicester' Model: Experiential Study of Group and Organizational Processes*. Occasional Paper no 10. Tavistock Institute of Human Relations. Slightly shortened version, 'Experiential learning in groups I: the development of the Leicester model; II: recent developments in dissemination and application', in E. Trist and H. Murray, eds *The Social Engagement of Social Science: A Tavistock*

Anthology, vol. 1, *The Socio-Psychological Perspective*. Philadelphia, PA: University of Pennsylvania Press/Free Association Books, 1990, pp. 165–85, 186–98.

(1991) 'Missionaries or mercenaries? Dilemmas and conflicts in voluntary organizations', Tavistock Institute of Human Relations Annual Review, 1990, pp. 10–12. Also in *Managing Voluntary and Non-Profit Enterprises: Resources File 3*. Milton Keynes: The Open University, 1992, pp. 65–7.

(1992) 'The therapeutic community approach – does it exist?', *Therapeutic Communities* 13: 127–29.

(1992) 'Compiti e processi produttivi delle comunità per adolescenti' ('Towards an organizational model for residential treatment of adolescents'), in C. Kaneklin and A. Orsenigo, eds *Il Lavoro de Comunità: Modalità de intervento con adolescenti in difficoltà*. Roma: La Nuova Italia Scientifica.

(1993) 'The human dynamic', in R. Stacey, ed. *Strategic Thinking and the Management of Change: International Perspectives on Organizational Dynamics*. Kogan Page, pp. 98–116.

(1993) 'Organizational consultation: a craft or a profession?', *Leadership and Organizational Development Journal*, 14: 31–32.

REFERENCES

Place of publication is London unless otherwise indicated.

Advisory Council for the Church's Ministry (1980) *The Continuing Education of the Church's Ministry: Report for the House of Bishops*. Church Information Office.

Aguilar Amilpa, E., Garduño Velasco, H. and Miller, E.J. (1982) 'Algunas tendencias en el manejo de sistemas hidráulicos en grandes urbes', in G. Guerrero Villalobos, A. Moreno Fernandez and H. Garduño Velasco, eds *El Sistema Hidráulico del Distrito Federal: Un Servicio Publico en Transición*. Mexico: Departamento del Distrito Federal, pp. 16.1–16.18.

Baillie, W. (1964) 'Control cabin management – monitored approach; control cabin management – the double check' (mimeographed). British European Airways.

Barry, W.S. (1965) *Airline Management*. Allen & Unwin.

Bertalanffy, L. von (1950a) 'The theory of open systems in physics and biology', *Science* 3:23–9.

—— (1950b) 'An outline of general system theory', *British Journal of the Philosophy of Science* 1:134–65.

Bion, W.R. (1948–51) 'Experiences in groups, I–VII', *Human Relations* 1–4.

—— (1952) 'Group dynamics: a re-view', *Int. J. Psycho-Anal.* 33:235–47.

—— (1961) *Experiences in Groups and Other Papers*. Tavistock.

Bott, E. (1957) *Family and Social Network*. Tavistock.

Brown, R.K. (1967) 'Research and consultancy in industrial enterprises: a review of the contribution of the Tavistock Institute of Human Relations to the development of industrial sociology', *Sociology* 1: 33–60.

Bullock Report (1977) *Report of the Committee of Enquiry on Industrial Democracy*. HMSO.

Carr, A.W. (1985a) *The Priestlike Task*. SPCK.

—— (1985b) *Brief Encounters: Pastoral Ministry through the Occasional Offices*. SPCK.

—— (1987) 'Irrationality in religion', in J. Krantz, ed. *Irrationality in Social and Organizational Life*. Washington DC: A.K. Rice Institute, pp. 76–89.

—— (1989) *The Pastor as Theologian*. SPCK.

—— (1992) *Say One for Me: The Church of England in the Next Decade*. SPCK.

Clark, D.H. (1964) *Administrative Therapy*. Tavistock.

Colman, A.D. and Bexton, W.H., eds (1975) *Group Relations Reader.* Washington DC: A.K. Rice Institute.

Colman, A.D. and Geller, M.H., eds (1985) *Group Relations Reader 2.* Washington DC: The A.K. Rice Institute.

Dartington, T., Miller, E.J. and Gwynne, G. (1981) *A Life Together: The Distribution of Attitudes around the Disabled.* Tavistock.

Davis, D. Russell (1964) 'Psychological mechanisms in pilot error', in A. Cassie, S.D. Fokkema and J.B. Parry, eds *Aviation Psychology.* The Hague and Paris: Mouton, pp. 12–23.

De Board, R. (1978) *The Psychoanalysis of Organizations.* Tavistock.

Department of Health and Social Security (1974) *Report of Committee of Inquiry: South Ockenden Hospital.* HMSO.

Dickson, J.W. (1983) 'Beliefs about work and rationales for participation', *Human Relations* 36:911–31.

Ecclestone, G., ed. (1988) *The Parish Church?* Mowbrays.

Emery, F.E. (1982) 'Sociotechnical foundations for a new social order', *Human Relations* 35:1095–122.

Emery, F.E. and Trist, E.L. (1960) 'Socio-technical systems', in C.W. Churchman and M. Verhulst, eds *Management Sciences, Models and Techniques,* vol. 2. Oxford: Pergamon, pp. 83–97.

Etzioni, A. (1964) *Modern Organizations.* Englewood Cliffs, NJ: Prentice-Hall.

Evans-Pritchard, E.E. (1940) *The Nuer.* Oxford University Press.

Fox, A. (1968) Review of Miller and Rice, *Systems of Organization, Journal of Management Studies* 5:241–6.

Freire, P. (1973) *Pedagogy of the Oppressed.* New York: Herder & Herder.

Freud, S. (1913) *Totem and Taboo,* in James Strachey, ed. *The Standard Edition of the Complete Psychological Works of Sigmund Freud,* 24 vols. Hogarth, 1953–73, vol. 13, pp. 1–100.

—— (1921) *Group Psychology and the Analysis of the Ego.* S.E. 18, pp. 69–134.

Fromm, E. (1960) *The Fear of Freedom.* Routledge & Kegan Paul. (Published in the United States in 1941 as *Escape from Freedom.*)

Goffman, E. (1956) *The Presentation of Self in Everyday Life.* New York: Doubleday.

—— (1961) *Asylums: Essays on the Social Situation of Mental Patients and Other Inmates.* New York: Doubleday Anchor/Harmondsworth: Penguin, 1968.

Goldthorpe, J.H., Lockwood, D., Bechofer, F. and Platt, J. (1967) 'The affluent worker and the thesis of *embourgeoisement*: some preliminary research findings', *Sociology* 1:11–31.

REFERENCES

Habgood, J. (1983) *Church and Nation in a Secular Age*. Dartington: Longman & Todd.

Heckadon, S. (1973) *Los Asentamientos Campesinos: Un Experiencia Panameña en Reforma Agraria*. Guatemala: UNICEF.

Heider, F. (1958) *The Psychology of Interpersonal Relations*. New York: Wiley.

Heimann, P. (1952) 'A contribution to the re-evaluation of the Oedipus Complex – the early stages', *Int. J. Psycho-Anal*. 23:84–92. Reprinted in M. Klein, P Heimann and R.E. Money-Kyrle, eds *New Directions in Psycho-Analysis*. Tavistock, 1955, pp. 23–38.

Herrick, R.W. and Carr, A.W. (1975) *Organisation for Training in the Context of the Task of Ministry*. Chelmsford Cathedral Centre.

Higgin, G.W. and Bridger, H. (1964) 'The psycho-dynamics of an inter-group experience', *Human Relations* 17:391–446. Reprinted as Tavistock Pamphlet no. 10, Tavistock, 1965.

Hopper, E. and Weyman, A. (1975) 'A sociological view of large groups', in L. Kreeger, ed. *The Large Group: Therapy and Dynamics*. Constable, pp. 159–89.

Jaques, E. (1951) *The Changing Culture of a Factory*. Tavistock.

—— (1955) 'Social systems as a defence against persecutory and depressive anxiety', in M. Klein, P. Heimann and R.E. Money-Kyrle, eds *New Directions in Psycho-Analysis*. Tavistock, pp. 478–98.

—— (1970) *Work, Creativity and Social Justice*. Heinemann.

Jennings, P.R. (1976) 'The amplification of agricultural production', *Scientific American* 235, 3:180–94.

Khaleelee, O. and Miller, E.J. (1983) 'Making the post-dependent society'. Unpublished paper.

—— (1984) *The Future of Work: A Report of the West Yorkshire Talkabout, July–November 1983*. Work & Society.

—— (1985) 'Beyond the small group: society as an intelligible field of study', in M. Pines, ed. *Bion and Group Psychotherapy*. Routledge & Kegan Paul, pp. 353–83. This vol., ch. 13, pp. 243–72.

Klein, M. (1928) 'Early stages of the Oedipus complex', in *Contributions to Psychoanalysis, 1921–1945*. Hogarth, 1948, pp. 202–14.

—— (1946) 'Notes on some schizoid mechanisms', in M. Klein et al., eds *Developments in Psychoanalysis*. Hogarth Press, 1952, pp. 292–320.

—— (1952) 'Some theoretical conclusions regarding the emotional life of the infant', in M. Klein, P. Heimann, S. Isaacs and J. Riviere, eds *Developments in Psychoanalysis*. Hogarth, pp. 198–236.

—— (1959) 'Our adult world and its roots in infancy', *Human Relations* 12:291–303. Also in M. Klein, *Our Adult World and Other Essays*. Heinemann, 1963, pp. 1–22.

Lawrence, W.G. (1979) 'A concept for today: management of oneself in role', in W.G. Lawrence, ed. *Exploring Individual and Organizational Boundaries*. Chichester: Wiley, pp. 235–49.

—— (1980) 'Citizenship and the work place. A current case study', in B. Sievers and W. Slesina, eds, *Organisationsentwicklung in der Diskussion. Offene Systemplanung und partizipative Organisationsforschung*. Arbeitspapiere des Fachbereichs Wirtschaftswissenschaft die Gesamthochschule Wuppertal, no. 44, pp. 65–98, Wuppertal.

—— (1982) *Some Psychic and Political Dimensions of Work Experiences*. Occasional Paper no. 2. Tavistock Institute of Human Relations.

Lawrence, W.G. and Miller, E.J. (1976) 'Epilogue', in E.J. Miller, ed. *Task and Organization*. Chichester: Wiley, pp. 361–6.

—— (1982) 'Psychic and political constraints on the growth of industrial democracies', in M. Pines and L. Rafaelsen, eds *The Individual and the Group: Boundaries and Interrelations*. vol. 1, *Theory*. New York: Plenum, pp. 399–404.

Lawrence, W.G. and Robinson, P. (1975) 'An innovation and its implementation: issues of evaluation', document no. CASR 1069, Tavistock Institute of Human Relations (unpublished).

Levinson, H. (1972) *Organizational Diagnosis*. Cambridge, MA: Harvard University Press.

Lewin, K. (1936) *Principles in Topological Psychology*. New York: McGraw-Hill.

—— (1946) 'Action research and minority problems', *Journal of Social Issues* 2:34–46.

—— (1947) 'Frontiers in group dynamics: I. Concept, method and reality in social sciences; social equilibria and social change', *Human Relations* 1:5–41.

—— (1950) *Field Theory in Social Science*. New York: Harper Bros.

Lupton, T. (1976) '"Best fit" in the design of organizations', in E.J. Miller, ed. *Task and Organization*. Chichester: Wiley, pp. 23–149.

McGregor, D. (1960) *The Human Side of Enterprise*. New York: McGraw-Hill.

Main, T. (1975) 'Some psychodynamics of large groups', in L. Kreeger, ed. *The Large Group: Therapy and Dynamics*. Constable, pp. 57–86.

Maslow, A.H. (1970) *Motivation and Personality*, 2nd edn. New York: Harper & Row.

Menninger, R. (1972) 'The impact of group relations conferences on organizational growth', *Int. J. Group Psychother.* 22:415–32.

REFERENCES

Menzies, I.E.P. (1960) 'A case-study in the functioning of social systems as a defence against anxiety', *Human Relations* 13:95–121. Reprinted as Tavistock Pamphlet no. 3, Tavistock, 1961, and in Menzies Lyth, 1988, pp. 43–85.

—— (1965) *A Note on Driving and Road Accidents*. British Safety Council. See also Menzies Lyth, 1989, pp. 123–57.

Menzies Lyth, I. (1988) *Containing Anxiety in Institutions: Selected Essays*, vol. 1. Free Association Books.

—— (1989) *The Dynamics of the Social: Selected Essays*, vol. 2. Free Association Books.

Merton, R.K. (1957) *Social Theory and Social Structure*. Glencoe, IL: Free Press.

Miller, E.J. (1959) 'Technology, territory and time: the internal differentiation of complex production systems', *Human Relations* 12:243–72.

—— (1975) 'Socio-technical systems in weaving, 1953–1970: a follow-up study', *Human Relations* 28:349–86.

—— , ed. (1976a) *Task and Organization*. Chichester: Wiley.

—— (1976b) 'Role perspectives and the understanding of organizational behaviour', in E.J. Miller, ed. (1976a), pp. 1–18.

—— (1976c) 'The open-system approach to organizational analysis, with special reference to the work of A.K. Rice', in G. Hofstede and M. Sami Kassem, eds *European Contributions to Organization Theory*. Assen/Amsterdam: Van Gorcum, pp. 43–61. See this vol., ch. 1, pp. 3–23.

—— (1976d) *Desarrollo Integral del Medio Rural: Un Experimento en Mexico*. Mexico DF: Fondo de Cultura Económica. Second impression, 1985.

—— (1977) 'Organizational development and industrial democracy: a current case-study' in C. Cooper, ed. *Organizational Development in the UK and USA: A Joint Evaluation*. Macmillan, pp. 31–63. See this vol., ch. 1, pp. 3–23; ch. 11, pp. 195–216.

—— (1978) 'Some reflections on the role of the diplomatic wife', *Diplomatic Service Wives' Association Newsletter*, Spring 1978: 13–27. This vol., ch. 7, pp. 132–45.

—— (1979a) 'Autonomy, dependency and organizational change', in D. Towell and C. Harries, eds *Innovation in Patient Care: An Action Research Study of Change in a Psychiatric Hospital*. Croom Helm, pp. 172–90. See this vol., ch. 12, pp. 217–37.

—— (1979b) 'Open systems revisited: a proposition about development and change', in W.G. Lawrence, ed. *Exploring Individual and*

Organizational Boundaries: A Tavistock Open Systems Approach. Chichester: Wiley, pp. 217–33.

— (1980) 'The politics of involvement', *Journal of Personality and Social Systems* vol. 2, nos 2–3: 37–50. Also in A.D. Colman and M.H. Geller, eds *Group Relations Reader 2*. Washington DC: A.K. Rice Institute, 1985, pp. 383–98.

— (1981) 'The role of the wife of Head of Mission', *Diplomatic Service Wives Association Magazine*, Spring 1981, 13–27.

— (1983) *Work and Creativity*. Occasional Paper no. 6. Tavistock Institute of Human Relations.

— (1985) 'OPUS Conference Report: "After 1984: New Directions?", September 28–29, 1985,' *Bulletin* no. 20–21, Part II. OPUS. See this vol., ch. 14, pp. 273–80.

— (1986) 'Making room for individual autonomy', in S. Srivastva and Associates, *Executive Power*. San Francisco, CA: Jossey-Bass, pp. 257–88. See this vol., ch. 15, pp. 284–315.

— (1989) *The 'Leicester' Model: Experiential Study of Group and Organizational Processes'*, Occasional Paper no. 10. Tavistock Institute of Human Relations.

— (1990) 'Experiential learning in groups I: the development of the Leicester model; II: recent developments in dissemination and application', in E.L. Trist and H. Murray, eds (1990) *The Social Engagement of Social Science: A Tavistock Anthology*, vol. 1, *The Socio-Psychological Perspective*. Philadelphia, PA: University of Pennsylvania Press/Free Association Books, 1990, pp. 165–85, 186–98.

Miller, E.J. and Armstrong, D. (1966) 'The influence of advanced technology on the structure of management organization', in J. Stieber, ed. *Employment Problems of Automation and Advanced Technology: An International Perspective*. Proceedings of a conference held at Geneva by the International Institute for Labour Studies, 19–24 July, 1964. Macmillan, pp. 318–31.

Miller, E.J. and Gwynne, G.V. (1972) *A Life Apart: A Pilot Study of Residential Institutions for the Physically Handicapped and the Young Chronic Sick*. Tavistock. Social Science Paperback edition, 1974.

— (1973) 'Dependence, independence, and counter-dependence in residential institutions for incurables', in R. Gosling, ed. *Support, Innovation and Autonomy: Tavistock Golden Jubilee Papers*. Tavistock, pp. 133–49. This vol., ch. 3, pp. 67–81.

REFERENCES

Miller, E.J. and Rice, A.K. (1967) *Systems of Organization: Task and Sentient Systems and Their Boundary Control*. Tavistock. See this vol., ch. 2, pp. 32–66.

Money-Kyrle, R.E. (1961) *Man's Picture of his World: A Psychoanalytic Study*. Duckworth.

OPUS (1980–89) *Bulletin* nos 1–29. OPUS.

Pederson-Krag, G. (1951) 'A psychoanalytic approach to mass production', *Psychoanal. Q.* 20:434–51.

Ranade, W. and Norris, P. (1984) 'Democratic consensus and the young: a cross national comparison of Britain and America', *Journal of Adolescence* 7:45–57.

Reed, B.D. (1978) *The Dynamics of Religion*. Dartington: Longman & Todd.

Rice, A.K. (1951) 'The use of unrecognized cultural mechanisms in an expanding machine-shop' (Glacier Project – III), *Human Relations* 4:143–60.

—— (1953) 'Productivity and social organization in an Indian weaving shed', *Human Relations* 6:297–329.

—— (1955a) 'The experimental reorganization of non-automatic weaving in an Indian mill', *Human Relations* 8:199–249.

—— (1955b) 'Productivity and social organization in an Indian weaving mill – II: a follow-up study of the experimental reorganization of automatic weaving', *Human Relations* 8:399–428.

—— (1958) *Productivity and Social Organization: The Ahmedabad Experiment*. Tavistock. Reprinted, New York and London: Garland Publishing, 1987.

—— (1963) *The Enterprise and its Environment*. Tavistock.

—— (1965) *Learning for Leadership*. Tavistock.

—— (1969) 'Individual, group and intergroup process', *Human Relations* 22:565–84. Also in E.J. Miller, ed. *Task and Organization*. Chichester: Wiley, 1976, pp. 25–46.

Rice, A.K., Hill, J.M.M. and Trist, E.L. (1950) 'The representation of labour turnover as a social process' (Glacier Project – I), *Human Relations* 3:349–72.

Rice, A.K. and Trist, E.L. (1952) 'Institutional and sub-institutional determinants of change in labour turnover' (Glacier Project – VII), *Human Relations* 5:347–71.

Rioch, M. (1979) 'The A.K. Rice group relations conferences as a reflection of society', in W.G. Lawrence, ed. *Exploring Individual and Organizational Boundaries*. Chichester: Wiley, pp. 53–68.

Robb, B. (1967) *Sans Everything: A Case to Answer*. Nelson.

Schein, E. (1965) *Organizational Psychology*. Englewood Cliffs, NJ: Prentice-Hall.

Schwartz, H.S. (1983) 'Maslow and the hierarchical enactment of organizational reality', *Human Relations* 36:933–56.

Shapiro, E.R. and Carr, A.W. (1991) *Lost in Familiar Places*. New Haven and London: Yale University Press.

Silverman, D. (1968) Review of Miller and Rice, *Systems of Organization*, *British Journal of Industrial Relations* 6:393–7.

—— (1970) *The Theory of Organizations: A Sociological Framework*. Heinemann.

Sofer, C. (1961) *The Organization From Within: A Comparative Study of Social Institutions Based on a Sociotherapeutic Approach*. Tavistock.

South East Thames Regional Health Authority (1976) *Report of Committee of Inquiry, St Augustine's Hospital, Chartham, Canterbury*. Croydon, Surrey.

Srivastva, S. *et al.* (1975) *Job Satisfaction and Productivity. An Evaluation of Policy Related Research on Productivity, Industrial Organization and Job Satisfaction: Policy Development and Implementation*. Cleveland, OH: Case Western Reserve University, Department of Organizational Behaviour.

Stern, E. (1982) *Welfare Crises in Britain: A Preliminary Assessment*. Occasional Paper no. 1. Tavistock Institute of Human Relations.

Sullivan, M.W. (1977) 'Toward unsnarling the Foreign Service "wife problem"', *Foreign Service Journal*, April–May 1977.

Trist, E.L. and Bamforth, K.W. (1951) 'Some social and psychological consequences of the longwall method of coal-getting', *Human Relations* 4:3–38.

Trist, E.L., Higgin, G.W., Murray, H. and Pollock, A.B. (1963) *Organizational Choice: Capabilities of Groups at the Coal Face under Changing Technologies*. Tavistock.

Trist, E.L. and Murray, H., eds (1990) *The Social Engagement of Social Science: A Tavistock Anthology*, vol. 1, *The Socio-Psychological Perspective*. Philadelphia, PA: University of Pennsylvania Press/Free Association Books.

—— (1993) *The Social Engagement of Social Science: A Tavistock Anthology*, vol. 2, *The Socio-Technical Perspective*. Philadelphia, PA: University of Pennsylvania Press.

Trist, E.L. and Sofer, C. (1959) *Exploration in Group Relations*. Leicester: Leicester University Press.

REFERENCES

Turquet, P.M. (1974) 'Leadership: the individual and the group', in G.S. Gibbard, J.J. Hartman and R.D. Mann, eds *Analysis of Groups*. San Francisco, CA: Jossey-Bass, pp. 337–71.

—— (1975) 'Threats to identity in the large group', in L. Kreeger, ed. *The Large Group: Dynamics and Therapy*. Constable, pp. 87–144.

Wilson, A.T.M. (1951) 'Some aspects of social process', *Journal of Social Issues*, Supplementary Series, no. 5.

Winnicott, D.W. (1960) 'Ego distortion in terms of true and false self', in *The Motivational Processes and the Facilitating Environment*. Hogarth, pp. 140–52.

—— (1971) *Playing and Reality*. Harmondsworth: Penguin, 1980.

Wittkower, E. (1949) *A Psychiatrist Looks at Tuberculosis*. National Association for the Prevention of Tuberculosis.

INDEX